The

MODERN WITCHCRAFT

Book of

Moon Magick

+=≡ *The* ≡=+

MODERN WITCHCRAFT
Book of

Moon
Magick

YOUR COMPLETE GUIDE TO
ENHANCING YOUR MAGICK *with the*
Power of the Moon

Julia Halina Hadas

**Author of *The Modern Witchcraft
Book of Astrology***

Adams Media

New York   London   Toronto   Sydney   New Delhi

Adams Media
An Imprint of Simon & Schuster, LLC
100 Technology Center Drive
Stoughton, Massachusetts 02072

First Adams Media hardcover edition March 2024

ADAMS MEDIA and colophon are registered trademarks of Simon & Schuster, LLC.

Simon & Schuster: Celebrating 100 Years of Publishing in 2024

For information about special discounts for bulk purchases, please contact Simon & Schuster Special Sales at 1-866-506-1949 or business@simonandschuster.com.

The Simon & Schuster Speakers Bureau can bring authors to your live event. For more information or to book an event, contact the Simon & Schuster Speakers Bureau at 1-866-248-3049 or visit our website at www.simonspeakers.com.

Interior illustrations by Sara Richard
Interior images © 123RF; Getty Images; Simon & Schuster, LLC

Manufactured in the United States of America

1 2024

Library of Congress Cataloging-in-Publication Data has been applied for.

ISBN 978-1-5072-2187-7
ISBN 978-1-5072-2188-4 (ebook)

DEDICATION

To the moon and stars in my own life, Ryan.

Acknowledgments

First and foremost, thank you, Ryan, for your endless love and support. Without your wisdom, I wouldn't be where I am today. Your insight balances, grounds, and centers me, and your support makes this work possible. I love you to the moon and beyond.

Thank you, Kate Davids and Arc Literary, for your guidance and for bringing this agreement together; Eileen Mullan, for coming to me with this project; Laura Daly, for your insightful and eloquent editing; and everyone at Adams Media, for your dedication and hard work. I'm constantly astonished at how you all manage to do it all!

Anyone who publishes today stands on the shoulders of giants. Thank you to all the witchcraft, moon, and astrology authors and generations past who observed, researched, and shared their lunar insights. Among these are Dorothy Morrison, whose *Everyday Moon Magic* guided my own lunar rituals as a teen; Yasmin Boland, whose *Moonology* constantly inspires; and Steven Forrest, whose *The Book of the Moon* is poetry as much as it is an educational astrological work. And thank you to Paul Bogle, who guided my passion for astrology and the meaning of the moon signs back when we worked together in the days of The Mystic Dream.

❖═ CONTENTS ═❖

PART TWO
SPELLS and RITUALS for EVERY MOON 83

CHAPTER 8: SPECIAL OCCASION MOON MEDITATIONS 143

CHAPTER 9: SEASONAL MOON SPELLS 161

CHAPTER 10: MOON SIGN SPELLS 187

CHAPTER 11: MOON DEITY SPELLS 219

Introduction

The moon has guided and nurtured human life since antiquity. Her movement in the star-adorned night sky marks the passage of time, and her endless power and striking luminescence can help your witchcraft practice become even stronger. From infusing water with moonlight to conducting new moon meditations, witches both ancient and modern have turned to the moon to enhance and support their practice. In *The Modern Witchcraft Book of Moon Magick*, you will learn how to integrate the moon into your spellwork and develop a sacred connection to this celestial body—a connection that you can tune into at any moment for psychic insight, effortless magick, and powerful healing.

Whether you are a witch who has worked with the moon for ages or someone who has always been enthralled by the moon's beauty and now wants to tap into her energy, *The Modern Witchcraft Book of Moon Magick* will help you seamlessly integrate the power of the moon into your practice. In Part 1, you will learn exactly how the moon can infuse your witchcraft with even more potential and how to harness the power of special moons like the eclipses and supermoons. Then you will learn what to expect from the moon when it's in each astrological sign so you can plan your spellwork appropriately.

In Part 2, you will find dozens of spells for every lunar occasion, whether you want to gain insight into your life, heal from spiritual issues, or find balance and peace. You will also learn how to choose crystals that are especially beneficial in moon magick. Plant the seeds for long-term financial growth and stability with the Apple Seed Spell, or cast the Cocreation and Cooperation Support Spell during the waxing gibbous moon when you need an energetic boost for your moon-magick intentions. Make your own Seed Planting Paper to capture your lunar intentions and help them grow and thrive, or try a meditation to pause, reflect, and relax. *The Modern Witchcraft Book of Moon Magick* will also help you uncover ways to be flexible with your lunar timing when necessary, and show you how to call in the moon's correspondences with herbs, deities, and symbols to boost the effectiveness of your spells.

The possibilities of working with the moon in magick are endless. When your witchcraft is in sync with the moon, your spells will manifest effortlessly, your psychic senses will flow with ease, and you will find yourself connected to the universe in a very unique way. Tune into the moon's special power and discover how it can support your healing, encourage your growth, and help you manifest your dreams.

PART ONE

UNDERSTANDING the MAGICK of the MOON and WITCHCRAFT

The moon is intrinsically connected to witchcraft. As she orbits the earth, reflecting the sun's light, she ceaselessly changes shape, entrances us, and illuminates both the nighttime landscape and our inner, spiritual realms. Changing form and even disappearing a couple of times a month, the moon provides witches with times for rest, times for growth, and times for release. As she moves through the astrological signs, she can bolster spells, whether to summon abundance or to banish and protect. And when the moon passes in front of the sun during a solar eclipse, she reminds us that with the right timing and the right alignment, even a comparatively small body is powerful enough to cover the light of a star, our sun. In fact, such occasions often ask us to "align" in our lives, inviting a time of powerful healing and change, a cosmic, life path–altering kind of magick.

By incorporating the moon's phases, seasonality, history, and even a tad of lunar science into your spellwork, you can manifest beyond your wildest dreams. By learning about the history of the moon, you will understand the intrinsic connection you have with her, as well as how her magnetic pull empowers your personal zodiac sign and other astrological aspects. Equipped with a solid understanding of the moon in all her phases, you'll feel empowered to cast any spell, on any lunar occasion.

Chapter 1

WITCHCRAFT AND THE MOON

When you think of witchcraft, it's hard *not* to think of the moon. After all, what image is more iconic than the silhouette of the witch on a broomstick with the moon at her back? Beyond that stereotypical image is a very meaningful connection, however. Modern spiritualists and witches bathe in the moon's light, charge moon water, host lunar rituals and parties, and practice moon meditations under her guiding luminescence.

These practices may go back, essentially, since the dawn of humankind. Our ancestors used the moon to keep time, guide travel across land and sea, plan hunts, and perform rituals to ensure success. The moon was a deity who guided and defined our very existence. And given that the moon helped nurture the evolution of life on earth, it is only natural that all creatures—human, plant, and animal alike—bask under her ethereal glow.

In this chapter, you will learn how the moon evolved and, in turn, helped earth's creatures evolve under her nurturing light. With this foundational knowledge, you will begin to understand how the moon influences you, those around you, the spells you cast, and even the herbal allies and tools you use in your spells.

THE MOON AND EARTH

The moon was most likely formed at least 4.5 billion years ago when a massive object collided with young earth (fittingly, scientists have named the object Theia, after the titan mother of Selene, goddess of the moon in Greek mythology). As a result of the impact, enough debris flew in to space to coalesce and eventually form the moon. Basaltic rock samples have confirmed the similarities between the makeup of earth and the moon, so scientists know that the moon indeed was made in part from earth.

When it originally formed, the moon was closer to earth—and still, to this day, it moves away from earth about 1.5 inches each year. Without the moon, life on earth would be very different. Over time, the exchange of gravity between the earth and the moon has steadied the seasons, lengthened the days, and inspired the tides, creating the world as we know it today (we'll discuss these topics in more depth in the next sections).

Today, the moon takes about 27 days (27.322 days, to be exact) to orbit the earth. However, because the earth is also moving during that time, the moon has to make up for the lost space, and takes 29.5 days to complete a lunar cycle from new moon to new moon, since the lunar cycle depends on the angles made with the sun. The moon's orbit around earth is actually elliptical—meaning it isn't a perfect circle but is slightly long, like an oval.

Lunar Tides

Tides can take on many forms—from soothing water lapping at a sandy shoreline to water crashing furiously against rock. Tides might be gentle, withdrawing and exposing more of the shoreline and revealing shells beneath—or they can roar in and envelop the beach and surrounding areas.

While the moon's gravity is substantially weaker than earth's, its impacts are not meager. As the moon moves around the earth, its gravitational force displaces ocean waters slightly every day. High tides—water pulled by the moon's gravity—happen where the moon's pull is strongest, on the parts of the earth closest to and farthest from (or opposite) the moon. But all that water has to be displaced from somewhere—and the displacement creates low tides on the sides of earth 90 degrees out from the high tides. When the earth, sun, and moon line up just right at the time of the new and full moons, the combined gravitational forces create even more dramatic high and low tides, called spring tides. When the moon and sun form a right angle about 7 days later (coinciding with the first and last quarter moons), the gravitational pull of the sun partially nullifies the moon's, causing the calmer, more moderate changes known as neap tides.

Billions of years ago, when the moon was closer to earth and young earth's spinning was more rapid, these tides would have been more extreme. The lashing of the moon-wild ocean would've chipped away at the coastline, stirring essential minerals into the water as if mixing a cosmic potion. Some scientists believe this process played a critical role in the evolution of life on earth and still to this day impacts ocean life.

Seasons and Length of Day

The moon's gravitational exchange with the earth influences not just the tides but the seasons and length of day too. Because the earth's axis is tilted at 23.5 degrees, the poles point away from or toward the sun during different parts of the year, giving rise to the seasons. How does the moon come into play? If it weren't for the moon, our experience of the seasons might be more extreme. That's because the earth's tilt is not actually 100 percent fixed—it has a slight wobble. (Imagine a spinning dreidel or a dropped coin's spiral movement in the moment before it lies flat.) The moon's gravitational pull helps stabilize this wobble and, in turn, stabilizes the flow of seasons.

What's more, over time, the moon's pull on the earth has slowed the speed of the earth's spinning, making our days longer. Evidence found in fossils shows the earth used to have a much shorter day.

LIFE UNDER THE MOON

Given the moon's impact on the tides, seasons, and length of day—even her possible contribution to evolution—it is of little surprise that all of life on earth is intrinsically in tune with the moon. All of modern life has evolved under the moon's light, alongside the sun's. The circadian rhythm—the biorhythm of the daily, 24-hour cycle—is well known. Research is now also expanding into how biorhythm relates to the lunar cycle, the 29.5-day circalunar rhythm of life.

Sea Creatures and Lunar Phases

The most evident example is marine organisms. The tides created by the moon impact the life cycles of countless sea and ocean creatures: Nesting and newborn turtles use the moonlight to safely navigate the shores at night when temperatures are cooler and the threat of predators is lessened; oysters and other shellfish open and close with the phases of the moon and the resulting ocean currents. The moon's impact on the ocean and its ethereal light amidst the dark of night also inspires marine creatures to mate, birth, eat, or migrate.

The Moon and Other Wild Animals

Who hasn't heard the myth that wolves howl at the moon? Lunar impacts on mammals and non-ocean creatures may be less obvious, but the moon is integrated into their daily lives as well. For example, in a study published in *Ecology Letters*, a team of ecologists watched the behavior of lions' typical prey in relation to the lunar cycle. They noted that wildebeests oriented their activities based on moon phases, keeping themselves harbored in a safe space during the dark moon. During the full moon, they were more adventurous, traveling into areas where encounters with lions were more likely. Animals with stellar night vision (such as lions) might have an advantage with the dark moon shadowing their presence, but the full moon casts light on the unknown landscape and on potential predators. With greater visibility, wildebeest and other animals can more safely forage, mate, or travel.

Of course, the moonlight's effect can look different for each creature. Some birds' feeding and migration patterns coincide with the lunar cycle. Even some of the smallest creatures—dung beetles—navigate by moonlight as they wheel balls of dung away from competition and predators.

Plant Life and the Moon

Plants operate in tune with the moon too. A Mediterranean plant called a joint pine weeps droplets of fluid that refract moonlight, and those ethereal sparkles attract nocturnal pollinators' attention. Many night-flowering plants also rely on moonlight to attract moths and other nocturnal pollinators—a process that's essential for the continuation of their species.

You may have also heard of gardening with the moon—that some phases are better for planting, pruning, and harvesting for the overall growth of a plant. While science hasn't shown that phases of the moon impact plant growth, many gardeners swear by it, insisting that the waxing-to-full moon increases the movement of sap in plants and the waning moon slows it down. Chapter 5 includes more details about lunar gardening practices.

Moonlight and Human Behavior

Thanks to electricity and digital devices, it can be hard to imagine the impact of lunar light in modern human society. But we, too, are still in tune with the moon. Many people who work in hospitals or police departments report an increase in incidents during the full moon, though official data is inconclusive. Research at large is still uncertain as to the moon's influence on humans, but at the very least the moon may impact our sleep by way of its light affecting our levels of the hormone melatonin. Perhaps future research on human circalunar rhythms will reveal more about how we evolved in tune with the moon.

Part One: Understanding the Magick of the Moon and Witchcraft

THE MOON IN HUMAN HISTORY

Since the dawn of human life on earth, the moon, sun, and sky have defined daily living. Early humans watched and mapped the passage of the moon across the sky to define time, and to this day, folklore still exists on what a ring around the moon might mean (precipitation), and on the moon's call to plant or harvest certain crops. The moon's daily changes and the lunar cycles' correspondence with the seasons (three to four moon cycles, or lunations, per season) helped our early ancestors anticipate the coming and going of seasons.

Early Lunar Timekeeping

Researchers have long speculated and debated as to what the first evidence of human lunar timekeeping might be. To some, cave paintings of animals and the night sky (such as those found in the famous Lascaux caves in France) were a show of early human creativity and a natural example of the moon's capacity to inspire. These drawings may have also been ritualistic and spiritual in nature, to grant blessings and luck in hunts—perhaps the first recorded lunar spells and rituals! Research published in 2023 in *Cambridge Archaeological Journal* observes that notations of lines, dots, and Υ's in some of these cave drawings coincided with animal activity and the lunar cycle. This could mean humans were actively timekeeping and planning using the moon 37,000–42,000 years ago.

Regardless of when ancient timekeeping began, the moon would have also aided hunting, the gathering of food, and nighttime travel. Since it was capable of casting a snowlike glow across a luminous landscape, the moon would've been key to many nightly activities. Our ancestors were in tune with and aware of the moon—they lived by the moon, the sun, and the seasons. With that in mind, it only seems natural for the moon to be personified as a deity.

The Moon As a Deity

With the agricultural revolution and the creation of writing, records of specific moon deities emerged, recording connections among the moon, timekeeping, and the fertility of life. To countless ancient cultures, celestial bodies were gods, and the moon was one of the most prominent. For example, in ancient Sumeria, the moon god Nanna (or Sin) was one of the most prominent deities. Nanna was seen as an old man or cowherd and was often associated with the bull or the cow (an ancient fertility symbol).

Through his children and wife, Nanna was also connected to fertility, abundance, and the dead.

The phases of the moon held meaning to ancient cultures and guided when to perform rituals and rites of all kinds. For example, the Egyptian moon deity Khonsu (whose name means "traveler") was a god of healing, fertility, and time. He was often petitioned at the appearance of the waxing crescent for fertility, for both women and animals.

Even though with the founding of permanent settlements many humans switched to sun-predominant worship, the moon still held vast importance:

● With no electricity, the light of the moon allowed for night travel.

● Seafaring required the study of the moon, tides, and stars for safe traveling.

● As more and more cultures settled down, the moon's cycles had importance for the fertility of not just humans and livestock, but also crops. When a ring appeared around the moon, it meant rain was soon to follow. (To this day, many farmers still harvest and plant based on the moon's guidance.)

As Christianity spread and the power of the church grew in Western culture, in many cases nature-based deities, including the moon gods, were shunned in favor of Christianity's single deity. To create reliance upon the church, leaders forbade people from accessing the healing power of nature and the moon. Worship of moon deities went underground, and healers lived on the outskirts of society, where they still used the moon for travel, gardening, harvesting, and so on.

The moon still guides religious traditions today: Many of the world's largest religions observe holidays that align with the phases of the moon. Ramadan lasts from crescent moon to crescent moon; Easter occurs on the Sunday after the first full moon following the spring equinox; many full moons mark Jewish holidays. In China, the lunar new year holds vast importance, and at the midautumn moon festival, the lunar goddess Chang'e, who drank an elixir of immortality and flew to the moon, is celebrated and left offerings. In both religious and secular ways, harvest moon festivals are still celebrated to this day.

While astronauts' landing on the moon may have demystified some of the moon's qualities, it also strongly reaffirmed our connection to her.

India and China have both recently named spacecraft after their respective lunar deities. The moon's mystifying light has inspired poets, scientists, and more. And now the moon is experiencing a revival of worship as modern witches incorporate this celestial body into their practice.

THE MOON AND WITCHCRAFT TODAY

The moon has always been associated with spells and rituals, and while that practice may have changed appearance over the years, witches today still heed the call of the moon.

How the Moon Aids Witches

Witches are connected to the moon in countless ways. For example, many modern witches:

- Manifest their desires based on the moon cycles, for example, by casting intentions at the new and full moons;

- Throw lunar parties and coven gatherings under the full moon;

- Meditate to align with lunar power;

- Use moon-charged water in their spellcrafting;

- Let the phases of the moon guide them regarding when to cast spells, heal, and reflect;

- Charge crystals and conduct healing rituals by the light of the full moon;

- Plant, nurture, and cultivate healing herbs based on the phases and cycles of the moon;

- Use the 29.5-day cycle from new moon to new moon to work on habits and monthly goals to take steps toward their dreams;

- Use the moon's phase, sign, and seasonality to guide reflection and focus.

In short, witches use the moon to access a deeper level of magickal power and healing. They acknowledge that the moon is both part of us and a source of power for spells. Some witches are so closely aligned with the moon that they see their own energy and psychic sensitivity grow and wane with its cycle.

Embracing Dark and Light

The moon's cycle reflects the polarity of dark and light that is well known to witches—the unknown and known, the spiritual realm and waking reality, the subconscious and conscious. Like the dark moon witch goddess Hekate, who holds the keys to secrets and mysteries, moon witches are unafraid to explore and find their power in the dark. They understand that there is a cycle and a time for everything under the moon. The moon's phases advise and illuminate: she offers a time for rest and retreat, times for growth and change, and time to shine in our power.

Empowering Women in Western Astrology

In modern times, the moon has held an especially important role associated with the reawakening of the goddess in a patriarchal society. While the moon has had an array of gender associations over time, to some, her themes call others to honor the power of the feminine. In Western astrology, the moon is seen to be feminine and represents the soul, the subconscious, early childhood, and patterns of nurturing. Her cycles often bring the subconscious into consciousness.

An Enduring Symbol

In some sense, the moon is our relative, made from earth and star dust, just like us. And as she has been there for our ancestors, she will be there for us and for many future generations—a looming light in the sky that connects everyone to the past, present, and future. As in the harvest moon gratitude rituals observed in generations past, you can use the moon to connect to ancestors, or to spirits beyond the veil. Through the careful, nurturing hand of the moon, all can come to manifest.

Chapter 2

THE MAGICK OF THE MOON PHASES

As the moon performs her celestial dance with the sun, she reflects not just sunlight but also the themes and energy of life. Each moon phase offers special opportunities for manifesting what you want in life. You may have heard of manifesting with the moon—setting intentions at the new moon, releasing with the full. Perhaps you've taken the occasional full moon bath or two. But there is even more magick to be had. In this chapter, you will learn more and sharpen your knowledge about the magick of the moon phases, from the new moon through the waxing phase to the full moon and the waning.

You will also learn about special lunar events—lunar and solar eclipses, supermoons and micromoons, blue and black moons—and how (or whether) you should use them in magick. The power and potential of every phase and alignment awaits you. Learn about them and you'll be able to effortlessly live in tune with the moon and her messages.

THE MAGICK AND MEANING OF THE MOON PHASES

The phases of the moon offer power in terms of both symbolism and magick. As the moon moves around the earth, it reflects the sun's light and casts the lunar phases back down to earth.

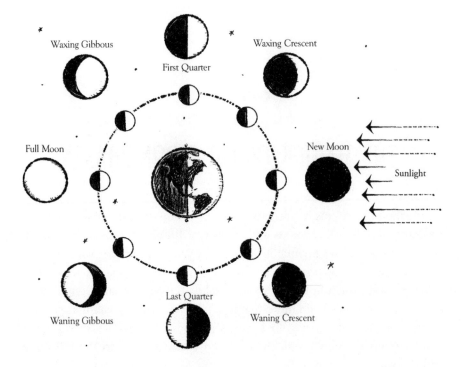

Waxing Gibbous

First Quarter

Waxing Crescent

Full Moon

New Moon

Sunlight

Waning Gibbous

Last Quarter

Waning Crescent

The moon's cycle can be broken into eight main phases, each with its own meaning and magick: the new moon, the waxing crescent, the first quarter, the waxing gibbous, the full moon, the waning gibbous, the last quarter (sometimes called the third quarter), and the waning crescent. Some of these moons belong to the waxing phase, a time of growth as the moon swells in light. Others belong to the waning, when the moon lessens in light and shape, a period of decrease and release. (Note, the individual phase images shown in each section represent the Northern Hemisphere.) Beyond the themes of waxing and waning, the lunar cycle also interplays themes of dark and light—the unknown and subconscious, and the conscious awareness and physical reality.

There are many ways you can use the themes of the lunar cycle in your witchcraft: Manifest based on the phase's tendencies, working with the phase to nurture and bring a desire into the world; alter spells to harmonize with the phase of moon for added celestial power; or use the themes of the phase for daily reflection and focus as you connect to the moon's myth and meaning. As you make your way through this book, you'll find your own unique ways to cocreate with the moon.

New Moon

Overarching themes: Alignment, Intention Setting, Insight, Manifestation, New Beginnings

The lunar cycle begins with the new moon. At this time, the moon is absent from the night sky and the gemlike stars shine ever brighter in her absence. The new moon is one of the energetic highlights of the lunar cycle. The precise moment it occurs is when the moon reaches a 0-degree alignment with the sun and is situated between the sun and earth. This positioning means the moon rises and sets with the sun in the sky. Because her absence often lasts a day before and after the exact alignment, and because the new moon is an important energetic marker for the entire cycle, many practitioners find the energy of this phase accessible for a total of 3 days.

This time of divine, cosmic alignment finds the two most significant celestial bodies in our night sky "meeting": the sun (consciousness, identity, ego) and the moon (subconscious, emotion, the soul). We can therefore connect to both the celestial energies above and within. Use this time to reflect on what your soul is calling for.

Straddling times of waning and waxing phase energy, the new moon is an occasion of celestial alignment that witches use in very personal ways: Some use it for rest; others for intention setting. To mirror the absence of the moon from the sky, you might want to use the time to take an energetic break to restore the vitality that will allow you to take action with the waxing moon. In other words, simply rest and prepare for the coming growth of moonlight. It's a great time to take a cleansing salt bath, purify your energy, rest, or meditate and read tarot cards to gain insight and information. With the dark night sky looming above, occult themes may feel more accessible now, which is why this is also a favorable time to start new magickal studies or strengthen your psychic skill set, investigate past lives, and explore your inner truth.

On the other hand, you might feel called to cast intentions for manifestation. The lunar cycle is beginning anew, and there is boundless cosmic energy hurtling forward, propelling the moon to grow in light again. You might want to use this energy to call forth a new desire or goal that can increase along with the waxing phase, or set one or more intentions to focus on for the entire lunation, or cast spells for rebirth and new beginnings. The meeting of the sun and moon is also a great time to cast magick related to alignment, such as balancing the sun and moon within or energetically aligning to a new life vision. The astrological sign of the new moon can offer particular beneficial potential around certain themes; for example, we can use the aligned Taurus new moon and sun to manifest money and long-term abundance (this will be discussed more in Chapter 4). And the combined energy of the sun and moon as they travel together across the daytime sky can empower *many* spells. With your energy aligned, you can channel this cosmic power for any number of magickal efforts.

So, it's the new moon. Should you rest or manifest? It's up to you how to use the time—perhaps it's both! Also, with each lunar phase, you may feel different. Part of working with the moon is to be in tune with your intuition and feelings and the ebbs and flows of life. There is a cosmos of energy at hand to use how you deem best. Just as a plant needs the right balance of soil, light, water, and pruning to thrive, so too do your actions within the lunation cycle need a good balance of rest and action. Trust that you will know what to do when, and that the universe will provide the right energy to nurture any intentions into reality.

Dark Moon or New Moon?

In the modern era, the day marked on calendars and datebooks for the new moon heralds the moment of the moon's 0-degree alignment with the sun. However, you may have also heard of the term "dark moon." When mixing common and scientific language, astrology and witchcraft, "dark moon" can take on many different meanings. In this book, "dark moon" refers to a part of the waning phase, one with its own distinct energy. You will learn more about it at the end of this section.

Waxing Phase

Overarching themes: Increase, Growth, Action

As the moon grows from new to full, increasing in light, we travel through the waxing moon phases. In the Northern Hemisphere, the moon appears to grow from right to left—a backward *C*. In the Southern Hemisphere, the moon grows from left to right, starting off as a proper *C*.

Moon Phases Northern Hemisphere

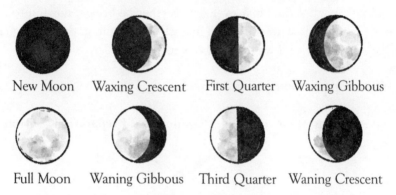

New Moon   Waxing Crescent   First Quarter   Waxing Gibbous

Full Moon   Waning Gibbous   Third Quarter   Waning Crescent

Moon Phases Southern Hemisphere

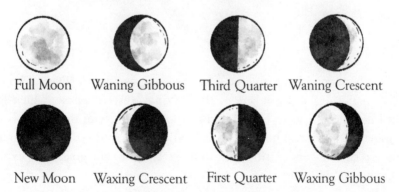

Full Moon   Waning Gibbous   Third Quarter   Waning Crescent

New Moon   Waxing Crescent   First Quarter   Waxing Gibbous

This waxing moon period, the first half of the lunation cycle, lasts about 2 weeks. During this time, each moonrise happens later in the day than the last. At the time of the new moon, the moon rose with the sun; by the time of the full moon, moonrise coincides with sunset. As the moon's light grows in the sky, so too does your sense of power.

Magickally, this is an auspicious time for any spells or intentions that require increase, growth, or momentum. The waxing period is filled with the energy of productivity, so try to put action behind your words. As your dreams move into the waking, conscious realm as the moon grows from new to full, shift energy toward your intentions and goals. Use the nurturing light and energy of the growing moon to support your endeavors as they are realized into physical reality.

While any effort toward growth and increase is favorable at this time, the waxing part of the lunar cycle can further be broken down into individual phases, each with additional magick and meaning: the waxing crescent, first quarter, and waxing gibbous moons.

Waxing Crescent

Overarching themes: Hope, Planning and Preparation, Action, Courage

As the moon begins to reemerge, growing as a small sliver of hopeful light in the night sky, it enters the waxing crescent phase, which lasts until the moon reaches half illumination. The energy of this phase is vulnerable but eager and hopeful, with limitless possibilities. This is a time to develop courage and faith, begin to move toward your goals, and explore the potential of your dreams.

Like sprouted seedlings growing beneath the earth and pushing to reach the surface, spells and intentions cast at the new moon start their initial phase of growth during the waxing crescent phase. And just as a plant needs the right conditions to grow, these intentions need nurturing. Continue to feed the energy of your spells and take the first steps to support their fruition. Preparing can help your endeavor feel real and bolster your faith. Keep the vision of your dreams alive and create space for them to manifest.

Magickally, this is a time to instill hope and excitement. Create and repeat affirmations and visualizations of hope and a sense of possibility to help support the manifestation of any magick. Develop an action plan and the guts to go after what you want. Take those first steps. When you attend to your courage and confidence during the waxing crescent, they can grow with the waxing moon and prepare you to take action. Because your energy will be vibrant, excited, and aligned, you will attract more favorable outcomes.

First Quarter Moon

Overarching themes: Overcoming Challenges, Tensions, Balance, Action, Integration

Following the waxing crescent, the first quarter is marked by a half-lit moon. A transitional moment from one phase to the next, the first quarter moon lasts about 1 day before sliding into the waxing gibbous phase. It marks the halfway point on the moon's journey from absence to fullness—and the midway point of your manifestation. With the moon half lit, the darker half of the cycle (the unknown and unmanifest) is balanced with the lighter half, where we begin to encounter material reality and, with it, the boundaries of the physical.

At the time of the half moon, the positions of the moon, sun, and earth form an angle that astrologers call a square, and this arrangement is known for clashing energy. With earth as the reference or central point, the moon and sun are at 90 degrees from each other—a right angle. Squares create energetic friction between the two celestial bodies involved. Challenges and blockages may arise, or energy could be stalled.

The newness and excitement of the new moon has begun to wear off, and you may feel tested. While this period can feel uncomfortable, it also offers the potential for amazing growth if you can push through or compromise. A time of crossroads, the first quarter moon is also an opportunity to rethink your intentions—or to continue with determined action. You may have to pivot, adapt, or integrate, providing a chance for creativity, overcoming, and strengthening. Check in with your progress now. Check tarot cards for insight, cast a spell to move you beyond this crossroads, or focus on balance.

At this time, there is a sense of not knowing. Sometimes the half moon period includes taking risks; sometimes, you may not be sure what waits on the other side, like the dark half of the moon. You may find yourself with no choice but to make decisions and gamble—roll the dice. But luckily there is magick for that; cast spells to turn luck and chance in your favor.

Waxing Gibbous

Overarching themes: Integration, Cocreation, Excitement, Endurance, Growth

As the moon grows past half illumination, we exit the challenging energy of the first quarter and enter into the energy of cocreation. This phase covers the moon's growth in light from half full until the moment of culmination at the full moon. This is the last phase of the waxing cycle, so work any last waxing moon magick for growth and increase now.

Following the challenges and decisions of the first quarter, the waxing gibbous moon is a time to implement any lessons you deem insightful, and to adjust, making any necessary tweaks to your moon magick. Cross your t's and dot your i's. In the spirit of integration, another aspect of the waxing gibbous moon is partnership and cocreation. Whether in love, business, or creative partnerships, or even in spiritual alliances, partnership is especially favorable now. This phase is a great time to exchange ideas and insight, combining energy to form something greater, whether with the universe or with another person.

"Gibbous" means "bulging," which matches the moon in both appearance and energy now. Success and abundance are within reach. The magick and momentum are swelling into power. In the face of something new, beautiful, and exciting, bolstered by the radiant power of the bright moon, your own fears, anxieties, and doubts might arise. If so, acknowledge these feelings for what they are. Push forward, or decide to take a different path and reinvest that energy in a new idea instead. If you stay the course and integrate wisdom or join forces, the combined energy can create something greater than you imagined.

If you find your battery running low, allow the moonlight to refill it for you, or do a spell for stamina or endurance. Recommit to your goals, using the buzz of energy to fill you with inspiration and excitement. As the moon bulges at this time, so too may your psychic senses, energy, and emotions. If so, channel that passion and power to supercharge your lunar spells.

Full Moon

Overarching themes: Celebration, Power, Culmination, Release, Manifestation

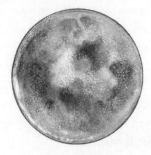

At long last, the moon is fully illuminated. During this time, the moon rises at sunset and sets at sunrise, taking her place as queen of the night and crown jewel of the dark sky. The moon appears full for about 3 days. As one of the key significant markers of the lunation cycle, each full moon radiates a particular energy based on the sign in which it occurs that tends to linger and frame the experiences of the whole month. Many practitioners feel the full moon's energy throughout the days before and after the moment of fullness, allowing a handful of days (or nights) to execute full moon magick.

At the time of the full moon, the moon is directly opposite the sun in the sky, with earth right smack in the middle. This is an astrological angle called an opposition and is exactly what the name suggests: The two celestial forces may seem to conflict. While the opposition can create challenges and the heightened energy can give raise to outbursts of emotions (as full moons are often known for), the energy *can* also become harmonious through awareness and balance within the polarity.

The full moon is also a time of culmination and celebration. Like farmers harvesting wheat under the full moon, we may reap the rewards of efforts sowed during the waxing phase, or receive guidance, signs, and insights that the fruits of our labors are on the way. Even if things have not yet culminated, abundance can very much still arrive in the future. The moon in her full radiance can inspire a sense of power that some witches channel to supercharge their magick. Psychic powers, creativity, and emotions may feel intensely called upon now—it is easy to feel a connection with the full moon and its power within our lives. Since we can see the moon throughout the night, we might also work or bathe in the moon's light, or even just gaze at her beauty in wonder. If you like the energy of the full moon, it may be worthwhile to charge any special items, such as your favorite stones, under the moonlight.

As the full moon straddles the boundary between the waxing and waning phases, some witches feel called to release and forgive and focus on self-care. With the results of the waxing phase at hand, you might release expectations now and preemptively celebrate and give gratitude to Mother Moon. Just as the moon fully reflects the sun, insight on your waking life may also be illuminated now. What has the moon revealed for healing and change? Listen to her messages. Since this is a moment of final culmination, whatever patterns or wounds are exposed or brought to moonlight can begin to be healed.

Depending on where a moon falls in your astrological chart or what's going on in your personal life, each full moon can feel different. The moon invites us to strengthen our intuition, tune into ourselves, and depending on how this specific lunar cycle has impacted us, decide whether it's time for self-care or for manifestation magick. A multitude of efforts can be empowered now.

Waning Phase

Overarching themes: Release, Decrease, Banishing

As the moon's light decreases in the sky and fades into darkness, we travel through the waning phase. The moon wanes from right to left in the Northern Hemisphere and the opposite way in the Southern (see images earlier in this chapter). Rising a tad later each and every night, she makes her way to once again rise and set with the sun at the new moon. Magickally, it's a time for rest and release, and for efforts that require decrease and banishment.

The full moon has brought everything to surface; the waning moon period is when we digest this information. While the waxing moon required active effort, the waning moon is a time to reflect, release, and integrate the lessons of the lunar cycle. We experienced growth; now comes a period of rest and relaxation.

In the waxing phase, the soil has been tilled and the seeds sown and nurtured. It is time to let those plants become ready to harvest on their own time, if they aren't already. Like energetic gardeners in tune with the cycles of the earth and the moon, now we prune: cut back what didn't work or is no longer needed. Or we sow efforts focused on internal and spiritual matters, tending to our own roots/nutrients like the beneath-ground plants and roots the waning phase favors. Break bonds; let go. Cleanse and release. Make room in both your energy and your life for the new blessings and magick of the next lunar cycle. As the moon wanes, efforts to decrease things are favorable, such as: to extinguish bad habits and unwanted influences and shrink debt and insecurity. It's time to end whatever we are ready to forgive, move on from, or transform.

Adapting Your Magick to Any Phase

There are times when you need to work magick that simply cannot wait, even though it might not seem to match the moon phase. Try your hand at adapting your magickal intentions to suit the themes of the sky. For example, if you're working on spells for focus, in the waxing phase you might cast spells to increase focus, peace, and willpower. In the waning phase of the moon, you might instead seek to decrease distractions, the number of tasks you need to do, or the wandering of your mind. Just as the moon shows us many sides, our moon-magickal intentions can have many facets we can take to support our end aims.

This phase can be further divided into separate stages, each with its own nuanced astrological energy and magick: waning gibbous, last quarter, and waning crescent, as well as an additional aspect called the dark moon.

Waning Gibbous

Overarching themes: Gratitude, Reflection, Release, Sharing, Acceptance

Following the full moon, glorious in all her radiance, comes the waning gibbous phase. The moon's light will now decrease until it's once again halfway lit at the last quarter. Though the moon is still in the brighter part of her cycle and the full moon's aura of culmination and energy still linger, the inevitable decline is in sight and inspires reflection.

As you reflect, release, and harvest the longer-term results of your lunar labor, this is a time to give thanks for harvests yet to come. When you harvest plants, you are also often collecting seeds for the future: The knowledge you glean now can set the tone for the next lunar cycle. What have you learned? What can you take with you? What is blocking you, and what should you begin to let go of? Now is the time to examine the experiences and psychic insights brought by the full moon.

Since you're still in the brighter half, you may yet feel empowered to cast more lunar magick. This moon is nicknamed the disseminating moon, and to disseminate is to spread widely—so focus your magick to spread blessings and knowledge. This is an echo of the partnership themes of the waxing gibbous moon: Share and help others in the spirit of gratitude.

As the moon pulls back from her full power in this phase, you may feel the call to pull back as well. Work in tandem with the energy of the moon. Relax and regroup your energy after the excitement of the full moon and the push of the waxing phase. Cleanse and begin to release.

Last Quarter Moon

Overarching themes: Surrender, Forgiveness, Letting Go, Balance, Crossroads

When the moon has waned to a half circle, it is the last quarter moon. Just like the first quarter's, the last quarter moon's light is in balance, half bright and half dark, for about a day. This time, however, the moon is receding into the darker part of her cycle. At this halfway point, we, too, are moving from one energy to the next, and alongside that movement comes a sense of looming finality. This phase bridges the gap from light into dark, and soon the moon's light will be overcome by darkness.

The waning gibbous was a time to reflect on the forthcoming decline of the moon's light. In that lighter part of the phase, you could still feel the lingering of the moon's luminous strength. Perhaps you gleaned insight and sought any last manifestations or blessings. At the last quarter, another balance between dark and light, you are at a tipping point, about to embrace surrender and fully let go. The waning phase's themes of release begin to sink in, and you now have to make a decision about what to let go and what to keep holding. Like a caterpillar casting a cocoon, you are called to turn inward to matters of the spirit and metamorphose toward new energy.

Like the first quarter moon, the last quarter brings a square, a right angle between the sun and the moon. Tension might be present, mainly in the internal and spiritual realms. Analyze any internal conflicts or revelations that arise for insight as to what it is *really* time to let go. The last quarter moon will help you let go of anything you have been holding on to. Use this tipping point to reveal stuck energy that has hung around and blocked you. With this insight, you can cast spells to eliminate bad habits, nip repeating patterns in the bud, vanquish critical self-talk, and more.

Waning Crescent

Overarching themes: Banishing, Endings, Spirituality, Peace, Psychic Senses

Once the moon has slipped past half illumination, we have reached the waning crescent phase of the cycle. Also called the balsamic moon, the moon is more in darkness than in light and will continue to decrease, a thin crescent slowly vanishing in the sky. This is the last official phase of the lunar cycle before it begins anew.

The waning crescent is associated with letting go, banishing, and making peace. While this is a time of decrease, it is also packed with powerful healing, allowing us to reconnect with matters of the spirit. The nickname "balsamic" hails from the word "balsam," used to refer to a healing or restorative substance (the word "balm" is a close relative), and also to resin burned as incense in spiritual, religious, and magickal ceremonies. Healing and restoration match the themes of this time: soothing, repair, and a return to spiritual matters.

Darkness overcomes the cycle, returning us to the world of mystery and shadow. This is a time of endings and surrendering to the divine and the inevitable cycles of the moon—and of life. The theme of death is effervescent in the air, but a sense of peace accompanies it. You might be able to analyze your ego and repeating patterns at this time. This time is mystical in nature, and the veil between worlds can feel thinner, marking a particularly advantageous time to connect to spirits, ghosts, and ancestors, and to develop mediumship skills or related psychic senses.

Use this time to surrender, to connect to the psychic realm, to heal, or to clean house so that you may be ready for the divine alignment of the new moon. If you have low energy at this time, focus on rest and letting go. You are on your way toward a new journey; reflect on what remains to be resolved, diminished, healed, let go of, ended, changed, or transformed.

Dark Moon

Overarching themes: Mystery, Limbo, Transformation, Shadow Work, Banishment

Over time, language and terminology can change and hold multiple meanings in various disciplines. The dark moon is one such example in modern witchcraft. When witches use the term "dark moon," it can mean many things. First, it can be a name synonymous and interchangeable with "new moon." Second, some witches refer to the entire 3-day period of the moon's disappearance from the sky as the dark moon, using the term "new moon" for the first glimmer of the waxing crescent. Still, others use the term "dark moon" to refer to the period of darkness at the very end of the waning crescent, when we cannot see the moon but it hasn't quite hit the 0-degree alignment with the sun (the new moon)—a time when the moon is not visible in the sky, but isn't yet growing toward something new.

No one way is right or wrong. In this book, "dark moon" refers to the very end of the waning phase, right before the new moon aligns with the sun. On a modern calendar, it's easy to see when the new moon will occur (and thereby determine the dark moon a day before) so we can tune into the powerful astrological alignment of the new moon.

Regardless of what definition or terminology they use, many witches acknowledge a distinct energy they refer to as the dark moon—a time of profound shadow work and inner alchemy. It is tucked under the wing of the waning crescent, an extra phase hidden among the traditional eight. The energy is that of limbo—the time in between the moon's death and her rebirth. Here, energy transforms and banishing is at its most powerful. It's a space between worlds, where witches may access mysteries and the unknown.

If you have anything that really needs to be nipped in the bud, this is the time to do it. The dark moon is also a key time for what is often called shadow work: facing your inner shadow—your fears, insecurities, ego, and the parts of yourself that are repressed and hidden but, nonetheless, unconsciously impact you. In the hands of a lunar witch, anything can be transformed at this time.

USING THE MOON PHASES IN MAGICK

Now that you have learned about the phases of the moon and their spiritual and energetic potential, you are ready to integrate them into your magick. You can cast spells, bolster a single desire through each and every phase with meditations, perform card readings at optimal times, or cast supporting spells to aid your goals. Or you can choose to cast unique spells for every single lunar phase to fill your month with moon magick. You can also use the moon phases to discern which day will be most beneficial for a specific spell you wish to cast, propelling your magickal results to new heights. Or simply use the ebb and flow of the moon's cycle to reflect on life themes and live in harmony with her magick. Connect to the energy of these phases for transformation in your personal life, your healing, and your manifestation.

But more information about the moon phases awaits you. As the moon dances with the sun across the cosmos, sometimes the alignment is so perfect that you can experience a luminescent supermoon or an eclipse.

SPECIAL LUNAR OCCASIONS

In ancient times, eclipses were surrounded by mystery, fear, and chaos. Some ancient astrologers could predict them, and they were seen as important harbingers or omens, especially for kingships and empires. Many myths surrounded these lunar occasions: in Norse mythology, a giant wolf created by the trickster deity Loki was said to have swallowed the sun; the ancient Greeks thought an eclipse heralded the anger of the gods, foretelling a time of destruction. When the moon turned bloodred at the lunar eclipse, it often brought fear and worry. The Inca believed the color came from a bloodthirsty jaguar attacking the moon, turning it red with blood, and would shake their spears to deter the predator from attacking earth. Many cultures took up activities to defend the sun or moon against being attacked or swallowed up.

Today, our ever-expanding knowledge of the universe can explain the occurrence of special lunar events such as solar and lunar eclipses, as well as blue moons, black moons, and supermoons. Despite full understanding of why these events happen, the magick and wonder of these occasions remains. Uncover the magickal potential of these special lunar alignments and how to use them in your moon magick.

Eclipses
Sometimes the alignment of the new or full moon is such that the moon blocks our view of the sun, or the earth casts a shadow across the moon,

changing our view of its shape or color. These are called eclipses, and they're often known as times of energetic shake-ups, causing intense life changes—spiritual jolts that may put you back on your life path or guide you to a new one. Solar and lunar eclipses often occur in pairs, and together they create a period of intense energy, often referred to as "eclipse season," that can emphasize certain life themes.

It's understandable that eclipses can cause such shake-ups, because they are the meeting of the two most definitive celestial bodies in our existence on earth: the sun and the moon. In astrology, the sun represents identity—our conscious awareness or ego, creative life force, unique individuality, and how we express our life's purpose. The moon resonates with the realm of feeling—our intuition, emotions, subconscious, and soul. Depending on your astrological birth chart (calculated from the moment you were born), some eclipses may influence you more than others—some might be more tumultuous, some empowering; one might whiz on by like a smooth breeze, while another may create a metaphorical tornado around you.

Furthermore, every eclipse occurs in a certain astrological sign. In addition, there is a 6-month period between a new moon in any given sign to a full moon in the same sign (or vice versa). This means we can see the reverberations of an eclipse's impact for 6 months and beyond—in some cases, even 18 years later when another eclipse might occur in the same position! Understanding the sign an eclipse will occur in can help us prepare for and understand its energetic significance. As with any celestial alignment, awareness can help us be prepared and perhaps even turn the ebb and flow of energy into opportunities, healing, and new beginnings.

To Do or Not to Do Eclipse Magick?

When it comes to eclipses, magick can be tricky. Some practitioners caution against casting eclipse magick because the energy is considered wild and unpredictable. Others find it powerful. The decision can also depend on how you define "magick"—for example, eclipses may be favorable times to work on healing, reflection, and meditation. Ultimately, it rests on how you feel!

As always, you can tailor your approach to suit your needs. For some, a given eclipse can cause a lot of turmoil. You might find new obstacles in your path that make the energy unpredictable. In such cases, it may be best to reflect, release, and focus on new paths, avoiding magickally stirring the cauldron of the cosmos at a time when energy can run amuck. Other practitioners feel the time is extra powerful. A given eclipse may be a welcome time of supercharged power. Perhaps the themes revealed to you, you are ready to embrace. You might consider doing some eclipse magick to tune into the power at hand and embrace it in the next phase of your life.

In general, though, or when in doubt, eclipses are opportune moments for meditations and healing rituals and cosmic soul alignment. Cleanse your energy, soak in a healing bath, read the cards. Tune into your soul and spirit, and trust your intuition and how you are feeling. In the long run, eclipses are often healing in nature. They offer an opportunity to return to your soul's journey, guiding you (sometimes not so gently) on to better routes and destinations.

Solar Eclipses

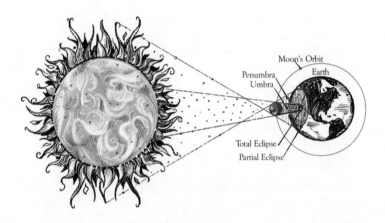

While named "solar" eclipses, these occurrences are still very relevant to witches practicing moon magick. Solar eclipses occur when the moon comes between the earth and the sun, blocking out part of the sun from earth's perspective. Solar eclipses only occur during new moons, and they can happen between two and five times a year, usually closer to every 6 months. Since the passage of the moon is relatively fast, a solar eclipse only lasts a few minutes or even just a few seconds. A solar eclipse is typically paired with a lunar eclipse during the full moon preceding or following it, and sometimes even both!

To see a solar eclipse, you must be somewhere in the area where the moon will cast a shadow when it moves in front of the sun. Because the moon's shadow is small compared to the size of the earth, each solar eclipse is only visible in specific parts of the world. But, visible or not, an eclipse's energy can be felt across the globe. There are three types of solar eclipses:

- **Partial:** The moon passes partially in front of the sun, leaving a crescent of the sun visible.

- **Annular:** The moon passes directly in front of the sun, but it's at its apogee (the furthest point from earth in its elliptical orbit), so the moon is too far from the earth to completely block our view. It leaves a ring of the sun visible, a halo of light.

- **Total:** The moon completely covers the sun for a matter of moments.

A solar eclipse often sets us on a new path, closing one door and opening another. Some call a solar eclipse a supercharged new moon, a time of amplified new beginnings. This can mean all that comes with closing one chapter: closure, insight, realizations—plus everything that comes with opening a new book entirely: new directions, big decisions, changes, or realignment with one's life path.

Since solar eclipses tend to bring about a rebirth of sorts, they are great for embarking on significant new life pathways (which eclipse seasons often reveal). If you decide solar eclipse magick is the path for you, set intentions. Craft a vision board. Align to the cosmic energy via guided meditations, crystal healing, singing bowls, or another favorite modality. Prepare by brainstorming, dreaming, and creating an action plan. Release the old just before the moment of alignment, and set forth on a new path. It is time to step through the celestial portal and create anew.

Lunar Eclipses

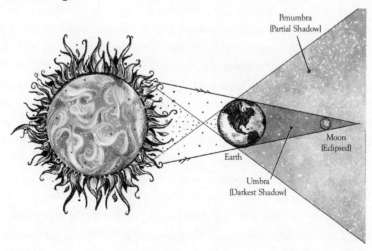

A lunar eclipse occurs when the earth comes between the sun and the moon in such a way that it casts its shadow upon the normally bright and vibrant full moon. The shadow usually makes the moon appear a foreboding red color. Visible only from the night side of the earth, lunar eclipses happen, on average, three times a year. During a lunar eclipse, two different parts of the earth's shadow (called the penumbra and the umbra) may be cast across the moon, and this is what differentiates the three types of lunar eclipses:

- **Penumbral:** The full moon passes through the penumbra, or outer shadow, of the earth. This can be very subtle, dimming or discoloring the moon only slightly.

- **Partial:** A portion of the full moon passes through the umbra, the darker, central part of earth's shadow. Only part of the moon changes color, appearing red, orange, brown, or even yellow.

- **Total:** The full moon fully passes through the umbra, and the shadow discolors the entire moon to a dark, burgundy red. Of course, in entering and leaving the umbra, the moon also has to pass through the penumbra, so a total lunar eclipse is the longest event of the three, lasting as long as 2.5 hours.

As with solar eclipses, some witches believe lunar eclipses are not the best time for magick due to the associated unpredictability or erratic energy. Others feel a lunar eclipse can present an immensely powerful time to cast life-changing, powerful manifestation magick. If a solar eclipse is a supercharged new moon, then a lunar eclipse is a supercharged full moon. The heightened emotions of the full moon can be doubly so. Conflicts and disproportional outbursts might occur as a result.

Since the full moon is a time of culmination, the magnified energy of a lunar eclipse can bring dramatic ends. Old wounds and hidden patterns are revealed, creating a sense of vulnerability but also offering profound healing. A lunar eclipse, with its pull on your senses, can be a good time to check in and see how you feel about the direction of your life. Your psychic abilities and sense of connection with the spirit realm may also be magnified at this time. Just as the clash of energy at the full moon can offer the opportunity for insight and balance between forces, so can the lunar eclipse be a powerful opportunity for personal growth and transformation.

Supermoons and Micromoons

Eclipses are not the only unique phenomenon humans experience as a result of lunar and solar alignments. Because the moon's orbit around earth is elliptical (oval-shaped) and the earth is not perfectly centered within it, some points in the moon's orbit are closer to the earth, and some are farther away. Essentially, the moon's distance from earth depends on where it is in its orbit. The point in the moon's orbit that's closest to earth is called its perigee. The point farthest from earth is its apogee.

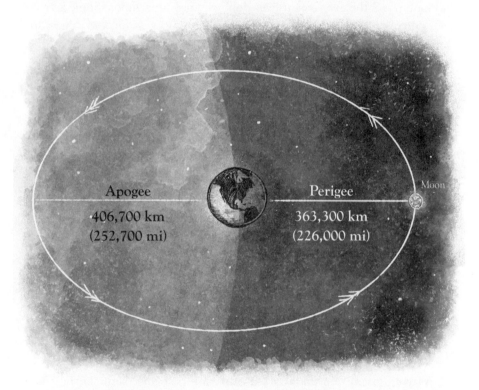

Apogee
406,700 km
(252,700 mi)

Perigee
363,300 km
(226,000 mi)

Moon

When the moon hits the part of its orbit closest to earth, it's called a perigee moon, or a supermoon. When a moon is at its apogee (its farthest point from earth), it's an apogee moon or micromoon. Micromoons are not usually a significant factor in witchcraft—but see if you notice an energetic difference during one!

Supermoons

Three to four times each year, a full moon perfectly lines up to occur at the moon's perigee. A full moon at its perigee—often called a supermoon—can appear 14 percent bigger than at its apogee. While this size difference may be hard to perceive with the naked eye, the supermoon also appears a significant 30 percent brighter than the micromoon. Since the moon is closer to earth, its gravitational pull is also stronger and can cause higher-than-usual tides. When it happens at a new moon, some astrologers might call it a super new moon and the moon's energy might feel more magnified around new moon themes at that time.

It is well known that many witches and moon lovers get excited about a full moon, and the excitement feels doubled for a supermoon. Some astrologers do not place any specific significance on this occasion, and others do. Tune into your senses and discern its importance for yourself. With the moon at its closest point to earth and at its full phase, the energy may feel electric—more emotional and powerful—and thus further empower your work for moon manifestation. The sense of celestial gravity may be magnified like the lunar light is magnified. Since the moon reaches its apogee and perigee at least once per cycle, if you feel a pull at the supermoon, consider noting when the moon reaches its perigee during other phases, and begin to explore how it impacts your feelings, psychic senses, and magick.

Blue Moons and Black Moons

Despite the term "moon" being a close relative of "month," the average lunar cycle lasts a tad shorter than a month by our calendar: about 29.5 days. As a result, every once in a while a month has more than one new or full moon. A repeated full moon is called a blue moon, whereas an extra new moon may be called a black moon. The excitement of an extra moon certainly adds a feeling of luck. But there are actually a few different meanings for these "extra" moons. They have three main usages:

- **Astronomical:** Normally a season (winter, spring, summer, fall) has three full or new moons. When there are four, the third full or new moon is called the astronomical blue or black moon. This may have significance for farming practices, since the combined meaning of the season and the moons has agricultural significance (as will be explored in Chapter 3). Such an event occurs once every 2–3 years.

- **Calendrical:** A calendrical blue or black moon is the second full or new moon in a calendar month. This definition originated from a mistake in the 1946 edition of *Sky & Telescope* magazine and has become popularized in modern times. Because the moon's cycle is 29.5 days and most months are 30 or 31 days long, calendrical blue and black moons each happen every 2–3 years.

- **Astrological:** These blue and black moons are not formally recognized, but they're similar in nature to their calendrical and astronomical siblings. An astrological blue or black moon is the second full or new moon in a zodiacal season. In a typical zodiacal season, such as Taurus season, there is one new moon in Taurus and one full moon in Scorpio (see Chapter 4 to understand more about moon signs). But if, for example, the new or full moon straddles the start of Taurus season, the season can contain a complete lunar cycle. In this example, there would be either two full moons in Scorpio during Taurus season, or two Taurus new moons. The new or full moon straddling the end of Taurus would be a black or blue moon.

Blue and Black Moons in Magick

To some, the magickal weight of these moons may not be significant, since the lunar cycle always remains the same. But there *are* alternative ways of looking at it. A blue or black moon can inspire a sense of second chances, emphasized or repeated energy, wonder, magick, or good luck. When seen as times of repeated energy, blue and black moons can be used to amplify intentions, perhaps ones previously set. A blue or black moon can be a second chance for an intention that didn't work out in the past— an energetic redo. As with all lunar practices, blue moon and black moon magick can be conducted in a few different ways. Each type of blue or black moon offers the chance to amplify magick:

- The calendrical blue or black moon relies on the weaving of the lunar cycles into our human-made calendar, so consider using such energy for self-made and manufactured success.

- An astrological blue or black moon (the second new or full moon occurring in the same sign) offers the chance to revisit that moon's energy.

- An extra lunation cycle in a season can mean more time to work with the combined seasonal and moon energy.

- Some consider the blue moon to be especially powerful, a special alignment for luck and success, power and prophecy.

- With many of our lives being planned around months (such as with business or personal monthly goals), a calendrical blue moon may emphasize an illuminated, energetically supercharged month.

- If you are a new moon manifester, the black moon may be an extra-powered opportunity for planning for the future. Since a new moon is a great time to align to new energy, the black moon can help you align to some powerful and long-lasting dreams.

- Some practitioners also believe that the black moon offers a time focused on truth—realizing personal truth, confronting hidden themes, or gaining insight into mysteries in general. If you feel the same, use black moon time to journey inward.

Regardless of which type it is, the blue or black moon is the result of lunar and solar cycles weaving together. In the case of a blue or black moon, there is certainly a sense of the unexpected. Your perceptions and preferences are key to deciding how to use these moons.

Chapter 3

SEASONAL MOON SPELLCASTING

The moon has a direct influence on the experience of the seasons on earth, and understanding the flow of the seasonal energy and how that intertwines with your moon magick can add another dimension to your spells. Moon magick is interwoven with the flow of the seasons. And, like lunar cycles, seasonal cycles give us times to grow, celebrate, release, and reflect.

In this chapter, you will learn about the turn of the seasons (celebrated as the Wheel of the Year) and the seasonal moons that fall within them. Armed with this knowledge, you will understand the interrelated nature of lunar and green (earth-based) magick. The natural merging of the earth's and moon's cycles will energetically empower your spells in tune with the universe and your place in the cosmos.

WHEEL OF THE YEAR

Many modern witches and pagans use the Wheel of the Year to celebrate the flow of the seasons and their magick. The Wheel of the Year is a cycle of holidays and festivities that celebrate the natural solstices, equinoxes, and cross-quarter days (halfway points between the solstices and equinoxes). This cycle helps us attend to the transition of seasonal energy. Like each lunar cycle, the Wheel of the Year highlights the ebb and flow of light and darkness. Throughout the year, the time in a day remains 24 hours, but the minutes that belong to daylight and those that belong to night vary. The degree and type of change depend on location—the closer to the earth's poles we are, the greater the seasonal change in light, and the Northern and Southern hemispheres experience opposite seasons.

Understanding the flow of the seasons and the markers on the Wheel of the Year can add another dimension to your moon magick. As you learn about the days the Wheel of the Year celebrates, you'll uncover the ways they are similar to the phases of the moon. When you are in tune with the cycles of the moon and of life, you can accomplish so much with your magick.

Winter Solstice

Northern Hemisphere: December 20, 21, 22, or 23; Southern Hemisphere: June 20, 21, or 22

The winter solstice is the first official day of winter and marks the longest night of the year. On this day, often called Yule in the Wheel of the Year, the nighttime hours reach their peak length, overpowering the hours of daylight and bringing introspection within the dark. Many people observe religious and secular holidays around this time, giving gratitude for each other in the midst of winter's scarcity and celebrating the strength that is found in connection.

Most of life is in hibernation or resting during the winter solstice. Trees are leafless, and their energy is withdrawn deep within, preparing for spring's time of regrowth and new life. This seasonal energy invites witches to rest, reflect, and prepare their energy. Marking the start of the winter season, the moons in this time frame highlight themes of strength, spirituality, reflection, healing, and rebirth.

In the long night, the moon's light becomes even more pronounced and impactful, providing the perfect energy to work alchemical and transformational magick, or to nourish and rest your lunar soul. The themes of the winter solstice parallel those of the new moon, as astrologer Steven Forrest establishes in *The Book of the Moon*: In this period of darkness, there is rebirth and renewal, and the light will begin to regrow. Intentions will also grow from this day forth to the summer solstice, just as they do during the moon's waxing phase. In the winter lunar cycles, create a vision of what you might like to summon with the growth of light; lay the energetic and magickal foundations that will soon make those possibilities tangible.

Imbolc

Northern Hemisphere: February 1 or 2; Southern Hemisphere: August 1 or 2

Imbolc is a cross-quarter day: a celebration halfway between winter and spring, halfway between the winter solstice and the spring equinox. Also called Candlemas, Imbolc is a light festival, traditionally celebrated by lighting candles to guide spring back. And the lighting of candles certainly resonates with the steady growth of daylight noticeable at this time. Like the waxing crescent phase, Imbolc is the first emergence of light after a period of darkness, and like the candles lit at this time, it restores inner light and hope. Energy is beginning to stir and awaken toward purification and preparation. Moon cycles still carry themes of winter, but they also bear spiritual renewal and the beginnings of eagerness and new dreams.

In the spirit of Candlemas, you may feel called to work with candles and themes of light in your moon magick. Lemon is a great ingredient for Imbolc moon magick, as it is associated with the moon, purification, and restoring hope and joy. Use lemon in homemade cleansing washes, renewing dishes and drinks, and spells related to hope. Connect to new dreams and aspirations with a childlike sense of excitement and possibility.

Spring Equinox

Northern Hemisphere: March 19, 20, or 21; Southern Hemisphere: September 22, 23, or 24

The spring (or vernal) equinox is the first official day of spring. It's one of 2 days of the year that hold a balance (as equal as possible) between daylight and nighttime hours. This heralds the growth of spring and warrants reflection on the balance between dark and light. From this day forth, the daylight hours will grow until their peak at the summer solstice.

The spring equinox is a transition into a phase of nurturing, excitement, and the promise of abundance. While the energy of the earth was withdrawn in winter, it is flowering now. Blossoms, birds, bees, and butterflies will soon dance in the dewy spring air, and the earth is fertile with potential. It's a time of rebirth and renewal, bringing blessings of both spiritual and physical growth and vitality. In tandem, the spring moons herald beauty, youth, new beginnings, and fertility. The beginnings of romance and love seep in too.

Like the first quarter moon, this day holds a close-to-equal balance of dark and light, and it marks a transition into the light half of a cycle, where abundance and growth will soon be in sight and favor cocreation and partnership. There is balance between the calls of the material or waking reality and the realm of spirit. As we step into the equinox and the season of spring, it's time for energy, vitality, and decision-making. Spells that use eggs, flowers, and seeds are fitting choices to bless your lunar efforts now. Anything can blossom with the blessing of the spring moons.

Beltane

Northern Hemisphere: May 1 or 2; Southern Hemisphere: Nov 1 or 2

With spring in full force and heading toward the heat of summer, the cross-quarter day called Beltane celebrates the passion and lusciousness of life. A fire festival of sensuality, love, lust, fertility, and well-being, it is a time of cocreation; energies merge to create newness and summon abundance. And, just as the rest of nature buzzes with energy now, fae folk are also thought to be more active. Go outside and celebrate the luscious, verdant life around you. Enjoy luxurious earthly delights and invigorate your wild side! This is a time to engage the senses and explore the sensuality of living. The moons of this time carry themes of spring, but with extra emphasis on beauty and love.

This day mirrors the waxing gibbous moon: Past the equinox, daylight has surpassed night, and the energy favors partnership. As during the waxing moon, combining forces now can result in something bigger and better than originally imagined. At Beltane, this idea can take a more sensuous edge. In the spirit of partnership, connect with nature allies, and use fresh ingredients in your spells, or cast magick for love or for cocreating with the universe. With the growth of spring, and with the light continuing to grow toward the next solstice, the time is right to bless endeavors.

Summer Solstice

Northern Hemisphere: June 20, 21, or 22; Southern Hemisphere: December 20, 21, 22, or 23

The summer solstice is the longest day of the year and heralds the start of summer. The Wheel of the Year calls the celebration of this day Litha. The hours of daylight are at their peak. The sun is in its full power and at its highest point in the sky, sharing its radiance and the blessings of strength, abundance, and manifestation. Bringer of optimism and positivity, the summer solstice marks a time of play and love. With the sun at the height of its cycle and the full moon reflecting its light, myriad efforts can be accomplished during summer lunation cycles.

The summer solstice matches many themes of the full moon: It's a time of radiance, celebration, culmination, power, and manifestation. Like the Strong Sun Moon that may shine around this time, the sun radiates in its full power, empowering efforts of manifestation. But from this day forth, the daylight will wane ever so slowly, until a sense of balance is again reached at the autumn equinox. The energy of the year now begins to turn toward themes of culmination, with the harvest cycle within sight.

Lammas

Northern Hemisphere: August 1 or 2; Southern Hemisphere: February 1 or 2

Lammas celebrates the first harvest. A cross-quarter day also called Lughnasadh, Lammas marks the beginning of harvest season and celebrates the halfway point between summer and fall. The harvest moons begin to rise now, as seeds and intentions sown earlier are in the first wave of harvest. The beginning of bounty is celebrated, offerings are given to ensure plenty in the remaining harvests, and thanks are shown for the blessings to come. A celebration of the grain harvest, Lughnasadh brings reflection on how grains of the past sustain the future. This is just the start of harvest season, however. What still remains to harvest? What goals do you still want to reach?

As during the waning gibbous moon, at Lammas the prominence of light has started to diminish, and energy turns toward waning and gratitude. Results of efforts may still come, and this potential inspires the drive to work hard, but there is a sense of an end nearing. Now, during the first of three harvests, a full moon has extra significance, providing light long into the night for those working to collect the bounty of the earth. Connect to the land and ancestors. Offerings given in gratitude now can bolster spirits to aid your remaining moon manifestation efforts. Use the abundance of the harvest grains by casting spells that work with grain, or even by baking.

Autumn Equinox

Northern Hemisphere: September 22, 23, or 24; Southern Hemisphere: March 19, 20, or 21

The autumn equinox marks the transition from summer to fall and, with it, the arrival of the darker part of the year, when loss, letting go, death, and transformation take hold. The celebration of this day among modern pagans and witches is often called Mabon. The second of three harvests, the equinox is still a time of thanks (many witches make corn dolls in the spirit of gratitude), but the energy turns toward decline. Like the spring equinox, this day brings a close balance between daylight and nighttime hours. But from this day forward, the darker hours overtake the hours of light. It is a time to turn inward and think about themes of balance and darkness. Reflect on which spiritual and physical aspects of life need to be brought to equilibrium before the final harvest.

With its themes of balance, the autumn equinox mirrors the last quarter moon phase. Like the half-lit last quarter moon, Mabon brings a temporary balance between light and dark before we descend into a darker part of the cycle. The myth of Persephone returning to the underworld at this time reflects our own transition into darkness, for at this time themes of loss and surrender start to arise as we journey inward for the colder months of the year. Spells and practices related to introspection, spiritual cleansing, and banishing do well now.

Samhain

Northern Hemisphere: October 31; Southern Hemisphere: April 30 or May 1 or 2

Samhain is an especially important day for many witches. Like Imbolc, Beltane, and Lammas, it's a cross-quarter day, halfway between two seasons. It marks the third and final harvest celebration, a time when the nighttime hours are visibly longer than the daylight. Samhain is a time of bounty, but also of loss. Ancestors and lost loved ones are remembered and honored, and in perfect tandem, the full moon that falls on or near this day is sometimes nicknamed the Blood or Hunters Moon. What better lunar cycle to connect to themes of sacrifice and loss?

Like the waning crescent phase of the lunar cycle and the dark moon, Samhain brings themes of darkness: endings, banishment, and letting go. It's the end of a cycle; we fully wane into the dark. Our perception of the "veils" between worlds feels thin—psychic information that pertains to mediumship and fortune-telling is easier to access within our consciousness with death all around, and so are connections with the dead, ghosts, and witchcraft spirit guides. The moon around this time will most certainly highlight your intuition. Many incorporate ancestors or bones into their magick or give offerings to their ancestors' memory. Often called the witch's new year, Samhain is a time to release what no longer serves you.

MONTHLY MOONS

Each month's lunar cycle has a special name and meaning. Drawing on seasonal activities, events, themes, and animals, these names mark the passage of time with the lunar cycles through the seasons. Many of the monthly moon names commonly referenced today hail from the Algonquian tribes in North America, which colonial American farmers adopted and adapted into their own calendar system. Some names hail from other Indigenous tribes, and some may have Celtic or English origins. Various other cultures have also developed unique nicknames to reflect each moon's seasonal significance. Oftentimes, these names apply to the whole lunation cycle, not just the full moon.

Connecting with the monthly moons can help you tap into seasonal magick and live in tune with the moon and with nature. Combined with seasonal themes, energy, and happenings, each monthly full moon holds power and meaning that can help you cast prolific moon magick. Perhaps in developing your own connection to the moon, you'll also be inspired to make your own secret monthly moon names.

Following, you will find a summary of themes for each month, capturing the seasonal significance of each lunation, along with a list of moon names commonly referenced today. Because these names have roots in various cultures, it's important to thoughtfully consider any names you use and to honor the names' history and your place within it. Be sure to show gratitude and respect for indigenous peoples of the land where you live and their practices. Try researching names local to your land, making sure to respect Native practices—after all, if you don't live in an area with snow, Snow Moon may not be an apt lunar name!

In the list of themes and names that follows, you might notice some names repeated in multiple months. That's because lunar names are generally based on seasonal themes and the lunar cycle doesn't perfectly align with the January-through-December calendar. For example, a full moon could happen at the very start of the month one year and at the end of the month in another. Seasonal themes could be very different at those two times. A perfect example of this is the Harvest Moon. This name is given to the full moon closest to the autumn equinox, so the Harvest Moon could arrive in either September or October in the Northern Hemisphere.

Another result of the months and the moon cycles' imperfect alignment is that full moon names can vary year to year. Every so often, a year has 13 moons instead of 12. In this book, the lunation cycles and moon names are organized by common month times for each hemisphere (since they experience opposite seasons).

January in the Northern Hemisphere, July in the Southern Hemisphere

Full Moon Is Called: Wolf, Cold, Ice, Winter, or Old Moon

The "Wolf" name of this moon hails from the howling that pierces the silent winter nights this time of year. Whether wolves' calls are social, for hunting, or due to traveling closer to towns in search of food, this moon's themes hold the same spirit as the sound: They emphasize survival, strength, and confronting scarcity. The Wolf Moon can also inspire us to call to our own packs, as many of us lean on one another for support and comfort in the cold, or exchange gifts of appreciation following the winter solstice. Thoughts of ancestors and the past and feelings of gratitude rise to the surface in kind.

Also often called the Cold Moon, Ice Moon, Winter Moon, or Old Moon, this lunar cycle comes amidst the onset of winter, a time of reflection. With the promise that daylight will once again grow, this lunar cycle can also inspire a sense of new beginnings, turning of corners, and healing—a time to sow metaphorical seeds. This cycle reminds us that the death of winter is vital for new life to grow.

Summon strength, endurance, and protection now. Cast money spells to endure through the winter months and inspire luck in the new year, to grow with the eventual return of longer daylight hours. Work magick around your own "wolf pack": your chosen family, home or shelter, ancestors, or spirit guides and allies. Use the lunar light to give thanks and heed guidance from your guides on the other side, who can be your source of strength and help you navigate this season of scarcity as you turn inward for spiritual and magickal growth.

February in the Northern Hemisphere, August in the Southern Hemisphere

Full Moon Is Called: Snow, Wolf, Ice, Storm, Hunger, Wild, Chaste, or Quickening Moon

The thick snowfall that this lunation cycle brings to colder climates inspires the nickname Snow Moon. We are still in the midst of winter, so the Wolf Moon's themes of winter scarcity continue, now accented by storms. In warmer zones, Storm Moon, Hunger Moon, and Wild Moon might better reflect a sense of stormy weather before the rebirth of spring, while the nickname Chaste Moon reflects a sense of purity and innocence.

Tucked inside warm abodes, with this moon we often experience a focus on home activities as our energy is still turned inward, or to efforts in the astral realm, or to banishing and protection. At the same time, this month also brings the celebration of Imbolc, a light festival calling forth the coming of spring. It's a time of purification and renewal of hope. Slowly, the daylight hours' increase is becoming more and more apparent as we head toward the spring equinox. New beginnings and renewal are just around the corner, and with them a time to cleanse and prepare.

You may sense that the theme of this moon varies depending on whether it occurs at the start or the end of the month. Refresh your energy and focus on magickal efforts around both the home and the spirit. Think about what you wish to rebirth, renew, and refresh in your life, and do the corresponding magickal work (whether banishing, cleansing, or healing) to prepare. Use the remnants of wintertime energy to do any leftover internal work, and begin to reconnect to childlike energy to nurture your soul and refresh your sense of possibility. You are ready for renewal.

March in the Northern Hemisphere, September in the Southern Hemisphere

Full Moon Is Called: Worm, Chaste, Storm, Windy, Death, Sugar, Sap, Raven, Crow, or Seed Moon

Named for the worm trails that appear as winter thaws away, or for the larvae peeking out of their winter tree-bark abodes, the Worm Moon brings nature's energy wiggling back to the surface. The lunar names Storm Moon, Windy Moon, and Death Moon hint at shaking the last remnants of winter weather, while Seed Moon, Sugar Moon, and Sap Moon indicate a time to plant and the sweet energy of spring.

The Worm Moon could be the last full moon of winter or the first of spring, depending on when in the month it arrives. Regardless, this lunation brings the promise of spring: thawing ground, sprouting bulbs, and the reemergence of life. Rejuvenation, fertility and regrowth, and coming prosperity anoint the spring breezes. Reconnect with your sense of imagination in preparation for a fresh, boundless start at the turn of the season.

Magickally, this is a time to refresh your mindset and reconnect to your inner child, whether for vitality, a limitless perspective, or renewed sense of joy, possibility, and hope. Creativity and excitement are boundless; for a better chance at achieving success and prosperity in the long run, give them direction. Alongside the melting of the snow or the fresh spring rains, water cleansings can help renew your spirit. Collect dew after the full moon to add to magickal baths and enchanting lunar mists. With rebirth and restoration in the air, efforts toward health are especially blessed. Heed the name of the Seed Moon, and plant and prepare the seeds of your magickal goals to germinate toward boundless growth.

April in the Northern Hemisphere, October in the Southern Hemisphere

Full Moon Is Called: Pink, Seed, Egg, Hare, Windy, Planter's, Meadow, Fish, Waking, or Flower Moon

Like the eager, early-rising pink wildflower blossoms of the wild ground phlox for which it is named, the Pink Moon brings the full swing of spring. Following the change of seasons last month, spring—and all of nature with it—is fully awake now. Alternative names Egg Moon and Hare Moon highlight the birds-and-the-bees fertility of this time, promising multipliable abundance for whatever you sow with this moon. The energy is bright and excitable.

Welcoming the onset of spring, this moon cycle is great for new beginnings. It bridges the energy between spirituality and growth in the physical realm too. Health, happiness, and spiritual attunement are favorable and—as with all springtime moons—themes of love, youth, and abundance also arise.

Lunar spells for excitement, fertility, health, renewal, and new beginnings are all great choices for the Pink Moon. This springtime moon favors efforts toward love and beauty. Cast spells for glamour, youth, attraction, and vitality. Perhaps a blush-making spell can turn your energy (and cheeks) pink like the moon's namesake. If the saying "April showers bring May flowers" rings true for your area, cast water blessings, washes, and beauty baths blessed by moon water or rainwater. All of life is in growth now. Celebrate this lunar cycle by noticing what's growing—whether it be edible violets, other flowers, or another seasonal symbol, the egg—and including this abundance in your meals and in your magickal workings.

May in the Northern Hemisphere, November in the Southern Hemisphere

Full Moon Is Called: Flower, Faery, Goddess, Hare, Milk, or Dyad Moon

The May moon is usually named the Flower Moon, which is apt for the bountiful plethora of blossoms that this lunar cycle brings. Other names— Faery Moon, Goddess Moon, and Dyad Moon—highlight the liveliness of nature and of fae spirits at this time. Fittingly, the start of this month also marks Beltane—a time of zest and sensuality, and also a time when the fae are thought to be more active. Creative energy and abundance are plentiful. The fertility of nature is evident all around, providing fruitful soil with which to nurture your lunar intentions. The air is filled with enchantment and with the enticing aroma of the spring blossoms that drift through the breeze. Efforts related toward love and well-being, and even toward divining psychic insight from nature (for example, by reading tea leaves) do well now. The energy is electric and filled with excitement, both in magick and in life.

In line with the name of this cycle, you might want to explore magick that includes flowers. Cast spells for love and beauty, and explore your sensual side. With earth regrowing now, connect to nature spirits or leave offerings for them under the ethereal full moon, when you can be sure they will be active. In the spirit of the nickname Milk Moon, take a milk-and-flower bath for beauty and renewal. Use this moon to bless your endeavors with creative, prosperous, or alluring energy. Partnership spells, whether for personal or romantic relationships, are also favorable.

June in the Northern Hemisphere, December in the Southern Hemisphere

Full Moon Is Called: Strawberry, Dyad, Rose, Honey, Partner, Hot, Green Corn, Strong Sun, or Mead Moon

Like the luscious red berries that ripen around June, the Strawberry Moon welcomes the happy, loving, and harmonious energies of the start of summer. This cycle is also called the Rose Moon, Mead Moon, Honey Moon, or Partner Moon; summer love and sweetening are in the air. With the hot summer sun around the corner, who can resist this energy?

Bridging the transition from lovely spring to summer, positivity and vitality are on the horizon, and all of nature is hard at work balancing rest and play—from bees busy at work in flowers to grain growing in the fields. Depending on the time of the month this moon arrives, the Strawberry Moon may be close to the summer solstice, the longest day of the year.

The themes of this lunation revolve around love and relationships in addition to the abundance and prosperity that come with summertime growth. Focus your lunar efforts on happiness, love, and success. Productive energy is accessible and will help you reap rewards in the coming harvest moons. In spirit of the Honey Moon, create and bless honey jars to sweeten your desires toward you. Use strawberries to enchant harmony and positive energy. Happiness for both yourself and your relationships are great lunar focuses, as well as spells for commitment to a relationship, fidelity to goals, or general prosperity and abundance.

July in the Northern Hemisphere, January in the Southern Hemisphere

Full Moon Is Called: Buck, Mead, Wort, Herb, Blessing, Thunder, Hay, Horn, or Summer Moon

The full July moon heralds a time of coming into personal power amidst summer. Like the deer who regrow their antlers this time of year (from which this moon gets one of its nicknames, Buck Moon), you are crowned with spiritual and physical strength and insight. Following last month's summer solstice, we are still in the blazing energy of summer, but the focus slowly transitions to spiritual matters.

Also called Wort Moon (meaning Herb Moon), this lunation cycle brings our herbal allies to full growth; they are ready to be harvested for spiritual and healing purposes. Hay is cultivated now, an important form of sustenance for animals, and summer storms bring revitalizing rains and electrifying lightning flashes, paralleling the spark and flow of our personal power and spiritual insights during this lunar cycle.

Despite the passing of the longest day of the year, summer is still in full swing, even though harvest season is around the corner. The energy is restored and relaxing. You may feel more connected to your sense of purpose and magick. Reflect on your personal goals in preparation for the harvests to come. Whether spiritual or physical, magickal efforts around strength, vitality, personal power, and goals resonate with this lunation.

Connect with the herbal allies and spirits that give this cycle the name Wort Moon as you work to harvest and dry herbs for your healing and magickal work. Craft herbal blends and teas for dreamwork, astral travel, or prophecy.

To connect to the alternative name Blessing Moon, choose this time to bless endeavors of all kinds. Try to attain insight to help you leap toward the achievements and goals that will make your spirit sing.

August in the Northern Hemisphere, February in the Southern Hemisphere

Full Moon Is Called: Barley, Corn, Grain, Sturgeon, Wort, Fruit, or Herb Moon

Often called the Barley Moon, Corn Moon, or Grain Moon, this lunation heralds the start of harvest season. It is sometimes also called the Sturgeon Moon, for the bounty of sturgeon available in the Great Lakes during this season. Either way, the theme of this lunation cycle is definitely abundance. Full moons are especially important during harvest season, providing added light and time to gather the earth's bounty. The month begins with Lammas, the start of harvest season, which bodes the waning of summer; harvest is a time to gather, share, and celebrate with friends and chosen family, and to give thanks to land spirits, ancestors, and spirit allies.

While prosperity is at hand, so is wisdom: Each piece of grain invites reflection on the sustenance of not just the body, but also the mind, spirit, and emotions. When harvesting for today's provisions, we're often also collecting the seeds of the future. The theme "You reap what you sow" can inspire us to reflect consciously on how our efforts (magickal or otherwise) of today might create the potential of tomorrow.

Since it's just the start of harvest season, there is still time to utilize the boost of seasonal moon energy to manifest results. Cast spells for plenty and prosperity, give thanks, reflect on patterns to cleanse, and name what you wish to manifest with the remaining harvest lunations. Since it's associated with a grain harvest, this moon is a lovely time to engage in kitchen witchery and explore the magickal benefits of what you ingest. Bake bread and break it to share with others—an act of offering, reconciliation, gratitude, and abundance. Spells that involve grains (oats, barley, corn), corn dolls, food, and even beer offerings and beer baths are great moon-magick choices.

September in the Northern Hemisphere,
March in the Southern Hemisphere

Full Moon Is Called: Wine, Sturgeon, Corn, Barley, Nut, or Harvest Moon

This lunation brings another key harvest, coupled with the transitional energy of the end of summer and the forthcoming fall. In the full swing of harvest season, we gather crops that give their names to this moon—nuts, barley, and corn, for example. Grapes are also harvested; hence the nickname Wine Moon. In fact, if this is the full moon closest to the autumn equinox, then it will also be called the Harvest Moon (see next entry).

Regardless of its name, this cycle continues the theme of gratitude we observed in August. However, with the turn of the seasons, our attention may turn toward the home for protection and to create a cozy environment for winter. The energy of life begins to turn inward, inviting reflection on the coming dark months and soaking up the last rays of summer. Wisdom and truth may be more accessible now, bridging dark and light.

Work spells for confidence as you call in any last big manifestation efforts for the remainder of the harvest. Magickally prepare your home for the colder months. Give gratitude for abundance. As the season turns, turn your focus inward toward spirituality and develop inner awareness. Cast spells using the ingredients the moon is named after, such as nuts or barley. If it coincides with the corn harvest, this lunation will be called the Corn Moon, a wonderful time to incorporate corn, perhaps in the form of cornmeal, corn bread, or corn husks, in your magickal workings.

Grapes, too, are great ingredients for magick this lunar cycle, as they're not only in season but also associated with the moon, abundance, prosperity, and garden harvest magick, as well as powers of the mind, such as trance work. In fact, wine has often been used to alter consciousness to commune with deities, making it an appropriate offering to show gratitude for the abundance of this time.

Part One: Understanding the Magick of the Moon and Witchcraft

September or October in the Northern Hemisphere, March or April in the Southern Hemisphere

Full Moon Is Called: Harvest Moon

Every so often, there are 13 full moons in a year. Since the Harvest Moon is the name given to the full moon closest to the autumn equinox, it has its own entry here alongside the 12 months, for 13 total moons. Because the Harvest Moon can fall in either September or October, consider the meanings of the entries before and after in tandem with this one.

The Harvest Moon is the peak of harvest season, and it's a special lunation honoring the cycles of the moon and earth. This full moon allows agricultural workers extra hours of light to harvest the abundance of the season. But whether you're a farmer, a gardener, or a witch in tune with the ebbs and flows of seasonal energy, this moon focuses on plenty and gratitude. With one final harvest left, manifestation is still possible. But now, close to the celebration of Mabon, the focus shifts to what you have sown and reaped these past lunar cycles, encouraging you to slowly tune into your inner landscape. Reflect on the balance of dark and light.

What would a Harvest Moon be without magickal celebrations to appreciate and give thanks for the bounty? Pumpkin is a seasonal favorite— it's plentiful this time of year, and very versatile. Cook up a pumpkin-related dish or stir a delicious pumpkin-spiced drink.

Be sure to share the results of the harvest with those around you. Make up a plate for friends or family, or give offerings to ancestors, land spirits, and moon deities. Cast spells for abundance well into the winter months, and consider what you are grateful for and what you still wish to manifest. Then turn inward to reflect as you head into the darker part of the year.

October in the Northern Hemisphere, April in the Southern Hemisphere

Full Moon Is Called: Hunter's, Harvest, or Blood Moon

With the turn of seasons to colder weather, animals prepare for food scarcity. One of the names of this moon hails from hunters using the light of this final harvest-season moon to track down prey to preserve meat for the winter. Since this moon and Samhain are the last of the harvests, harvest themes still apply. Whether called the Blood Moon, Hunter's Moon, or Harvest Moon, this lunation cycle focuses on sacrifice: the sacrifice of the land for the harvest; the sacrifices necessary to sustain the cycle of life; the sacrifices of those (witches and ancestors) who came before us; and our own inevitable endings. With all of life, there is a give and take. Samhain occurs around this time, and we enter the darker months of the year. It's a time of power for many witches—shadow work and personal alchemy are more tangible, divinations are cast, psychic abilities and communication with the realm of spirit feels easier.

For Hunter Moon magick, spells or rituals that focus on the cycle of life and giving gratitude for that exchange of energy are especially important. Divination, spells, and psychic rituals connecting to the dead, reflecting on lessons from the past, or using bones (such as for charm or bone casting) do well now. You can even make your own magickally empowered bloodred ink with pomegranate!

Some call Samhain the witches' new year, and the full moon near Samhain is a powerful time to focus on cleansing and banishing for personal alchemy in the new year. What do you wish to lessen in your life with the turn toward winter? Extinguish bad habits. Banish old energy and repeating life patterns that have kept you stagnant.

November in the Northern Hemisphere, May in the Southern Hemisphere

Full Moon Is Called: Mourning, Frost, White, Beaver, Hunter's, Larder, or Snow Moon

The lunation cycle following Samhain fully embraces the waning of the year and the coming of winter. The name Mourning Moon hints at the transitional energy of loss and letting go, while Frost Moon signals the onset of winter and cold weather and White Moon evokes early snow. Like the beavers preparing their winter abodes or the Indigenous tribes who set traps for them (giving this lunation cycle one of its names), you might use this time to prepare your own abode and stock up on sustenance. Themes of darkness may remain from Samhain, and that makes this lunation a good time to access the psychic realm and do divination or dreamwork. This cycle's energy is like that of each month's waning moon: Letting go and embracing the darkness allows for healing and transformation.

Following the hard work of the harvest season, this lunation cycle may provide a much-needed rest before the coming solstice. If so, focus on inward matters, such as learning, meditation, psychic development, or taking up new areas of study that catch your interest and feed your soul. If the weather of your geography keeps you at home, hearth magick and abode-focused or home-protection spells are favorable to cast now. Magickally and physically prepare your home or space, and make it a nurturing, safe environment. Finish up any lingering projects so that you may turn your attention inward and focus on rest and restoration.

December in the Northern Hemisphere, June in the Southern Hemisphere

Full Moon Is Called: Long Night's, Snow, Cold, Oak, or Wolf Moon

During the longest nighttime hours of the year, the full moon illuminates the dark night sky, much like your soul guides the way during the cocoon time of winter. If it occurs near the winter solstice, this full moon may be called the Long Night's Moon, heralding a time of darkness and spiritual alchemy. Other names—Snow Moon and Cold Moon—focus on the change of weather. The name Oak Moon heralds themes of strength through this time of scarcity. The oak tree has had a prominent role in human history; its acorns have provided sustenance, and religious items have been carved from its wood. The oak also provides protection, magick, strength, good luck, and blessings. This magickal tree often lives to be ancient, reminding us that, despite the cold, we have the strength and magick to endure and deep roots to connect us.

Many facets of this lunation cycle may guide your moon magick, depending on when the full moon occurs. When it heralds the start of winter, this moon is a time of silence, loneliness, and peace that inspires spiritual introspection. As dark hours overtake the day, the moon's light feels more powerful, tugging at our emotional, subconscious, and spiritual landscapes for transformation.

At the same time, depending on its nearness to the winter solstice, this moon may also remind us that the daylight hours will slowly begin to grow again. You may feel called to cast magick for strength to endure the winter and for prosperity as the Wheel of the Year restarts. With the rebirth of the light and with your inner alchemy inspired, you might take up hobbies and ruminate in the creative energy of rebirth. Spells or meditations connecting with the oak may also help summon strength and connection with this moon's namesake ally.

Chapter 4

MOON SIGN MAGICK

As the moon moves through the chasm of space, orbiting the earth and illuminating the night sky, she also moves through sections of the sky associated with the zodiac signs. In astrology, many people study the moon's movement through these signs (also known as moon signs). In witchcraft, these meanings can enhance your spellwork. Astrology is the study of celestial and heavenly bodies and how their movements correspond to happenings in the human world. In ancient times, astrology was a way to divine the messages of the gods and find meaning in the stars. The moon still holds an esteemed place in Western astrology today, and that's what you'll learn about in this chapter.

Astrology is intrinsically connected to witchcraft at its roots. By learning about the moon's meaning within astrology, you'll come to understand even more about this celestial body, what her movements through astrological signs mean for you and your spellwork, and how her power can be used for healing and manifestation. You will also learn what to do during the void-of-course moon and even ponder the effects your own moon sign might have on your magick. You will master not only how to time your moon spells and take advantage of opportunity periods, but also how to work in tandem with specific themes the moon is inviting you to explore, and to live in tune with the stars, sky, and earth. Then you will be able to access the magick of the moon at any time for profound, powerful, and healing moon magick.

THE MOON IN ASTROLOGY

In astrology, the celestial bodies of our solar system, including the moon, correspond to life themes and archetypes. Since the moon holds sway over earth's tides, it is of little surprise that she is associated with the classical element of water. In astrology, the moon is seen to represent the realms of feeling (psychic and emotional), the subconscious, nurturing and being nurtured, and the most intimate self.

The moon helps us map out our emotional and intuitive landscapes, and it illuminates the subconscious realm. It allows for profound spiritual healing to clear the way for manifestation. Through the moon, we can unlock the deepest, most vulnerable parts of ourselves, bringing the hidden to the surface. Emotional responses often arise from the subconscious, communicating information—based on triggers, needs, or cues—that helps us navigate life. In your birth chart (which shows the position of the celestial bodies at the moment, time, and location of your birth and potentially communicates information about your life path, tendencies, healing, etc.), the moon can indicate how you were raised and nurtured, and thus how you like to be nurtured or how you elect to nurture those close to you—the most intimate parts of your being. Through the moon, we can access the past: uncover repeating patterns and past lives and even connect to ancestors. This echoes what we experience during harvest moons: The moon is particularly powerful in connecting to those who have come before us.

The moon is also associated with daily habits and adaptability—which makes sense when we consider how the moon changes form slightly every day but also follows predictable patterns. Her changes are a mirror for our own routines and ability to change as needed. This means that it's incredibly effective to use moon-magick spells to work on habits—habits that build the way for lifelong change.

THE MOON THROUGH THE SIGNS

While the moon is the celestial ruler of the Cancer zodiac sign, the moon has special meaning and magick in all of the signs. As the moon moves through the signs of the zodiac—each with its own meaning, mythos, and associated life themes—she encourages reflection and empowers magick with each sign's energy. You don't *have* to use these moon signs if they don't resonate with you—you can always empower your moon magick outside of signs and just use phases and other events. But as the moon moves into a new sign every 2–3 days, she expresses her power through the traits and themes of each particular sign. Since she rules the realm of emotion, the moon in different signs can impact how you feel as well as focus your reflection and guide your magick:

- In a **fire** sign (Aries, Leo, Sagittarius), the moon's energy can feel spontaneous and warm. This time favors efforts toward vitality and promotes self-expression.

- In a **water** sign (Cancer, Scorpio, Pisces), the moon is in her home element and is supportive and nurturing. This time promotes emotions and is fruitful for connecting to the realm of feeling and intuition.

- In an **earth** sign (Taurus, Virgo, Capricorn), the moon can feel more slow and steady and intentional. You might use this time to engage the physical senses and promote structure and long-lasting results.

- In an **air** sign (Gemini, Libra, Aquarius), the moon illuminates the mind, inspiring ideas. This time is effective for magickal efforts around communication and intelligence.

As you learned in Chapter 2, the new moon is not visible, because it is aligned between the sun and the earth. And the full moon occurs opposite the sun, with earth in the middle. For this reason, the new moon is always in the same sign the sun is in, and the full moon, because it's positioned opposite the sun, is always in the opposite sign. This makes it easy to know what sign a given new or full moon might be in—if it is Libra season (a time when the sun is shining through Libra, making everyone born at the time a Libra), then the new moon will be aligned with the sun (a Libra new moon), and the full moon will occur in the opposite sign, Aries. The moon moves through all 12 signs each lunation.

When you have a working knowledge of the moon's meaning through the signs, you can specialize and focus your full moon and new moon rituals, or even combine this information with moon-phase magick—for example, to conduct spells in the first quarter Taurus moon or the waning gibbous Capricorn moon.

Moon in Aries

When the moon is in passionate, emboldened Aries, the lunar energy has a fiery, enthusiastic, and impulsive flavor. The magickal ram who, in Greek myth, flew in to save two children is representative of Aries's leadership and bravery, and shows us the value of taking swift action in critical moments. The moon in this cardinal fire sign ushers forth courage, motivation, and victory in overcoming any obstacle—there is little the trailblazing, headstrong ram cannot initiate.

You might feel more productive and action oriented during this time. Use this energy to get things done, perhaps to take the first steps on projects that you've been avoiding or that have stalled. As the first sign of the zodiac, the Aries moon is great for beginning projects and for new beginnings in general, since it provides a sense of zest for a quick and powerful start. Now is the time to embrace a go-getter attitude in your moon efforts and develop the boldness to follow through. Use the lunar flame of this energy as the spark that lights the fire—whether that be for a project, love, or passion. Ruled by Mars, a planet of physical activity, the moon in Aries also favors looking into matters of health, the body, and physicality.

The new moon in Aries during Aries season (between March 21 and April 19) favors new beginnings, ventures, and restarts. Develop a plan of attack now for your Aries moon–favored magick goals. The full moon in Aries during Libra season (when the sun is in Libra, between September 23 and October 22) is a powerful time for passion and empowering many Aries moon efforts, but it also invites reflection in weighing between the sun in indecisive Libra and the moon in headstrong Aries. Growth can be found in balancing these two polarities; sometimes you need to be passionate and spontaneous, and other times you must consider multiple perspectives.

Aries Moon Magick

In magick, use the Aries moon for victory and success and to overcome any hurdle. Because the Aries moon can inspire physicality, consider magick to boost your vitality, vigor, and energy, or spells that incorporate movement. It's also a good time for spells boosting motivation, inspiration, and passion. If you have been lacking courage, the moon in Aries can help you feel more courageous and embody a go-getter attitude. Cast spells to get things moving and off to a powerful start, and follow your moon magick with action.

Moon in Taurus

When the moon shines in the sign of Taurus, themes of value arise. This may be related to finances, self-worth, or what you value in life. In older times, the bull, the symbol of this constellation, represented wealth, plenty, and fertility. Taurus is ruled by Venus, the planet of love and luxury, so you may be called to celebrate your own value and engage in indulgences and the pleasures of life. The moon in this fixed earth sign can provide fertile energy with which to grow almost any intention and a sturdy foundation to build lasting structures. With Venus's rulership, these "structures" could include long-term relationships, intimacy, or wealth. Money, abundance, and material security (including property) are illuminated now. While the fixed nature of the moon in this sign blesses long-term efforts, it also invites patience. As the story of the hare and the tortoise shows, to ensure success in the long run, sometimes it is worth it to move slower.

The Taurus new moon during Taurus season (when the sun is in Taurus, from April 20 to May 20) is a blessed time to plant seeds of any kind (in gardening or in energy) that will take a while to grow. Cast spells for anything you wish to last long-term—perhaps financial, romantic, or security goals. Conversely, the full moon in Taurus during Scorpio season (when the sun is in Scorpio, from October 23 to November 21) will paint a sharp contrast between two fixed energies: stable, comfortable Taurus and intense Scorpio. While the Taurus full moon is powerful for many Taurus themes, healing can be found in balancing the sun and moon: Are you too unmoving, or do you plunge into the deep side of the pool, unafraid to make a splash or drown? Since Taurus deals with wealth and Scorpio can relate to joint financial dealings, the Taurus full moon can be fruitful for magick that seeks to change your financial situation and debts. Taurus's long-lasting nature in relationships, coupled with Scorpio's passionate energy, can also make this a romantic full moon.

Taurus Moon Magick

With the moon in Taurus, it's time to work magick for money and long-lasting results. The fixed earth energy of this moon can bring stability into your magick, such as to secure finances, assets, and wealth in the long run. Work with greenery-, garden-, and earth-related magick. Shining through this Venus-ruled goddess sign, the Taurus moon invites you to engage your senses in your magick and incorporate a pinch of sensuality, perhaps even using aromatic flowers, for efforts related to self-value and beauty. In partnerships, focus on curating intimacy to create long-lasting connections. Goddesses associated with cows, the moon, and Venus, such as Hathor or Ishtar, are allies to your spellwork now.

Moon in Gemini

When the moon moves into the Mercury-ruled air sign of Gemini, communication and ideas come to the forefront. Symbolized by the twins, this social, adaptable, quick-witted and excitable sign is about connecting, as well as the understanding, gathering, and exchange of information. So the moon in this sign favors communication, especially about feelings or things that excite you. This is a good time for socialization—engage your inner conversationalist. Since Gemini is the sign of the twins, siblings or sibling-like relationships can come into focus, and you might want to communicate with those you share a close bond with.

Whether you're writing, making small talk, sharing information, giving speeches, or teaching, reflect on how you communicate, how you use your words, and how you connect with the immediate environment around you. In fact, Gemini energy is great for both devising and expressing new ideas, and it may lead to recognition for your unique thoughts. Explore what excites your mind—innovation and inspiration may come more easily than usual during this time. Infuse new projects with excitement, or brainstorm problem-solving proposals. The Gemini moon can illuminate new information and messages of all kinds.

With the Gemini new moon aligned with the sun during Gemini season (May 21–June 20), the energy supports new beginnings in all Gemini-related endeavors. Start new projects, gather information, initiate ideas while socializing, and meditate and reflect on your communication patterns. The Gemini full moon occurs when the sun is moving through the zodiac sign of wisdom-seeking, adventurous, philosophical Sagittarius (November 22–December 21), offering the opportunity to find balance between these forces. The energy of this time will certainly be adventurous and excitable and favor spells for travel and innovation.

Gemini Moon Magick

The energy is youthful. At the same time, under the sign of the twins and the duality of the human spirit, the energy can also be fickle and excitable. In order to not let this lunar energy scatter your emotions, magickal focus, and mind, it is important to balance it within your heart. Use spells to summon communication and inspiration. Network and connect. Integrate your favorite form of communication into your spell, or work word magick—such as writing, speaking, inscribing a word onto a candle, or chanting. Spells connected to transportation, writing, siblings, and the exchange and gathering of information are all Gemini moon–magick themes. This moon's quickening energy can move things into motion magickally.

Moon in Cancer

When the moon is in its home sign, Cancer, it illuminates emotions, intuition, and the realm of feeling. Explore the deeper meaning of your emotions, but—like the crab pinching in attack or retreating into the waves—you'll also need to be wary of moodiness or an urge to withdraw or be overcome by emotion. The moon in Cancer can reveal your wounds, insecurities, and emotional needs; it also can provide a time to heal those injuries and empower yourself. The energy invites introspection and inner journeys beyond just emotion—this is a time for psychic endeavors and development of all kinds. You may also want to nurture yourself, others, and relationships. Check in with your aspirations: Which goals feed you and are balanced with your needs? Both Cancer and the moon highlight home environments, providing the perfect time to create spaces to be comfy, cozy, and secure—to create a shell of safety. The focus on home can include your relationships with family members, as well as love interests and other people you are close with. Now is a good time to connect; foster supportive, loving relationships; and resolve tensions.

The new moon in Cancer during Cancer season (June 21–July 22) is favorable for fresh starts and new beginnings in all Cancer-related endeavors. Cultivate closeness, support, or new beginnings in important relationships; refresh your goals; or start a new self-care regime. Conversely, the energy between the determined, stern Capricorn sun and the nurturing, protective Cancer full moon during Capricorn season (December 22–January 19) can certainly feel conflicted. Through awareness, these energies can be integrated: Seek the wisdom within your emotions, heal old wounds that might otherwise block headstrong Capricorn, and balance your new year's goals with self-care and nurturing in mind. Choose endeavors that feed (rather than drain) your soul.

Cancer Moon Magick

With the moon in its home sign of Cancer, any number of moon spells do well. Tune into the realm of feeling—whether that's your emotions or your psychic abilities and intuition. Cast spells to heal old wounds that arise, and find the deeper meaning in your feelings. Strengthen your psychic skills by practicing meditation and divination. Home protection, home harmony, and hearth magick do exceptionally well during the

Cancer moon. This includes kitchen witchery and nurturing both body and spirit through what you eat and drink. The Cancer moon will boost magick around nurturing relationships and curating support.

Moon in Leo

When the moon is in Leo, creativity, expression, romance, and playfulness permeate the air and your heart. Ruled by the Sun, Leo is about self-expression, talents, and sharing your warmth with others—the inner light that everyone has, radiating from the inside out. The moon reflecting the sun's light in Leo illuminates emotions and magick around these themes, connecting you with the inner flame that sustains your sense of self. Connect with what makes you glow, whether it be a person or a passion.

Leo is also a sign of leadership and warmth—ruling the heart, Leo invites heart-to-heart connection and inspires inner strength. The moon tends to encourage creative energy and romantic ventures, and in Leo this theme is amplified. You may be inspired to throw a party and celebrate yourself, or host a gathering and celebrate your friendships, relax, let loose, and have fun. Reflect on how you express yourself in the world, and become the star in your own life.

The Leo new moon during Leo season (July 23–August 22) strengthens new beginnings in all Leo-favored endeavors. Embrace a new sense of confidence, explore talents and other creative endeavors, or practice expressing yourself and sharing your warmth with the world. When the Leo full moon shines in Aquarius (January 20–February 18), themes of romance, self-expression, and celebration take center stage. The energy invites a bridge between individualized, eccentric Aquarius and connective, expressive Leo. Find your unique self in the balance, and do not be afraid to embrace it.

Leo Moon Magick

When the moon is in Leo, it is time to connect to your inner lunar radiance. Full moons inspire creativity, and the Leo full moon is an especially advantageous time to channel divine energy into your creative works and cast spells to develop talents. The Leo moon is also a good time to embrace your uniqueness and cast confidence spells, since Leo ignites your inner light. It can also boost efforts for self-expression. This extends to glamour magick—let your inner light shine out, giving your aura an enchanting, radiant glow to attract blessings, friendships, and gifts. The radiant moon in Leo also invites fun. Celebrate yourself through ritual, plan a vacation, or host a moon gathering and cast spells for friendship. In addition, with Leo ruling the heart, magick around inner strength does well now.

Moon in Virgo

When the moon shines through meticulous Virgo, it illuminates the everyday details of life. A mutable earth sign ruled by the communication-focused planet Mercury, Virgo's energy is detailed and organized, fruitfully combining her rulership of earth's domain (which covers physical matters) and Mercury's association with the mind. Highly intellectual, analytical, practical, and detail-oriented, the Virgo moon invites restructuring and organization of your emotional and material realities. This moon illuminates the efficiency and sustainability of daily schedules, habits, finances, and organizational systems—the little things that, when done every day, lead to long-term success and longevity.

This theme also extends to the body, nutrition, and health. With Virgo's commitment, physical habits, routines, and organization systems are more likely to endure the long run and prove efficient. Symbolized by the maiden, Virgo is about dedication to oneself, self-sufficiency, and self-improvement. Her energy of commitment also extends to romance and values. Virgo represents the helper who assists plant, animal, and human life alike, so the Virgo moon is also a good time to give back.

With the sun and new moon aligned during Virgo season (August 23–September 22), all Virgo-favored efforts will receive the blessing of the cosmos. Begin habits, start a new health regime, and curate long-range plans. The full moon in Virgo (during Pisces season, February 19–March 20) may illuminate mental clutter, which you can then cleanse with the waning moon. The Virgo full moon invites introspection about and balance between going with the flow and planning or organizing. This is a good time to cast magick for clarity, for breaking unhealthy habits and banishing a scattered mind, and for cleansing.

Virgo Moon Magick

When Virgo and the moon combine forces, it's a powerful time for working on habits and reorganization. This may seem mundane, but for any effort to manifest on the material plane, it requires a discerning eye for decluttering—to make physical and energetic space, as well as to plan the steps for many moon-magick intentions to become a reality. Work spells around the mind, mental clarity, and organization. Cleansing under this moon, such as with lemon and rosemary, will energetically refresh your space and invite mental powers and efficiency. Reset and reorganize your space (for example, your altar). Integrate healing herbs into your moon magick as a way to connect with plant spirits for aid and health.

Moon in Libra

When the moon shines through the sign of the scales, it's a time for beauty, balance, perspective, and cooperation. There is a certain charm and glamour to the luminous moon in this sign. It invites focus on personal aesthetics alongside the beauty within, without, and all around. The Libra moon illuminates the way you compose yourself and connect with others. It's Venus-ruled and is a cardinal air sign, and therefore the moon in Libra invites calm communication and curiosity to see all perspectives. Symbolized by the scales, Libra brings balance into view—whether the balance of life, relationship balance, personal balance, or even justice. This time is also a fruitful one to focus on partnerships, romantic and otherwise, and the ways we work together. The moon in enchanting Libra invites harmonious energy, which can facilitate cooperation and diplomacy.

The new moon in Libra (during Libra season, September 23–October 22) also invokes a favorable time for new beginnings and fresh starts in Libra matters of all kinds. Perhaps start a self-care routine, such as taking luxurious aromatic baths; try expressing yourself through style; or display more art around your home. The full moon in Libra (during Aries season, March 21–April 19) brings a contrast between balanced (and sometimes indecisive) Libra and the sun in fiery, rash Aries. You can cultivate growth through inviting balance between weighing all sides and taking immediate action when necessary. Plus, the partnership-oriented Libra moon in passionate Aries season could favor romantic outings, and provides an excellent time to enchant beauty products under the bright lunar light.

Libra Moon Magick

The Libra moon is a time to cast spells for harmony, balance, and justice. With the moon in this sign inviting different perspectives and peace, use magick to bring harmony and balance in interpersonal and social relationships. Enchant your spells and others with social graces—via your words, composure, and connection. The moon is associated with beauty and enchantment, and so is Libra—so use this time to bless beauty products or cast glamour through clothes, jewelry, beauty and skincare products, and more. The moon's romantic energy and Libra's partnerships focus make a favorable combination for love magick. Cast spells for cooperation to alleviate tension in situations where teamwork is required. In terms of balance spells, ponder how you can bring better balance into your life, take care of yourself, and be able to show up and thrive every day.

Moon in Scorpio

With a stinger that pierces right to the heart, Scorpio gets to the truth of things. Amplifying the moon's usual illuminating energy, the Scorpio moon can bring a time of revealing truths—in a (sometimes painful) way that often instigates transformation for personal growth. This moon prompts investigation of the ego, and deep inner shadow work comes with the territory. Scorpio's stinger tends to come out in moments of danger, and the emotional prodding of the lunar cycles may lead to a sense of vulnerability as your deepest emotions are exposed.

Connected to the realm of the occult, Scorpio also has an energetic favorability toward psychic abilities, the dead, mediumship, and divination. With the moon in Scorpio, this energy is only magnified, so it's an effective time to investigate the realm of mystery, explore occult themes, and strengthen your psychic abilities. Exploring the truth often goes hand in hand with intimacy. Scorpio is known for being sensual, making the Scorpio moon a time to get a bit sexy, passionate, and intimate with the rawness of life.

The new moon in Scorpio (October 23–November 21) provides a time for all Scorpio moon–favored endeavors to move forward with the blessings of both the moon and the sun. Conversely, the full moon in Scorpio amidst Taurus season (April 20–May 20) proves a sharp contrast between immovability and comfort on the one hand and revelation of hidden truths and uncomfortable (but necessary) change on the other. Find a balance between the two, and use the powerful Scorpio moonlight to empower all Scorpio-related efforts. This can also be a favorable lunation for financial focus, as Taurus provides the structure and stability of wealth while Scorpio is particularly auspicious for business partnerships.

Scorpio Moon Magick

The moon's cycles tend to bring the truth to light. Coupled with Scorpio's truth-seeking energy, spells for uncovering truths and getting to the heart of things do especially well now. Because Scorpio can encourage investigation of the ego and reveal inner truths, repeating patterns and karmic issues may be exposed—but this recognition allows them to be powerfully changed, transformed, and healed. The Scorpio moon also favors efforts of banishing and ending—important parts of transformation. The sharp stinger of this moon is also useful for cleansing and protection spells, which can help you maintain energetic boundaries. Scorpio also relates to financial partnerships, making it a good time to invest intelligently and cast spells to combat debt. For the psychically in-tune, cast spells for divination, and perhaps meditate to connect with the realm beyond the veil.

Moon in Sagittarius

With the moon illuminating the archer, whose arrow is aimed at the center of the galaxy, Sagittarius brings your eyes to the heavens, inviting questions about guiding beliefs, principles, and philosophies. For those with a talent for prophecy and the esoteric arts (such as astrology, the New Age, and alternative healing paths), the moon in Sagittarius is a blessed time for prophetic work and expansion. A mutable fire sign, Sagittarius craves adventure and exploration and can illuminate a sense of excitement and spontaneity. Ruled by Jupiter, the planet of expansion, luck, and benefactors, the Sagittarius moon can bless you with abundance and be used to expand your luck and connections. This moon sign also favors higher education—a perfect lunation for studying and learning about new paths.

The new moon in Sagittarius (November 22–December 21) blesses new beginnings or resets of all Sagittarius moon–related efforts. The full moon in Sagittarius happens during Gemini season (May 21–June 20), and the contrast between the archer and the twins invites reflection on the balance between gathering exciting information and actually transmuting it into meaningful wisdom. This period is definitely a lunation for travel and adventure as well.

Sagittarius Moon Magick

Connect to your higher self and spirit allies from above now for profound wisdom. In fact, the Sagittarius moon encourages exploration of prophecy and prophetic dreams in your moon-magick workings. A key aspect of magick is your sense of possibilities and your belief in what can happen. Sagittarius, his eye on the horizon, invites you to look at your guiding beliefs. Ponder the interplay of your belief systems and your moon-magick results. Cast spells and practice meditations to raise your sights beyond the horizon, and expand your sense of possibility in your magick. Ruled by Jupiter, the

Sagittarius moon also energizes spells for optimism and hope. You might invoke the Sagittarius moon for luck, abundance, expansion, positivity, and even favorable legal results. Finally, consider casting spells to connect you to benefactors to help your lunar dreams come true.

Moon in Capricorn

The moon in headstrong Capricorn shines a light on matters of motivation, determination, career, achievement, tradition, and ambition. Despite the moon's tendency to bring the emotional landscape to the forefront, in Capricorn, emotions may be more repressed. Instead, efforts related to physical reality take focus now. Represented by the archetype of sea goat (half fish, half goat) this sign is determined in nature. Its front hooves place a firm foot forward; it's a mountain goat, unwavering in climbing the steepest of inclines. Its back end is a fish tail, flexible and able to traverse land or water to attain goals.

Working with the Capricorn moon can help you do the hard work to get to your goals in the long run and climb the steepest of hills, regardless of the time it may take. Furthermore, this lunation is practical: It encourages you to work with what you have on hand. In general, efforts related to business, career, and achievement are favorable now. Connect to your goals. If you have had trouble achieving goals in the past, the Capricorn moon can provide a favorable time to cast supporting spells for self-control and discipline in order to have success this time around.

The new moon in Capricorn comes close to the new year in both the Northern Hemisphere and the Southern, when the sun is in Capricorn (December 22–January 19). Since the new moon and sun align at this time, it's a good idea to set long-term goals. The Capricorn moon can bless your ambitions with endurance and determination. Conversely, the Capricorn full moon occurs during Moon-ruled Cancer season (June 21–July 22), creating a sharp contrast between emotionally in-tune Cancer and emotionally repressed and achievement-focused Capricorn. Find the balance between them, and use the luminous moon to bless powerful Capricorn moon efforts. Use this time, too, to reflect on any new year's goals you set 6 months ago.

Capricorn Moon Magick

This is a time to cast spells for long-term goals, ambitions, and achievement. Energy cast now can grant the endurance and stamina to climb any mountain, regardless of the incline or the length of the journey. It can also be a good time to work magick on business, money, and working within structures—or even just adding structure to your life. This can include moon magick that deals with organizations, especially those with defined power structures. Family structures fall into this category too. The Capricorn moon finds comfort in tradition, so try incorporating traditions into your moon rituals. Continue to be practical, and consider spellwork that uses materials you already have on hand. Follow up spells with thoughtful everyday actions to affirm the energy you are casting. Since Capricorn is ruled by Saturn, you may also consider incorporating structural elements (such as pyramid shapes) and timing in your Capricorn moon spells.

Moon in Aquarius

Represented by the revolutionary cupbearer who rebelled against the gods and poured the cup's contents down to earth, the moon in Aquarius illuminates themes of liberation, breaking free from limitations, and innovation. This lunation invites you to move into realms beyond what you thought possible by breaking free of labels, old identities, or toxic, restrictive power structures. This theme also extends to limiting relationships, especially since Aquarius favors group dynamics over person-to-person ones. After all, the people you surround yourself with can influence your perceptions and the energy around you.

Aquarius is an air sign ruled by Uranus, and the moon in Aquarius blesses innovation and genius. With this lunar energy, you can move into new realms and realities that will expand your sense of possibility. Bearing visionary energy, the moon in this sign can help you visualize a better and different future, perhaps devoting yourself to a specific cause or purpose. The cupbearer pours out life-giving ambrosia; what do you pour out into the world?

The new moon in Aquarius (January 20–February 18) is a time for new beginnings and resets in all Aquarius-related themes: embodying a new identity, embracing a new open-mindedness that invites genius and innovation, or stepping into new group relations. The full moon in Aquarius occurs opposite the Leo sun (July 23–August 22). Finding balance between mental, independent Aquarius and expressive, dynamic Leo can mean embracing your own unique identity and eccentricities and inviting the realm of creative and innovative ideas. The waning phase following this full moon is an optimal time to release limiting old ties.

Aquarius Moon Magick

Aquarius is all about breaking limitations, so use Aquarius moon magick to cut old cords or restrictive patterns. Work with this lunation to embody new innovative beginnings or to cut away the restrictive energy of the past. Cast spells for genius, summon solutions to problems, and bring innovation into both your life and your magick. Since Aquarius is related to technology, spells that use or include technology can be favorable now.

On a larger scale, you might consider magick to support change, humanitarianism, and innovation for a better future. If you are ready to step into a different realm of being and manifest a better future for yourself, the Aquarius moon is a time to break free of limiting energy and step into the lunar doorway of a future beyond what you thought possible.

Moon in Pisces

The moon in watery Pisces highlights themes of psychic ability, healing, and going with the ebbs and flows of life. Represented by the fish, Pisces has the ability to dive deep—into spirituality, into the realm of the collective unconscious, or into old wounds. Pisces is in tune with the currents of life and seamlessly swims through them, teaching us to go with the flow. Pisces's association with music and channeling great works of art, coupled with the moon's inspiring tendencies, makes the Pisces moon a great time to tap into inspiration from the universe. Since Pisces is ruled by Neptune, dreams and fantasy are heightened at this time.

The new moon in Pisces (February 19–March 20) is an occasion for beginnings in all Pisces themes—for example, start a new meditation practice or embrace the idea of going with the flow. Try a new way to unwind and connect to the flow of life. The full moon in Pisces, however, occurs in opposition to the sun in Virgo (August 23–September 22)—seemingly creating a conflict between planning and overthinking and going with the flow. Harness the balance of these two forces for profound moon magick: The right balance can illuminate areas in your life for healing and letting go. With the full moon in psychic Pisces, you may experience amazing psychic insights—just be able to discern which are premonitions and which are fantasies. The water can get murky at times.

Pisces Moon Magick

Combining the moon's impact on sleep and Pisces's being ruled by the planet of dreams, this moon is a time to explore dream magick. Uncover your dreams' symbolism for psychic information or to uncover wounds to be healed. Cast spells about sleep and dreamwork. In fact, psychic work of all kinds is favorable now. In Pisces, the moon invites you to tap into your sense of feeling—not just your emotions, but the flow of energy around you. If you are a creative, try channeling psychic information into works of art. Casting moon magick while listening to tunes is great for the Pisces moon too. Healing is also available now: Soothe and invoke peace and harmony with the healing power of water. Cleanse away old wounds. Take a moon bath or drink a lunar tea and read the tea leaves. Investigate past lives. Meditate with the moon and tune into the collective unconscious.

Void-of-Course Moon

Beyond the moon moving through the signs, there is an extra astrological factor to consider: the void-of-course moon. Essentially, the void-of-course moon is transitioning; it's energetically between one sign and the next. In general, any new efforts started now are not likely to come to fruition. A more complex definition (and one of a few different precise meanings) is that the moon is void of course when she has made her last significant aspect (or angle) to a planet in a sign but hasn't yet moved into the next zodiac sign. The moon spends 2–3 days in each sign and is void of course about 12 times a cycle. But the void-of-course period is a different length each time, lasting anywhere from mere minutes to hours to a day. Unfortunately, this means that to know when the moon is void of course, it's necessary to check online or use an app, a planetary calendar, or an ephemeris. Luckily, those are all widely available today.

Since anything new started at this time is said not to come to pass, the void-of-course moon may not be the best time to cast spells. Instead, it may be more suited to rest. The moon still lights the course at night, despite being void of course. Use the time for meditation and reflection and connecting to the moon's energy. Accept the moon's offering of time to wait, rest, and think through spellwork before taking magickal action. Each person's relationship with the moon and magick is unique. Discover for yourself what does and doesn't work and how you feel about the void-of-course moon.

YOUR MOON SIGN AND MAGICK

Just as you have a sun sign, you also have a moon sign, the zodiac sign the moon was in at the time of your birth. Your moon sign can reveal information such as how you were nurtured or raised, how you like to be nurtured, and how you opt to nurture others when close. It can provide insight—about your emotional and subconscious landscape, your sense of feeling, and perhaps even your soul—to guide and illuminate your purpose. When it comes to magick, knowing your moon sign is not essential. But if you are able to get your hands on your birth chart (for which there are many free resources online), you may gain insight into what kind of magick is most comforting, healing, and nurturing for you. It can reveal the aspects of your intuitive and emotional nature that especially empower your lunar spells.

Astrology has many moving parts, and your moon sign is just one facet of a much larger puzzle. But reflecting on your own moon sign can be interesting and lead to insights as you consider moon spells and how the moon in each sign impacts you.

PART TWO

SPELLS and RITUALS for EVERY MOON

Whether or not you've realized it, the moon has always been there, influencing your spellwork. In Part 1, you learned the meaning and magickal potential of moon phases, eclipses, special occasion moons, and seasonal lunation cycles. Now it's time to learn the moon's correspondences with crystals, herbs, and other allies and uncover the power of the moon through spellwork.

The spells in this book are organized by overarching concepts: You'll find general spells, recipes, and meditations for the moon phases; special occasion moon rituals and reflections; seasonal moon spells and crafts; moon sign spells; and finally, moon deity spells. But most of these spells can be cast at any time. Once you feel comfortable working with the moon, trust your own intuition. Use the lists in Appendix A to guide you to efforts that match your desired intentions (for example, spells for clarity, money, or love).

The power of the moon is infinite. There are so many ways you can use the moon in magick, whether by simply connecting and tuning into her energy or by timing your spells or healing rituals to her phases and movements. Remember that your lunar practice is yours—let these spells exemplify ways you can work with the moon, and make them your own.

Chapter 5

LUNAR CORRESPONDENCES

Now that you have foundational knowledge of the moon, its phases, and its connection to astrology, it's time to turn your attention to the details of practicing witchcraft in tune with the moon. From moonwort to moonstone, a plethora of moon-magick ingredients can help boost your moon-magick efforts. You can even grow some ingredients in your own garden to deepen your connection to the earth and its celestial neighbors.

Dozens of natural objects and materials correspond with the moon. Call upon specific deities such as Artemis or Diana to enhance your connection to the moon. Meditate and cleanse your energy before lunar spellwork with a selenite stone. Include the scent of jasmine in your spells to boost the moon's power to provide love, abundance, and a strong sense of spirituality. In this chapter, you will uncover these and many other correspondences. You can use these ingredients to enhance and customize the spells in this part.

LUNAR GARDENING

Lunar gardening is a longstanding practice that, when adhered to, can help you tune into the magickal energy of your plants—especially those associated with the moon—on a deeper level. Plus, you can potentially grow plants to use in your moon magick.

To this day, many farmers and agriculturalists plant, harvest, and prune by the phases and cycles of the moon. Guided by the belief that the moon's gravitational force pulls upon the water tables underground and impacts the flow of sap and life force within a plant, many gardeners swear by planting with the moon. They seek the most optimal time to perform each task to get the best yield and potency they can. Scientists aren't yet able to definitively prove these theories—but as a moon witch you are concerned with the spirit of things, and there is little denying the energetic buzz that plants get under the empowering light of the full moon. Gardening with the moon is an opportunity to tune into and work in tandem with nature—and to supply yourself with magickal ingredients to use in spells.

Waxing Moon (New to Full Moon)

This is considered an especially fertile time to sow seeds of aboveground crops and plants, or to repot and transplant. During the waxing phase, it is believed that plants' energy and sap flow upward, making this a key time of growth for plants that have an aboveground yield. Some also believe that the combined gravitational pull of the moon and sun during the new moon draws underground water tables up so that plants are better able to absorb nutrients and water.

Waning Moon (Full Moon to New Moon)

Under the full moon, all of life seems to sing energetically at night. This can be a key time to harvest plants for their magickal properties if they have reached their full potency. With the shift of the cycle to waning, it is believed that plants' energy and sap move downward, favoring pruning (as plants may heal faster, with less loss of life in reaction to pruning), as well as planting bulbs and belowground crops. (These are better to harvest nearer the new moon.) Many lunar gardeners also weed during the waning phases, as the focus turns to reaping what has been sown.

Moon Sign Gardening

In addition to the position of the moon during its phases, some lunar gardeners go the extra mile and consider the sign the moon is in. Some moon signs are considered to be more fertile or fruitful in the garden, and others are called barren. Combined with knowledge of the seasons and phases, such gardeners select the most optimal gardening times available to them:

- **Fertile/Growth Signs:** In general, all three water signs—Cancer, Scorpio, and Pisces—are considered fertile, plus fixed earth sign Taurus. Capricorn and Libra are also considered fertile, but less so than those four. The moon in these fertile signs signals a time to plant and bless seeds, and to transplant.

- **Barren/Dry/No-Growth Signs:** All fire signs are considered barren: Aries, Leo, and Sagittarius. Gemini, Aquarius, and Virgo are also considered barren. These signs are seen as less favorable for growth—but remember, there are always several factors at hand when gardening! Barren moon signs indicate times to focus on maintenance: gathering, pruning, and getting rid of weeds and pests.

LUNAR DEITIES

To our earliest ancestors, the moon was a god. The moon defined the passage of time as it changed phases throughout the lunar month, lighting the nighttime sky and then disappearing. Despite the shift from lunar- to solar-dominant worship with the start of more permanent settlements, many moon deities are still honored and worshipped to this day. While many associate the moon with the perception of feminine energy, you will find that throughout the great expanse of human life, the moon has been associated with deities across the gender spectrum and, in some cases, with gods who have changed gender over time.

The variations on mythology surrounding the moon are truly endless. Some ancient cultures adapted and adopted moon deities from other societies, while others worshipped different deities for varying aspects of the moon. Some moon gods were considered the personification of the moon, others deities of the moon, and still more were simply associated with the moon.

In this section, you will find descriptions of some of the lunar deities commonly mentioned in modern witchcraft. The full list of moon deities you can connect with is much longer and exemplifies the endless potential of the moon's power. If you're interested in this topic, you can research more about moon mythology in general and moon-related deities for specific cultures.

Arianrhod

Arianrhod is a Celtic/Welsh goddess associated with the moon. Her name means "silver wheel," a possible reference to spinning and to the moon, the lunar cycle, or the lunar year. She gave birth to the spirit of the sun and the spirit of the sea. While little information on her survives, she is a very powerful goddess who rules magick and manifestation.

Artemis

Artemis is one of many ancient Greek goddesses identified with the moon. The Romans later associated her with the goddess Diana (see the section on Diana for more on this). Artemis is often depicted as a young goddess with a horned or lunar headdress, a bow (shaped like the crescent moon) and arrow for a hunt, and a stag or pack of hunting dogs at her side.

Artemis is goddess of the moon, counterpart to her twin brother Apollo, god of the sun. Daughter of mother Leto and father Zeus, she was born ahead of her twin, then turned around to help their mother birth him. In this midwife form, Artemis is sometimes referred to by the name Cynthia, connecting the moon to women and birthing.

Mistress of wild nature, Artemis assists in the growth and protection of vegetation and wildlife, creating close ties between the moon and living things. (Some impacts of those close ties are described in Chapter 1.) Artemis is a chaste goddess beholden to only herself, and her mythology is a testament to how working with the moon—in tune with the nature within and without and dedicated to our own mastery—can lead us, much like Artemis's arrows, to hit any target.

Cerridwen

Cerridwen is a Celtic moon deity and enchantress who keeps a cauldron of wisdom that contains secrets accessible only to witches and favored people under her care. Her cauldron can bestow inspiration and transformation, much like a witch's cauldron. The Celtic myth tells us Cerridwen had a beautiful daughter and an ugly son (a possible symbolism of dual energy), and to aid her son she brewed a potion to bestow knowledge of the universe. However, her cauldron needed to be stirred continuously. She employed her servant Gwion to stir the pot, but he took the potion for himself, perhaps by accident. A chase ensued, where Cerridwen transformed into various creatures. From this myth, we can glean the moon's connection with shape-shifting and the power to transform.

An herbalist with extensive botanical knowledge, Cerridwen's association with the moon also connects the moon with the power of herbs and healing remedies. Her cauldron points to a connection between witchcraft, the moon, and potions, and also informs us that transformation can often require constant work, just like her cauldron needed to be stirred for a year and a day.

Chandra

Chandra is the Hindu god of the moon, associated with fertility, vegetation, and plants. In Vedic astrology, Chandra is one of the nine planets. The name means "bright" or "shining" and is also used in Sanskrit to refer to the moon itself. In fitting association with the moon, Monday is considered Chandra's day. Chandra may have been depicted as both female and male at different times.

Chandra's actions are also closely connected to waning and waxing, since he represents the moon. In one myth, Chandra laughed at Ganesha and was thus cursed and wounded by him, giving way to the moon's waning. In another myth, Chandra married Daksha's 27 star daughters but favored one named Rohini. The other sisters complained, and Chandra was cursed to wane until Shiva came to the rescue. Chandra then had to compromise and visit one sister each night, waxing in glee as he approached Rohini and waning after having to leave her. At the end of the cycle, he was permitted to rest for 3 days—all of which gave rise to the lunar cycle and the 27 mansions of the moon in Vedic astrology.

Chang'e

Chang'e (also referred to as Ch'ang O and Heng'e) is a moon goddess still celebrated to this day in China's midautumn moon festival. A variety of myths surround her, but the overarching theme is that she drank an elixir of immortality that was meant for her husband, archer Hou Yi (or perhaps she drank both her share and his), and as a result, flew to the moon. In some versions of the story, this turn of events was an accident; in others, the flight represented a welcome means of escape. To this day, Chang'e remains known as Lady of the Moon and is often depicted on or near the moon, accompanied by a rabbit.

Coyolxauhqui

Coyolxauhqui is the Aztec goddess of the moon. She led her brothers, the 400 gods of the southern stars, in a rebellion against their mother upon hearing she was pregnant. However, they were defeated by their then-birthed brother, Huitzilopochtli, as he sprung forth from their mother fully grown and beheaded Coyolxauhqui. The moon is thought to be her severed head rolling through the sky.

Diana

Diana likely originated in ancient Italy as a goddess heavily associated with the woodlands, trees, and wild animals. Much of what's known about her beginnings has been overtaken by her absorption into practices and beliefs related to Artemis. A goddess of magick, Diana is a protectress of people who are enslaved or fleeing enslavement, people in childbirth, women, children, other disadvantaged people, wilderness, wild animals such as wolves, and more.

While she was probably not originally identified with the moon, she took on that association with it once she was identified with Artemis. Diana is often recognized as a part of a triplicity, alongside Hekate and Luna/Selene.

Hekate

Hekate is a powerful goddess associated with witchcraft, crossroads, and the moon—in particular, the dark moon. Her origins are not fully known, but she is referred to today as an ancient Greek deity. She has been depicted as a trifold goddess (three feminine figures facing outward in each direction of a three-way crossroads), or as a single figure holding two torches, or as a single goddess with three heads (sometimes including animal heads). She's often accompanied by hounds or snakes, or holds a key (she's considered a guardian of entranceways). In Rome, she was known as Trivia: "tri" meaning three and "via" meaning road. Many practitioners particularly connect to her during the waning and dark moon times.

Khonsu

Khonsu is an ancient Egyptian moon god often petitioned for fertility and healing. He was invoked to help women and livestock conceive, most often when he shines as the waxing crescent moon. His name translates to "traveler," for the traveling of the moon across the sky. Khonsu is seen to rule the passage of time and the human life span, connecting the moon with timekeeping and the cycles of life.

Through various stages of Egypt's history, Khonsu's image and associations have changed: At one point, he was depicted with cannibalistic tendencies. He later become associated with Mut as his mother and Amun as his father, creating a trinity wherein he represented the child (although he is also sometimes depicted with differing parents at different times). In art, he is often shown as a child mummy or, like Horus, with the head of a falcon, or with a crescent moon "horn" holding a full moon disc atop his head. Khonsu is also often associated with baboons. He shows the connection between the moon and fertility of life and shares some associations with another ancient Egyptian god, Thoth.

Kwan Yin

Kwan Yin (whose name has many variations and spellings, including Guan Yin and Kuan Kin) is a bodhisattva of compassion who has been adopted into many religions and is celebrated as a goddess. She is a deity of mercy and compassion who helps break cycles and is prayed to for miracles and assistance, and a wide variety of matters. While not necessarily a moon goddess, she is often depicted with the backdrop of the moon and celebrated during the lunar cycle.

Luna

Luna is the Roman embodiment or spirit of the moon, who, over time, became associated with the Greeks' Selene and balanced with Sol, the spirit of the sun. At this point in time, Luna and Selene are used interchangeably, and not much mythology exists about Luna on her own (see the section on Selene). In moon magick, she can be petitioned as the spirit of the moon.

Mama Quilla

Mama Quilla (also called Mama Killa) is the Incan goddess of the moon, and her name means "Mother Moon." She is the daughter of the Incan creator god and Mama Qucha, the goddess of the sea. Her sister is Pachamama, the earth, and sun god Inti is her husband and brother. She cries tears of silver and is considered a goddess and defender of women, marriage, and the menstrual cycle. Mama Quilla was tied to the Incan calendar, as it used the moon to keep time. It was believed that lunar eclipses were caused by her being attacked by an animal, and people would throw weapons and make noise to scare off the animal.

Mani

Mani is the Norse personification of the moon, sibling to sister Sol, of the sun. He steers the course of the moon and determines its phases, charged with keeping time. In myth, he and his sister Sol are endlessly pursued by wolves, and eclipses occur when the wolves catch up with them.

Nanna

Nanna, also known as Sin, is the ancient Mesopotamian and Sumerian god of the moon. He's one of the oldest gods of the pantheon and for a time was considered the main deity. He is usually shown as an old man with a lapis lazuli beard sitting upon a throne, or as a bull or cowherd. He is also represented by the number 30, for the days of the lunar month.

Nanna's family reveals more about his associations in ancient Sumeria: The fertility goddess Ningal was his wife, the sun god Utu (also called Shamash) was his son, and his daughters were Inanna (also known as Ishtar), goddess of love and sexuality, and Ereshkigal, queen of the dead. Thus, the moon was seen to have relation to fertility, love, the dead, and the sun. In fact, Nanna's role as father of the sun could be a marker of how, prior to the agricultural revolution and the start of civilization, the moon was more important than the sun to many traveling peoples. Throughout his ages of worship, he became known for his wisdom, and for being a protector of humanity, diviner, and master of time.

Selene

Selene is a Greek goddess of the moon, born to titans Theia and Hyperion. Her siblings are the sun god Helios and Eos, goddess of dawn. While there are many Greek moon goddesses, Selene and her Roman counterpart, Luna, are considered personifications of the moon. In Greek mythology, Selene carries the moon across the sky at night in a chariot pulled by a pair of winged steeds. She is often depicted riding sidesaddle on a white horse. Like many Greek deities, she had a few lovers, but the most prominent was Endymion. This lover distracted Selene from her tasks as moon goddess, so Zeus gave Endymion a choice: eternal youth in a permanent slumber—or death. He chose the eternal, youthful slumber. Each dark and new moon, Selene visited Endymion, and they produced many daughters together.

Thoth

You may have heard of Thoth as the Egyptian god who weighs a person's heart against Ma'at's feather to determine whether the soul will be allowed to proceed to the afterlife. Like Khonsu, Thoth is associated with the moon and the passage of time. However, Thoth is so much more than that—he is considered god of the moon, scribes, magick, sciences, messengers, knowledge, writing, and more. In ancient Egyptian mythology, he is credited as having invented writing and the calendar and having written the first book. His Egyptian name, Djehuty, means "he who is like the ibis," for the bird he is most commonly associated with. Like Khonsu, he is also associated with the baboon.

Thoth is a self-actualized deity closely associated with Ra, the sun god. In one myth he self-created as an ibis and laid the cosmic egg responsible, in Egyptian myth, for all of creation. He recorded for the gods, created new laws, and even taught Isis magick.

Triple Goddess

Trinities have always been seen as sacred. Many deities (the Tridevi, Hekate, the Morrigan, the three Fates, and even the Christian trinity) depict a divine triplicity. The Triple Goddess as it is known today is an archetype in Neopaganism and Wicca. Symbolized by the full moon with a crescent moon on either side, it is generally associated with the waxing, full, and waning or dark moon. Some associate the Triple Goddess with the trio of moon goddesses Diana, Selene, and Hekate.

Rather than one specific deity, though, the Triple Goddess is an archetype associated with many different concepts and deities, all aligned with the phases and expression of the moon. For a time, the three goddesses were correlated with the various perceived stages or cycles of a woman's life: maiden (waxing moon), mother (full moon), and crone (waning or dark moon), but many modern witches have found such labels restrictive. At large, the Triple Goddess and the triple moon can be seen to be more: the underworld, the earth, and the heavens; the three selves (id, ego, superego); the three souls of witchcraft; and the three phases of life (youth, adulthood, old age). To interact with this archetype, choose the meaning and representation that resonate best with you.

LUNAR SPELLCASTING INGREDIENTS

In witchcraft, each ingredient in a spell contributes a certain energy; each is an herbal ally alive with its own vitality and spirit. When aligned to a specific intention, these ingredients can amplify the power of your spells. The list that follows shows ingredients that are used in the spells later in this part, along with their correspondences and the themes they represent.

Some ingredients are especially associated with the moon, and others are not, but each has been included in this book because its energy is helpful for moon magick. For a full list or ingredients, their suggested uses, and even planetary associations, check out *Cunningham's Encyclopedia of Magical Herbs* by Scott Cunningham. Remember: Every ingredient grew and developed under the light and gravitational pull of the moon, so whether or not it is specifically associated with the moon, as long as it matches your intentions, it has the capacity to be profound in your lunar spellcasting.

Ingredients with Moon Associations

Ingredient	Key Themes
Aloe	Healing, Soothing, Protection
Blueberry	Abundance, Psychic Protection
Chickweed	Love, Fidelity
Coconut	Spirituality, Love, Inner Purification, Psychic Ability
Cucumber	Beauty, Peace, Healing, Youth
Eucalyptus	Protection, Healing
Gardenia	Peace, Love, Spirituality, Healing, Attraction
Grape	Fertility, Garden Magick, Mind, Dreams, Money
Iris	Purification, Wisdom
Jasmine	Love, Money, Abundance, Spirituality, Prophecy, Dreams
Lemon	Creativity, Fidelity, Friendship, Happiness, Joy, Longevity, Love, Purification
Lemon Balm	Healing, Love, Peace, Success
Melon (includes watermelon)	Healing, Purification
Myrrh	Healing, Spirituality, Cleansing, Protection
Poppy	Dreams, Fertility, Abundance, Love, Sleep/Rest, Money, Luck
Pumpkin	Abundance, Divination, Goddess Worship, Healing, Money
White Sandalwood	Wishes, Healing, Spirituality, Cleansing, Protection
Wintergreen	Cleansing, Protection, Healing

Other Useful Ingredients

Ingredient	Key Themes
Anise	Purification, Protection, Clarity, Psychic Ability, Spirit
Apple	Love, Healing, Longevity, Fertility, Wisdom, Magick
Basil	Love, Protection, Wealth
Bay Leaf	Protection, Strength, Prophecy, Healing, Purification, Wisdom, Success
Black Pepper	Protection, Purification, Banishment, Grounding
Blackberry	Abundance, Healing, Sensuality, Protection
Blue Cornflower	Psychic Ability, Wisdom, Love, Vision
Butterfly Pea Flower	Transformation, Love, Youth, Happiness, "Feminine" Energy, Spirituality
Cardamom	Love, Sex, Luck
Cayenne/Red Pepper	Passion, Heat, Jinx-Breaking, Repelling/Protection, Banishment
Chamomile	Money, Peace, Love, Purification, Communication
Cinnamon	Raising Energetic Vibration, Power, Lust, Love, Success, Spirituality, Psychic Ability
Clove	Comfort, Exorcism, Love/Sex, Money/Riches, Purification, Protection, Raising Energetic Vibration, Spirituality, Stopping Gossip
Cranberry	Action, Abundance, Protection, Love
Egg	Protection, Rebirth/New Life, Cleansing, Abundance, Healing, Divination
Garlic	Protection, Health
Ginger	Health, Healing, Love, Money, Abundance, Success, Power
Grapefruit	Purification, Positivity
Honey	Spirituality, Purification, Health, Harmony, Love, Sex, Happiness, Wisdom
Lavender	Love, Purification, Dreams, Peace, Longevity, Protection, Happiness
Lime	Healing, Love, Hex-Breaking, Protection
Maple	Love, Grounding, Longevity, Money
Milk	Love, Spirituality, Goddess Worship
Mint	Mind, Clarity, Abundance, Divination, Psychic Ability, Love, Protection, Calm

Ingredient	Key Themes
Mugwort	Psychic Ability, Dreams, Healing, Protection
Nutmeg	Luck, Money, Wishes, Health, Fidelity
Oak	Protection, Health, Money, Healing, Potency, Fertility, Luck
Onion	Protection, Healing, Cleansing, Money, Sensuality
Orange	Love, Divination, Well-Being, Luck, Money, Beauty, Purification, Creativity
Pear	Lust, Love, Longevity, Money
Peppermint	Mind, Abundance, Communication, Psychic Ability, Love, Protection, Peace
Pomegranate	Divination, Luck, Wishes, Wealth/Abundance, Fertility/Life Cycles, Youth, Protection, Creativity
Rose	Love, Healing, Spirituality, Beauty, Psychic Powers, Luck
Rosemary	Protection, Memory, Mind, Love, Clarity, Purification, Healing, Peace
Sage	Longevity, Wisdom, Purification, Protection, Focus, Spirituality
Salt	Grounding, Protection, Purification
Strawberry	Love, Harmony, Divination, Luck
Sugar	Love, Lust, Money, Abundance, Attraction
Thyme	Love, Psychic Awareness, Purification, Healing, Health, Courage, Peace
Violet	Hope, Luck, Love, Lust, Wishes, Peace, Healing, Faeries

MOON MINERALS, CRYSTALS, AND STONES

Some stones, such as moonstone and selenite, are thought to have a special connection to the moon. Working with these crystals can help enhance your intuition, healing work, and connection to the moon in your magick. You can also work with them to practice feeling energy, as guided in Chapter 6. In this section, you will find stones that are especially attuned to the moon, as well as a handful of others that contribute energy to the spells later in this part.

Minerals, Crystals, and Stones with Moon Associations

Material	Purpose
Aquamarine	Named after the great ocean blue, aquamarine favors smooth sailing across the high and low tides caused by the moon. It can be used for safe travel over the ocean, for calm, and for peace. It also inspires communication and truth.
Moonstone	Moonstone enhances intuition and inspires calm knowing. The most well-known varieties are blue and rainbow moonstone. A powerful stone commonly used for connecting to goddess energy, moonstone invokes creativity and inner power. Use moonstone to help with safe travel over waters and to help balance emotions to allow intuition and inner high-priestess energy to come through! Other varieties of moonstone include: • Black moonstone: Akin in color to the new moon, black moonstone is a powerful stone to work with during the new and dark moons. It has the traditional qualities associated with moonstone, and it also aids inner journeying, grounding, and protection. • Peach moonstone: Peach moonstone offers the traditional moonstone qualities, with a more emotionally balancing and joyful edge.
Mother-of-Pearl	The iridescent material found inside certain shells, mother-of-pearl is believed to contain the healing and soothing power of the sea. Like many other moon-associated stones and minerals, mother-of-pearl promotes intuition, expression, and emotional balance, and also helps with overcoming fear.
Pearl	Formed within shelled mollusks overtime, pearls have a special connection to the ocean and the moon. They are associated with tranquility (especially through transitions), sincerity and truth, and wisdom.
Selenite	Named after the moon goddess Selene, this salt crystal is great for lunar workings (especially cleansing, protection, and working with the higher self) and will keep any space, person, or item energetically clear.

Other Minerals, Crystals, and Stones

Material	Purpose
Amethyst	While not necessarily a moon mineral, amethyst is a popular meditative stone commonly used in moon magick and workings. Amethyst fosters connection with spiritual wisdom and aids in the development of intuitive abilities while also providing auric protection. A wonderful stone for stress relief, amethyst helps break addictive patterns and also invites peaceful rest.

Material	Purpose
Black Tourmaline	Black tourmaline is one of the premier stones associated with grounding and psychic protection. Black tourmaline neutralizes energy, making it great for empaths or for dealing with negative energy. It helps open the grounding channel, assisting with anxiety and worry and also clearing any blockages one may have in manifestation.
Citrine	Citrine will help connect you to your inner inspiration, and promote joy and happiness. This stone transmutes negative energy into positive, and attracts abundance as well.
Clear Quartz	When it comes to manifesting intentions, clear quartz is a wonderful stone for directing and amplifying energy toward goals. Use it for clarity, for memory, and to set intentions for a spiritual journey.
Garnet	A stone of passion, sensuality, and vitality, garnet helps people recognize their primal instincts and draws repressed emotions to the surface, making way for profound healing.
Green Aventurine	Green Aventurine is a wonderful stone to use for prosperity, and to bring in new opportunities. It helps one release attachment to outcomes, inviting in optimism and joy, as well as prosperity, good luck, and vitality.
Jade	Jade is a powerful stone for well-being, good fortune, and energetic balance. It helps to open one to life's abundance and transmute any blockages to prosperity. Wear for good luck, to balance your energies, or to aid in any healing.
Jet	Associated with the root energy center, jet is a calming and grounding stone. Jet acts like an energetic filter, clearing out negative emotions and energy, making it great for empaths. Formed from compacted, fossilized wood (with similarities to coal), jet provides insight and wisdom.
Labradorite	With an ethereal, entrancing flash, labradorite is wonderful for developing psychic abilities and working with the moon. It's a protective stone, keeping the aura intact and safe from others while intuitive abilities are developed. It is also an aid during times of transition and change.
Lapis Lazuli	Associated with the Sumerian moon god Nanna, lapis lazuli is a wonderful stone for psychic development and manifestation with the moon. It enhances intuition, inner knowing, communication, access to other realms, and healing of karmic cycles.
Pyrite	Pyrite is well known for its association with luck and prosperity, and is often used to bring in abundance of all kinds. Pyrite can also help promote physical vitality and well-being, and enhance will and inspiration. Energetically, this stone can help deflect negative energy, balance one's energy, and help ground.

Material	Purpose
Smoky Quartz	Smoky quartz protects and grounds, helping to filter out unwanted energy and providing a tether to the earth during moon magick and healing ceremonies.
Sunstone	Part of the moon's influence on earth comes from the sun! A crystal of confidence, strength, courage, and joy, sunstone works in tandem with moonstone for new moon and solar eclipse alignments.

DAYS OF THE WEEK

In modern witchcraft practices, many witches work with the days of the week. Hailing from Western astrology's ancient beginnings, where the celestial bodies were synonymous with the will of the gods, each day of the week was dedicated to one of the seven celestial bodies that could be seen with the naked eye—and this includes the moon.

Below, you will find a short reference list of the days of the week and their planetary associations. As you've learned in this book, there are many opportune moments for a variety of spells. This is simply another factor to consider. These may come in handy when favorable lunar timings are too far off, or to combine with your lunar magick for more potency. For example, a waxing gibbous moon in Libra on a Friday could be an opportune moment for love and partnership magic.

- **Monday** is the day of the week associated with the moon. Efforts around healing, the home, intuitive and psychic workings, and emotions can be especially successful then.

- **Tuesday** is Mars's day, and is great for boosting workings around vitality, physical energy, action, and passion.

- Ruled by the planet Mercury, **Wednesday** is a beneficial time for spells and magick around communication, information, research, technology, and efforts around speaking and writing of all kinds.

- **Thursday** is associated with Jupiter, often called the planet of expansion in astrology. This makes it a powerful day to focus on efforts related to abundance, new opportunities, luck, increase, and favorable outcomes when it comes to the law.

- **Friday** is Venus's day, and a great day to boost magickal workings for love, wealth/money, sensuality, beauty, and connection.

- Associated with Saturn, the planet of boundaries and restriction, **Saturday** generally favors efforts around time, structure, organization, systems, and boundaries.

- **Sunday** is associated with the sun, and is a good time to try witchcraft related to success, creativity, positivity, health, and any effort you want to bless.

COLOR AND MOON MAGICK

In witchcraft practices—or even so far in this book—you may have heard that silver or white is the moon's color. In magickal practices, color is associated with various celestial bodies, and even just general themes and energy for spells.

There is no hard-and-fast rule—many things influence the way you perceive and experience color, including culture. For example, in America, dollar bills are often green, and thus green is seen as the favorable color for money magick—but that is not the case in all cultures. So, always trust your personal judgment when it comes to color. In this section, you will find a basic list of colors and their perceived magickal associations, to help you choose the right colored candles, cloths, and more when it comes to your moon-magick spells and intentions.

- **White:** Cleansing, purification, clarity, spiritual matters, serenity, any effort when in a pinch

- **Black:** Protection, banishing, boundaries, mystery, power, endings

- **Red:** Sensuality, passion, desire, anger, vitality/physical energy, action, strength, repellant

- **Orange:** Road opening, success, creativity, motivation, sensuality, play, joy, energy, confidence, courage

- **Yellow:** Happiness, luck, inspiration, communication

- **Green:** Growth, money, healing, fertility, prosperity

- **Blue:** Psychic abilities, communication, peace, harmony

- **Purple:** Spirituality, power, control, harmony, wisdom

- **Pink:** Friendship, love, compassion, emotions

Chapter 6

LUNAR SPELLCASTING

From her waxing in power in the sky to her waning and vanishing into darkness, the moon holds vast potential for your magick. Since you have learned about the meaning of each phase, the electric "oomph" of eclipses and supermoons, and the qualities of the moon in each sign, you may be tempted to just jump in and start slinging spells. But there are some spell-working basics to learn first.

In this chapter, you will gather the fundamental information necessary to create successful spells, for moon magick or otherwise. Beginning moon witches will grasp the building blocks for powerful spells, while advanced practitioners can refresh themselves on the basics. You'll create a lunar grimoire to record your personal relationship with the moon, plan and arrange a lunar altar that works for you, and use the magick of words to speak your will into reality with affirmations and visualize the success of your lunar spells. With these moon-magick essentials, you'll be casting powerful moon spells in no time.

KEEPING A LUNAR GRIMOIRE

Many witches keep a journal or notebook called a grimoire or book of shadows. It's a place to record spells that have worked well for you, magickal information that you like to reference, and any other notes that can help you track or expand your spellcasting journey. Some prefer a casual journal, and others might use a binder with pages that they can remove or add as needed. Whatever style you prefer is the best choice for you!

Tracking Your Personal Experiences with the Moon

Your grimoire will quickly become a reference you can return to time and time again. The way the moon impacts you is deeply personal—the moon in one sign might amplify stress for you, while in another sign it could inspire calm or confidence. The effect might be the opposite for another witch. Just as the moon reflects the sun's light, she also acts as a mirror for your own personal life. Beginning to piece together how certain phases and signs impact how you feel and what is happening in your life can not only strengthen your magick but also cultivate a deeper connection with the moon within your witchcraft practice.

First, Record the Moon's Phase and Position

To begin filling in your lunar grimoire and start to notice threads and themes of the moon's influence, you'll first need to know the basic information about the moon at any given moment. For example, note:

● What phase is the moon in?

● What sign is the moon in? Or is the moon void of course?

● Are there any special moon occurrences, such as an eclipse season or a supermoon?

Many phone apps and websites have this information. You can also purchase a datebook that lists the moon's phase and zodiac sign for each day. When you capture this information, you can more easily go back and reference what experiences you had with a certain lunar phase or sign, what spells were cast, and how they manifested. As you record each meditation, spell, or experience, you'll slowly begin to piece together how the moon's position impacts your life, spiritual practice, and magick.

Record Other Details in Your Lunar Grimoire

Beyond the moon's placement, here are some possible details to record in your magickal grimoire, moon journal, or book of shadows. If this seems like a lot, start tracking one thing at a time, or choose the factors that seem the most important to you:

● How are you feeling at this time?

● Are you experiencing any key life events?

- What spells are you casting, or what intentions are you working on?

- Which parts of your lunar magick are working well? Which might need adjusting?

- Which herbal and crystal allies have been most effective for you? Which do you want to try next?

- What insights or impressions do you gain from your moon meditations or when you look up at the moon?

- Are you noticing any patterns standing out in your life?

You can write as much or as little as you want about these topics. The moon is connected to your emotional nature, so maintain your grimoire in whichever way feels right to you. As you pay more attention to how the moon impacts you, you'll begin to see overarching themes and take more notes that, in the long run, can benefit your magick. Plus, your grimoire can be a place to store special lunar recipes, rituals, and spells you want to repeat!

CREATING YOUR LUNAR ALTAR

An altar is a sacred place where you can cast your spells, perform rituals, and meditate. Over time, using such a space repeatedly helps to create a sacred, charged area that further amplifies your lunar workings. An altar is not *necessary* for your craft; the earth itself is an altar, and as a witch you should use what is accessible to do your work. But when it comes to moon magick, it can be useful to have a dedicated space to cast lunar spells or to charge your crystals and magickal items under the moonlight. If you are able to, take some time to create a dedicated space where you can sit down, meditate, and develop your sacred, inherent connection with the moon. An altar can be as small as a reused mint tin, or as big as a table, or larger. Whatever you have access to, you can make it work for you!

Where to Set Up Your Altar

Perhaps the best spot for a lunar altar is a place near a window, or even a windowsill where you can leave items to charge under moonlight. If you can see the moon through the window, that makes a great moon meditation and reflection spot! But any place will do—whether you can see the moon outside or not, your altar can always include a symbol of the moon to help remind you of its energy.

You can also create a moveable altar. Many witches make travel altars inside little tins to take with them on trips. A moveable altar could include a symbol or image of the moon, plus ritual items such as incense, salt, and crystals. Instead of a tin, you might use a tray (thrifted silver trays are terrific for lunar workings!). A tray gives you a firesafe surface to burn candles, and you can move it from location to location: Cast spells outside under the moonlight on your tray and then safely bring it inside—or bring a magickal tray with crystals and ritual items outside to charge under the moonlight! A moveable altar can also be as simple as a special cloth that you can open to perform spellwork on.

What to Include on Your Altar

The following are some items you probably want to have on your lunar altar. You can use these for meditation in addition to spellcasting:

- **Lunar symbol:** Artwork or a symbol or image of the moon can help you reflect on the power of this celestial body's energy. You could also consider a moon-shaped object, a tapestry depicting a lunar scene, or even the tarot card The Moon.

- **Incense:** Scent is powerful when it comes to altering the mind for meditation, and it can do a lot to set the tone for a room. Consider scents that help you relax, or choose a specific incense that helps you connect to the moon.

- **Devotional candle:** You may decide to make a devotional candle for the moon—a candle you light anytime you cast moon magick, meditate, or connect with the moon, then promptly snuff out when done. The colors white and silver traditionally represent the moon, but pick whatever color speaks to you best. You can "dress" or anoint the candle with Moon Oil or cleanse it with Moon Water (see instructions in Chapter 7), or even sprinkle the top of it with moon-associated herbs.

- **Crystal:** Gemstones such as moonstone and selenite are especially powerful for connecting to the moon. Holding a stone can do a lot to attune your energy for meditation and moon magick.

- **Tarot or oracle deck:** In working with the moon, you might find it helpful to pull a daily card to decipher the moon's daily message for you. The moon loves to communicate in symbols!

LUNAR SPELLCASTING ITEMS

In order to cast the lunar spells and rituals in this book, you will probably want to have certain tools on hand. These tools will help you perform your spells, and they'll also heighten your lunar magick. Remember that you do not need all of these—in witchcraft, any item can be sacred and you can always use what you have on hand. Here's a list of tools that might come in handy:

- **Bowl:** Given that the moon is connected to the element of water, a bowl can come in handy. Use it to create Moon Water or to hold water for other uses. For water scrying (gazing into water to receive visions or images and divine symbols for psychic information), a black bowl is especially useful.

- **Cup or chalice:** Whether it be Moon Water or a relaxing tea or cocktail you're sipping, drinking is a great way to connect with the moon via liquid. A cup is a vessel—a symbol of what you wish to hold in your life and blessings—and it can provide whatever will nourish your body and spirit. The moon's connection to water makes a cup or chalice a simple yet very effective moon-magick tool. It can be as simple or ornate as you wish.

- **Wand:** Some witches opt to use a wand to direct and magnify energy. A natural quartz point works, too, and in a pinch your pointer finger will work as well!

- **Selenite:** Named after the moon goddess Selene, with an iridescence that matches the moon, this stone is perfect in many ways for your moon magick. If you've read Chapter 5, you already know that selenite is a great lunar crystal and useful magickal tool for cleansing your energy before moon meditation or magick.

- **Candles:** Candles are a must-have for many moon witches! Candles are used for intention setting and prayers across a vast array of religious and spiritual practices, and when it comes to moon magick their light echoes the growing light of the waxing moon and lunar transformation. There are many types of candles you can choose from—votives, chime candles (short pillar candles), bigger pillar or jumbo candles, and glass-encased ones.

- **Candleholder(s):** If you're going to burn candles, you will definitely need some firesafe candleholders for safety. In a pinch, you can use sand contained in a bowl, but if you work with candles frequently, find a trustworthy and safe holder. You can also use a lighter to melt the bottom of a candle and affix it to a fireproof surface (such as a plate).

- **Cauldron:** A cauldron provides a safe space to burn herbs, charcoal incense, petition papers, and more. Like Cerridwen's cosmic cauldron, your cauldron is a space for magick and alchemy. You can often find small cast iron ones that will do the job at your local witch supply shop. A cauldron may not be necessary to get your witchcraft practice started, but at some point it's useful to invest in one if you find yourself burning items frequently. A cauldron often comes with a cover to easily snuff out fire. Consider a fireproof coaster to keep under the cauldron as well, as depending on what you burn inside it can get hot!

- **Mortar and pestle:** Often made from stone, a mortar and pestle consist of a bowl and blunt, club-like pestle to grind down resin and herbs to a powder. While not an immediately necessary tool in your moon magick, a mortar and pestle can come in handy further down the line as you experiment with making your own powders or incense.

- **Plate(s) or trays/serving dishes:** Plates and trays are versatile witchcraft tools: you can place crystal grids, candle spells, offerings, and more on them, and then move them around your space or house as needed. Plus, a plate or tray can also provide another layer of fire safety.

- **Jars and containers:** Instead of recycling that pickle jar, upcycle it for your witchcraft! Jar spells are common in witchcraft, and jars provide airtight storage space for store herbs, herb blends, oils, and more. There's no need to purchase jars—over time, you can collect all you need from everyday grocery goods. (Although, much to the chagrin of their partners, many witches find they can never have too many!)

- **Pen and paper:** When it comes to moon magick, having a pen and paper handy to write intentions and affirmations is essential. You can use them to craft petition papers to place under candles or to burn in your cauldron or above a fireproof dish.

- **Oils:** In witchcraft, oil is often used to anoint candles. Some witches make their own magickal oils by mixing a carrier oil, essential oils, oil infusions, and herbs aligned to specific ritual purposes and intentions, such as love or protection. You can also buy oils if you prefer. In a pinch, you can use kitchen oils—just be mindful of what they're made of. For example, for moon magick, coconut oil would be a great fit, since coconut is associated with the moon and spirituality.

- **Herbs:** Herbs are often used to "dress" candles after they have been anointed with oil, to add specific energy or intentions. A witch might do this by sprinkling a pinch of herbs atop a votive or glass-encased candle, or by rolling a standing candle in a blend of herbs so that the herbs stick to the sides of the candle. Adding aligned herbs helps empower and support your intentions, but it can also feed the flame, so be reserved in deciding how much to use, and take precautions with fire safety. Be sure to burn within sight and, if possible, use multiple layers of firesafe features, such as a candleholder, a plate, and a tray or lantern. Herbs can also be crafted into herbal blends; crushed down with a mortar and pestle into powder; added to baths, sachets and charm bags; and more. You can always use kitchen spices in a pinch, or even open up tea bags to get herbs until you build up your own magickal herbal collection. Just be mindful of safe herbal practices!

- **Pendulum:** Pendulums are useful divination tools. They can be used to answer questions, find lost objects, or even select items to use in magick when you are unsure. In modern witchcraft practices, many people use gorgeous pendulums carved out of stone or crystal they feel a connection with. However, you don't need to invest in one unless you want to—you can use a simple pendant on a necklace, or even get some charms from a craft store and make your own.

How to Use a Pendulum

To use your pendulum, start by uncovering what "yes" and "no" look like. To do this, hold your pendulum's string with your dominant hand, hovering the charm or pendant over the palm of your nondominant hand. Ask the pendulum to show you "yes," and see how it moves. It may take a while, but keep asking and be patient. Once you feel like you know your yes, ask the pendulum to show you "no." You can repeat this each time you use your pendulum, just to be sure. I've found everyone has a different yes and no, and discovering your own adds an extra magickal connection with your pendulum. Some people also decide for themselves what their yes or no might be, or craft a pendulum board (by drawing on paper) so the pendulum can swing toward the written answers. Some common movements include a clockwise circle for yes and counterclockwise for no, or a vertical line for yes and a horizontal line for no, or a circle for yes and a diagonal line for no, or any combination of those options. Working with a pendulum can be useful for guidance and divination, to read energy, and also to choose what lunar herbs and ingredients to use in spells when you aren't quite sure.

As you begin working with the moon, you may feel called to dedicate tools and items just for your lunar practice. While this isn't necessary, if you see yourself working with the moon in the long run, blessing and consecrating your tools to be attuned to the moon can strengthen your ritual magick.

GET READY TO PERFORM MAGICK

You have learned so much about the magick of the moon: its phases, eclipses, seasonal moons, correspondences, spellcrafting tools, and more. Now it's time to pick up several techniques often utilized in magick that are essential to pave the way to powerful moon spells. In this section, you'll uncover the steps to performing powerful lunar magick: how to prepare and plan for your spells, cleanse and ground your energy, practice visualization, and more. You will find all the information you need to cast powerful moon magick for any spell or meditation. As always, some tips might resonate more with you than others—let your intuition guide you, and uncover your own style of moon magick.

Prepare Your Tools and Environment

Before you grab your wand or light that candle, consider both the ingredients you'll be using and your mindset as you begin your spellwork. In particular, think about the following factors to help produce a calming, focused, and magickal lunar environment to support moon meditations or spells:

- **Scent:** Think about what helps you feel calm and centered. Is there incense or a particular scent that could calm you or boost your efforts? In addition to incense, many witches work with mists. In whatever form you choose, you can use scent to help calm your mind and bring focus before a meditation or ritual.

- **Sound/music:** Another important aspect of preparing for spellwork— and especially meditation—is sound. Some witches use an instrument such as a drum or rattle. There are also lots of great meditation music options available online, including on *YouTube*. Chanting is another great way to integrate sound vibration into ritual.

- **Comfort:** It may seem small, but it can be hard to meditate or focus when you are uncomfortable. Think ahead if you might need a blanket or a pillow so that you won't need to interrupt a ritual or meditation.

- **Drink:** Performing moon magick is a great excuse to hydrate. Even a simple cup of tea or nurturing water can help calm and center you as you breathe in the calming steam, aroma, and soothing warmth.

- **Light:** Bright lights can be distracting, but you'll need some light to see what you're doing. Consider the mood—would a small lamp work, or a few bright candles? The right light can help relax your vision and bring your focus to the magick at hand. Like the dark moon, you can cast your magick under the cloak of shadow.

- **Visuals:** Everyone learns and feels energy differently. Meditation doesn't have to mean sitting cross-legged and closing your eyes—it can also be done while gazing into a crystal or while looking at a painting or photo. If you are someone who enjoys visual elements, consider an image that you can use to connect to the moon—you can even use the tarot card The Moon.

- **Touch and movement:** If you're someone who appreciates movement, you might consider including a stone or crystal that's pleasing to hold (and also has great energy), or even incorporating some movement into your practice. For example, you could unwind before meditation by rolling your neck and shoulders and rotating your abdomen, or by taking a moonlit walk to connect to the serenity of moonlight.

- **Journaling:** Have your grimoire handy. You can write down anything that's on your mind to help clear your focus, or have it handy to record insights you get during ritual.

Once you've assembled your altar and tools, you might want to magickally prepare them for use in witchcraft. Here's a ritual you can do to empower your magickal tools with the moon's energy:

Lunar Tool Consecration Ritual

Through this ritual consecration, your moon-magick tools will be blessed with the power of the moon, making it easier to tune into her magick in the future. For best results, perform this ritual during a full moon so your items will be blessed with the moon's maximum power and potential. You can begin as the sun sets and the full moon rises.

You Will Need:

❭ Altar or ritual cloth

❭ Whatever items you wish to bless as lunar tools

❭ Lunar incense, such as jasmine, eucalyptus, or sandalwood

❭ Silver or white cord, ribbon, or yarn

❭ Moon Oil or Moon Water (see instructions in Chapter 7), or coconut oil or other oil of choice

Directions:

1. Begin by cleansing your energy and the energy of your items. You can do this with cleansing smoke (use the Lunar-Charged Cleansing Herbal Bundle in Chapter 7), with the cleansing suggestions later in this chapter, or by using sound, salt, or other methods.

2. Open your ritual cloth and put the items on it, or place your items on your altar's surface.

3. Light the incense and watch the smoke rise toward the celestial moon and her energy.

4. Visualize the moon interacting with the incense. See the moon's celestial light beam down, her rhythm calling to you. Feel the moon's

connection with you, and see her moonlight consecrate and shine through your skin, like liquid silver.

5. With your cord or ribbon, create a big circle (like the moon) that can encompass all your lunar tools.
6. Now that you are feeling charged up and connected to the moon, consecrate each item one by one: Hold it, anoint it with some of your lunar oil, pass it through the lunar incense, then lay it down within the circle and repeat the process with the next object.
7. When you are done, hover your hands above the tools. Visualize the lunar light above you, shining through your head, down your arms, and into the items. You may wish to say a chant: "The moon increases your power with every passing hour."
8. Allow the items to charge overnight. If they can catch the light of the full moon, that's especially powerful.

Prepare Your Mind and Energy

Now that you have considered what tools and elements you might need and prepared them for ritual, it's time to prepare your energy and mind for optimal moon-magick results. After all, you might not cast an effective money spell if your mind and energy are still wrapped up in the events of the day. The following are some meditative exercises and techniques to minimize distractions, focus and cleanse your energy, and align to the cosmos to cast powerful moon magick.

Center Yourself

To start a spell or meditation, it's a good idea to call your energy back to the present moment and also tune into your body and sense of psychic feeling. Your mind can run wild with thoughts and possibilities from the activity of the day, and centering is a great way to bring it back. Here's one way to do it:

1. Take three deep breaths into your belly. As you do so, feel the sensation of your stomach expanding and tightening with air, and listen to the sound of your inhalation.
2. Hold each breath for a few seconds, sitting in the silence of the moment.
3. Exhale, allowing your shoulders to soften, savoring the release of air. Notice the silence before breathing in again. With each deep breath, tune into your body.

4. Finally, bring your focus to your solar plexus—an energy center right below your breastbone, slightly above your belly. Breathe in for four counts, then hold for four, then exhale for four. (You might also try different arrangements of counts to discover works best for you.) With each breath, notice the solar plexus glowing with energy.

Cleanse Your Energy

Throughout the day, you move around and meet other people, and you can—intentionally or unintentionally—hold on to their energy or the energy of the environment. This can often also create energetic cords of attachment. When sitting down to meditate or do spellwork, it's a good idea to free yourself from that. Cleansing is like taking an energetic bath—cleaning off the psychic debris.

There are many ways to cleanse. Here are some effective options:

- **Pass a selenite wand or stick around your body.** These sticks are usually relatively inexpensive, and they're named after the moon goddess Selene (perfect for lunar spellwork!). Slowly outline your body with the selenite wand, focusing especially on the back of your neck, your head, and your heart. Do this slowly, with intention, and you might feel an energetic shift.

- **Try using cleansing sprays.** Many sprays contain cleansing essences, such as lemon. Simply spraying the mist through your aura and space can help cleanse the energy. You can even experiment with crafting your own sprays using a combination of purified/spring water, essential oils, and alcohol.

- **Burn herbs.** We can use herbs the same way we use incense: Let the smoke from the embers of an herb or herb bundle waft around the space. You might lightly burn the tip of a dried rosemary sprig, or craft the Lunar-Charged Cleansing Herbal Bundle in Chapter 7 to use for cleansing before moon magick. Just be wary of setting off any fire alarms, and open doors and windows for circulation!

- **Exhale.** Visualize using your breath to move energy. Breathe in cleansing energy with each inhale, and blow out unwanted energy, thoughts, or feelings with each exhale.

- **Try using water.** We shower and wash dirt off our hands with water, so why not psychic energy too? Water is connected to the moon and filled with healing, cleansing energy. You can spritz salt water around yourself, touch it to your skin, or visualize running water cleansing away unwanted psychic debris and thoughts.

These are just a few ways to cleanse your energy, but there are as many ways as there are stars around the moon!

Ground Yourself

When connecting with a celestial force, it is especially important to be grounded—meaning connected to the earth. In magick, it's easy to forget the importance of grounding, as most of our attention usually turns to manifesting. However, grounding is essential to making the energies you experience real and tangible in the physical world. It is also helpful to ensure you don't get overwhelmed by the lunar energy, which can (on occasion) reveal your deepest and most wild, vulnerable emotions. Here are some ways to ground yourself ahead of spellwork:

- **Take off your shoes and walk around outside.** The most simple and popular grounding technique is simply going barefoot outside, preferably on grass, dirt, or other natural materials.

- **Use a crystal or stone.** Hold a piece of hematite or black tourmaline, and tune into its energy. To ground, breathe deeply and bring your focus to where your body connects with the earth. You might slowly begin to feel the pulsing vibration of Mother Earth's gravity.

- **Visualize a grounding cord.** Some witches imagine a root or energetic grounding cord extending from the base of their spine down to the earth's core. Then they visualize exchanging energy with the earth—pulling energy up through the cord and sending some back down. This is a way to both draw energy up from the earth and ground and neutralize energy back down. Beyond helping you feel connected to the earth, this visualization can also source vitality and strength for your spellwork without draining your own energy.

Connect to the Moon

One way to begin the process of connecting yourself to the moon is simply by gazing at the sky—specifically, the numerous stars and vibrant moon that illuminate the landscape. You can hold a lunar crystal, such as moonstone or selenite, while you do this. Or, imagine yourself as a tree, your growing branches reaching up to the moon just as your grounding cord or root reaches into the earth. Or picture a pillar of light connecting you to the ethereal moon. Remember your connection to the moon, and visualize its pull upon you.

WORKING WITH ENERGY

In working with the moon, it will be important to identify how you feel energy. If you're a newcomer to witchcraft, that's something you may need to practice. Here are some ways you can begin to decipher what energy feels like to you:

- **Sensing crystal energy:** When holding a stone, slow your breathing and gently bring your awareness to where the stone rests in your hand. You might feel a hum or vibration, or an energetic shift within your body. Try feeling the energy of different stones by holding each one separately, taking deep breaths, and slowly tuning into the stone. Some crystals, you might not feel at all; you might connect with others instantly.

- **Feeling auras and energetic boundaries:** Everything has an energy that surrounds it—oftentimes, this energy is referred to as an aura. As you get closer to the aura, the energy often gets denser and more defined. One way to begin to decipher what an aura feels like is by experiencing the energetic boundaries of plant and crystal life. To practice this, go outside to some plants or select a few different-sized crystals. Place your hand a few feet away from a crystal or plant, and slowly bring it closer, noticing where (and if) you feel a shift in energy. You might experience a more definite buzzing of energy as your palm gets closer.

Once you know how to feel energy, you'll want to know how to send it too. Sending energy is one way you can communicate your intentions to plant spirits, such as candle-dressing herbs, in your magickal work. There are many different ways to send energy, but here is one simple method to start with for now:

- Perform one of the centering and grounding practices described earlier in this chapter. This is important to ensure you are not depleting your own resources.

- Visualize tree branches arising from your head and shoulders, all the way to the moon or even beyond the moon into the cosmos. The same way the leaves of earth photosynthesize energy from the sun's light, the leaves of your branches collect the ethereal moonlight and starlight, bringing that energy back down to you, down your head, shoulders, and arms. If it's easier, you can also simply imagine a beam of celestial, lunar light shining upon your head and down your arms.

- Now channel the energy out from you as you give it an intention or even visualize a color corresponding to your desired outcome. You can use this energy to communicate to plant and crystal allies what your goals are for your moon magick. You might notice an energetic response from them as you do so, or you can imagine your plant or crystal ally receiving or attuning to the energy the way a night flower opens up in the cosmic moonlight.

These techniques are great beginner steps toward working with crystals or herbs in your lunar magick—they'll help you recognize energetic responses from your allies and know when they are aligned with your intention. They'll also hone your ability to discern what energy feels like to you, and to sense differences in vibration. This information will allow you to assess which spells are more powerful for you at any given time, and which spells you might need to put more support and effort behind.

AFFIRMATIONS AND VISUALIZATION

You've now got a great foundation for conducting your spellwork. But as you begin manifesting with the moon, you might hit a few bumps in the road. Oftentimes, we get in our own way—we cast a spell not *really* believing it will work, or we are closed to or unaware of different (and perhaps better) possibilities, or we don't create room for our desires to manifest.

Witches work with energy, and energy follows the path of least resistance. Two ways to avoid getting in our own way are to create and repeat an affirmation, and to practice visualization. In fact, these can often become spells in themselves! Witches and non-witches alike can utilize these techniques to create the life they desire.

Write a Moon Affirmation

As you work with the lunar cycle, it is important to cast supportive energy to help your moon-magick intentions grow into reality. If you do not truly believe something can happen and do not create mental and physical space for it to exist, your spells can fall flat. Writing an affirmation can shift your mindset and make space for your desires to manifest into reality. An affirmation is essentially a statement repeated aloud or internally, phrased to *affirm* your desired mood, feeling, or result.

Working with an affirmation will help you align your mind, energy, and communication to your desires and speak them into reality. Affirmation can be a stand-alone practice or can be integrated as a powerful addition to your lunar spellwork. For example, throughout the waxing phase, repeat an affirmation related to spells you cast at the new moon. This practice can support your desires as they manifest with the growth of the moon's power. Here's how to do it:

- With a pen in hand and a piece of paper in front of you, consider what you wish to bring into this world. Jot down one or more words that match this intention, or simply write your desire. For example, you might start off with, "I want more money."

- Now try getting even more specific—is there a purpose you need this money for? Is there an exact amount you need?

- Think about the energy of how you want this to come to you. You may want it to flow freely, or effortlessly.

- Next, try writing your intention as though it is already happening, and from a positive perspective. Make it confident too. For example, "Money flows effortlessly and freely to me" is a general (and still potentially successful) affirmation, while a longer version can add even more context: "Money flows effortlessly and freely to me. I have plenty to pay my bills, save extra, and afford what I want." Go with what feels best to you at this time.

- When you have arrived at a powerful affirmation, you will feel it resonate and sing through your body. If you're having trouble coming up with ideas, find premade affirmations and use them as foundations for building your own.

- Next, consider how often you'll want to repeat your affirmation. It's a good idea to say it at least twice a day. But at the beginning of the moon cycle, it may be best to repeat it more often, as this is often when we need the most support to create space and change to allow our spell to manifest.

- Once you've decided on the affirmation and how frequently you want to repeat it, write the affirmation out on its own piece of paper. If you like, you can anoint it with Moon Oil (see Chapter 7) and place it somewhere you can see it. For example, you could use nice stationery and colorful ink and stick it to your bathroom mirror to make it easy to repeat the magickal chant in the morning when getting ready for the day and at night when preparing for sleep.

- Repeat your affirmation throughout the waxing phase, adjusting as needed. You can burn the paper at the full moon, if desired.

In addition to creating and repeating an affirmation, you may choose a magickal booster to hold or use while saying your affirmation. Some options include spraying a mist, perfume, or spray as you say your affirmation, or holding an aligned crystal as you say the words. You may even connect your affirmation to a specific symbol, sigil, or charm that reminds you of your magick and hold that object or place it in a visible location. Remember that your moon-magick intentions are real and tangible.

Visualizing

Have you ever daydreamed or imagined how something might look or feel if it were to happen to you? Then you have visualized! In magickal practices, conscious visualization can be a great tool to help call your desires to you and begin to make them real, and it's great for visual and kinesthetic learners. The key is to remain open to alternate possibilities and shift your visualization over time if needed.

By visualizing what a goal, manifestation, or spell outcome might look or feel like if it were to come true, you attune yourself to that energy, calling it toward you and supporting efforts cast at the new moon. Here's how to do it:

- Cleanse your energy or get your thoughts out by writing them out on paper. When ready, close your eyes and breathe deeply.

- Think about what you are trying to manifest into reality. Visualize its coming true—how does it make you feel? Connect with that emotion.

- Focus on the end result and let the universe work out the "how." Really feel it in your body. Imagine your senses—what will you see, smell, taste, or feel when this goal is manifested?

- Continue visualizing until you feel joy and excitement in your body at the possibility. When you feel ready, breathe the energy and visualization into your body and into every fiber of your being.

- You may especially wish to perform a visualization during the waxing phase, or even before a spell, to help strengthen and align to the energy—but it works for many moon efforts. You can even repeat the process each day and slowly allow the universe to show you more of the details of how that moon manifestation looks and feels.

You now have all the basic knowledge you need to prepare yourself physically and mentally for spellwork, focus and align your energy to your goals, and perform spellcasting. It's time to put this all together and begin conducting your own brand of moon magick.

Chapter 7

FOUNDATIONAL MOON PHASE MAGICK

As the moon waxes and wanes before the celestial backdrop of the sky, she offers both power and wisdom to guide your magick, healing, and focus—the growth of your soul as a moon-magick witch. In this chapter, you will uncover basic spells, rituals, and meditations that invite you to connect to the magick of each moon phase. These approachable, modifiable recipes will become the foundation of your moon magick, and they can easily be adapted to suit a variety of purposes and lunar occasions as you grow in your practice. Whether it's a meditation during the moon in Virgo or the quarter moon in Libra, use these spells to connect with each moon moment.

Through working with these lunar enchantments, you will get familiar with the power and magick of each moon phase and with the basics of making oils and bath blends, devotional candles, and more. You can use these workings throughout a lunar cycle to continue supporting one greater goal set at the new moon, or pick a single spell for whatever moon phase you are in, regardless of intent.

This chapter is broken down by lunar phase to give some initial structure to your magick. Once you have mastered working with the moon, let your intuition tell you what spells to do and when. As you advance in your practice, you can easily alter each spell to suit more specific desires, or even to fit the sign the moon is in, by swapping in corresponding colors, crystals, herbs, and other elements using the information in Chapter 5 and Appendix C. For example, if the moon is in Taurus, you might add Venus-ruled cardamom, rose, or vanilla into any of these spells. And of course, be very careful when using lighters or flames in any spells to ensure safety. A world of endless moon magick awaits you.

NEW MOON SPELLS

New Moon Alignment Crystal Meditation

Best Lunar Timing: New Moon, Solar Eclipse, Moon in Any Sign

Lunar Energy: Alignment, Empowerment, Inner Knowing

Access the magick of the new moon phase and attune your energy to the conjoined powers of the moon and sun with this crystal moon meditation. At the new moon, the moon and sun align in the same astrological sign—a cosmic, divine moment of synchronicity and harmony. In this meditation, you will use crystals to tune into the celestial energy of the new moon for empowerment and align the strength of the sun and moon within yourself. Use this meditation to tap into the energy of the new moon, or perform it before you cast spells or read the cards to empower your moon magick.

You Will Need:

> Moonstone, or another stone to represent the moon
> Moon sign crystal or mineral of choice, or a crystal related to your goal (see Appendix C)
> Oracle or tarot card deck, optional

Directions:

1. Sit in your sacred space and set the mood for meditation as you see fit (see Chapter 6). Be sure you're comfortable and relaxed and have cleansed your energy and cleared your mind.
2. Hold the moonstone in your nondominant hand and the other crystal or mineral in your dominant hand. Close your eyes. Breathe deeply three times, feeling the stones' weight in your hands, and slowly tune into their energy.
3. Visualize the sun and moon aligned in the cosmos and yourself on earth feeling their pull. Reflect on what sign the moon is in (see Chapter 4), and ponder the following questions, letting the moon guide you or using a tarot or oracle deck if inspired:

   ● What does the energy of this new moon feel like to me?

- What is something I need now in my life, or an issue that has arisen recently?

- What do I feel called to pursue at this time? What is the best way to utilize this energy for my life path and goals?

- What is the next step forward in my journey?

4. With the insights you collected in mind, again visualize the cosmos around you—the moon aligned with the sun and earth. Visualize your own inner sun (your inner light, warmth, and consciousness) and moon (your intuition, feelings, and soul that guides the way) aligned within you.

5. Breathe deeply three more times, feeling a sense of determination toward your new moon intention or goal and envisioning it becoming reality. Breath the celestial energy into your body, infusing every part of your being with this alignment and your new moon intentions.

6. Carry the moonstone or moon sign–related stone with you as you work on these aspirations. If desired, follow this meditation with the Intention-Setting Candle Blessing spell (the next spell in this chapter) to further empower your new moon goals.

Connect to Your Inner Moon

You can modify this crystal meditation to connect to and balance the energy of your own personal moon sign. To do so, use the moonstone, plus a moon sign–related stone for your personal moon sign. If you meditate holding both stones, you might find yourself tuning into a specific energetic feeling. This can help you become more familiar with and empower your inner moon sign and magick.

Intention-Setting Candle Blessing

Best Lunar Timing: New or Waxing Moon, Any Special Lunar Occasion, Moon in Any Sign

Lunar Energy: Intention Setting, Manifestation, Blessing

With the moon and sun in alignment, the cosmic forces at the new moon offer an opportunity to set intentions and cast them out into the world for success. In this simple intention-setting candle spell, you will bless your goals for the lunar cycle via a spark of light (the candle's flame) so they can grow alongside the waxing light of the moon. You can use this simple candle spell with any intention, with the new moon in any sign—feel free to even swap out the herbs and ingredients for corresponding moon signs–or intention-specific elements using the information in Chapter 5, Appendix B, and Appendix C. Try this as you bless one single goal, a list of lunar magickal desires, or even your monthly moon intentions.

You Will Need:

) Pen and paper (can use Seed Planting Paper—see Chapter 8)

) Toothpick or needle

) Small taper or chime candle

) Jasmine or sandalwood incense, optional

) Moon Oil (see instructions later in this chapter), coconut oil, or other oil of choice

) Sandalwood powder or ground nutmeg

) Dried rose petals

) Plate or surface to roll candle in herbs

) Candleholder

) Matches or lighter

Directions:

1. On the night of the new moon, gather your items before you on your lunar altar or in your sacred, meditative space, and dim the lights. You might wish to reflect on the moon sign energy (the sign that the moon is in at this time) to guide your efforts.

2. On the paper, write your lunar wish(es) or intention(s).

3. Visualizing your aspirations coming to light, use the toothpick or needle to carve into the candle a key word that captures your intention, such as "success" or "focus." You can also add your name, if you like, to help draw that energy to you. Pass the candle and paper through the incense smoke if desired.

4. Anoint the candle with oil, spreading it from the top of the candle toward the base (toward yourself), a metaphorical act for coaxing your intent your way. Also dab the corners of the paper with oil.

5. Sprinkle sandalwood powder or nutmeg and rose petals on a plate or directly on the paper. Then roll the candle toward yourself through the herbs, once again pulling your desires toward you. (If you use the paper as your rolling surface, you'll leave some herbs and traces of oil behind, which can add an extra layer of enchantment to your goals.)

6. Place the candle in the candleholder. Safely tuck the intention paper under the candleholder.

7. Hover your hands around the candle and above the paper. Visualize the moon and sun aligning toward the same direction in the universe, similarly pulling you toward your desired outcome.

8. With your intention in mind, light your match or lighter—a cardinal spark to start the growing light of your desires coming into manifest reality, to grow with the moon. Light the candle now, feeling empowered.

9. Gaze upon the light illuminating the darkness. Alongside the waxing of the moon in the coming days, your intention will begin to grow.

10. Allow the candle to burn all the way down. Afterward, you can fold the paper and keep it in a pouch with you, or leave it somewhere you will look at it every day—by your bed, on a mirror, or on your desk. At the time of the full or waning gibbous moon, you can burn the paper to let the energy transform or release as you reflect on what you learned during that lunar cycle.

Growing Your Moon Magick with the Phases

To match the growing light of the waxing phase, you can repeat this ritual with larger candles as the waxing phase goes on. For example, perhaps start with a tea light, then use a votive, then a taper candle, then a larger glass-encased candle. You can keep the candle dressing the same, or use Chapter 5 and Appendix C to incorporate herbs for the sign the moon is in, such as clarity herbs for the Virgo moon. This is an easy way to work continuously with your spell alongside the waxing of the moon to increase the energy of your intention in the world.

Moon Dust Blessing Powder

Best Lunar Timing: New, Waxing Crescent, or Quarter Moon; Monday; First of the Month; Moon in Cancer, Taurus, Leo, Sagittarius, or Capricorn; Supermoon; Solar Eclipse; Blue or Black Moon

Lunar Energy: Opportunities, Abundance, Luck

Many witches blow cinnamon powder, a well-known ingredient for fast luck and manifestation, through their front doors for blessings and luck on the first of the month. With added lunar-specific ingredients (jasmine for blessings, abundance, and spirituality; sandalwood for wishes, healing, and protection), this powder is perfect to blow onto your front door at the start of the lunar cycle, or every Monday (moon day), or at the start of each month to bring in lunar blessings and abundance with the lunar cycle. You can also use this mixture as a ritual powder to dress candles; to sprinkle on resumes, letters, or business cards for blessings; or to sprinkle a shape (for example, a pentagram or a circle) on your altar around a spell to boost its power.

You Will Need:

- ❯ Mortar and pestle
- ❯ 1 teaspoon dried jasmine
- ❯ 1 teaspoon ground cinnamon
- ❯ 1 teaspoon sandalwood powder

Directions:

1. Use your mortar and pestle to grind up the dried jasmine. Mix in cinnamon and sandalwood powder, stirring clockwise. With your finger, draw a symbol of the moon into the powder—for example, the crescent moon symbol used in astrology, or the Triple Goddess symbol mentioned in Chapter 5.
2. Place your hands above the powder and envision the moon's light casting down upon you and the powder, and guiding you to new pathways and blessings.
3. On the morning after the new moon (or on a Monday or the first day of the month), place a pinch or so of the powder in the palm of your hand. Open your front door, face it, and with your intention in mind, blow the powder onto or into your front door—a metaphor for drawing in blessings through your doors.
4. This recipe will create enough powder for a few different uses, as you'll only need a pinch for the spell. You can place into a vessel, like a small vial, to reuse as desired for candles or repeating this ritual regularly.

New Moon, New You Sea Salt Scrub

Best Lunar Timing: New or Waning Moon, Moon in Virgo, Moon in a Water Sign (Scorpio, Pisces, Cancer), Eclipses

Lunar Energy: Cleansing, Purification, Rejuvenation

Scrub away old energy and make way for the new with this cleansing salt scrub. The new moon, a time of cosmic alignment between the moon and sun, is perfect for stepping into new energy. With the moon's influence over the tides in mind, a sea salt cleansing scrub is a great way to connect to the moon and refresh your skin. Empowered with lunar ingredients—hex-breaking wintergreen, rejuvenating lemon, healing eucalyptus, spiritual coconut—and also purifying rosemary, this recipe is sure to refresh and revitalize your energy for a fresh slate. Craft this scrub at the waning or new moon, then use it throughout the lunation cycle as desired. Feel free to use the recipe below as an example and, guided by Chapter 5 and the appendixes at the back of the book, swap in ingredients that better suit your purposes and your budget. If you substitute other essential oils, remember to check that they're safe for skin use.

You Will Need:

❭ 3–4 teaspoons coconut oil (olive and grapeseed also work well in a pinch)

❭ 6 drops lemon essential oil

❭ 3 drops rosemary essential oil

❭ 1 drop wintergreen essential oil

❭ 1 teaspoon cut and crushed, dried eucalyptus leaf

❭ Jar with lid

❭ ½ cup sea salt

Directions:

1. Pour oils and eucalyptus into jar. Mix counterclockwise, thinking of their cleansing properties purifying away stagnant and unwanted energy.

2. Mix in sea salt and close the jar. Shake to mix further, imagining that your movement will help shake off unwanted energy and infuse the mixture for cleansing.

3. Use as part of your lunar bath time rituals or each time you shower to keep your energy refreshed and focused on the goal at hand. You can also use as a hand scrub anytime you wash your hands, to purify and cleanse your energy. For example, if you are working on habits or banishing negative thoughts, you can wash your hands with the scrub to cleanse away undesired energy as it arises! Scrub in a counterclockwise direction as you visualize its being cleansed away.

4. If desired, you can also add 1 or 2 teaspoons of muddled cucumber for refreshing, youthful lunar energy. However, you may need to add more sea salt to balance the added liquid, and you'll need to keep the

recipe refrigerated (which is also great for a soothing, cooling effect on the skin) and use before the cucumber goes bad.

Moon Oil

Best Lunar Timing: New Moon–Full Moon, Pisces, Cancer, Supermoon, Blue Moon, Eclipses

Lunar Energy: Psychic Power, Manifestation Lunar Connection

Magickally infused oils—which can be used to dress candles and anoint and bless crystals, spellcasting tools, and other objects—are a key component of many witchcraft practices. Infused with intention and favorable herbal essences, these oils allow you to bless a variety of tools for corresponding purposes and to further empower your magick. This is a basic oil recipe—once comfortable, you can refer to Chapter 5 and the appendixes at the back of the book to make your own recipes, using this one as a foundation. For example, while this oil will be empowered with the waxing phase, you could also craft a protection and banishing oil to use with the waning moon, using protective ingredients.

You Will Need:

) 6 drops lemon essential oil

) 12 drops jasmine essential oil

) 10 drops myrrh essential oil

) Pinch of sandalwood powder

) 2 tablespoons fractionated coconut oil (other carrier oils, such as olive or almond, can also work in a pinch)

) 1-ounce bottle

Directions:

1. On the night of the full moon, mix the essential oils, sandalwood powder, and carrier oil in the bottle. Allow to infuse during the waxing phase, and then leave out to charge under the full moon light.

2. Then it's ready to use! Keep it away from sunlight, and use it to anoint candles, crystals, and more for moon magick. Test a small amount of the oil on your skin for safety, and if all's clear, use it to help open your psychic senses: Anoint your third eye with oil, and meditate holding moonstone, labradorite, or lapis lazuli.

WAXING MOON SPELLS

Waxing Moon Reading

Best Lunar Timing: Quarter or Waxing Moon

Lunar Energy: Insight, Problem-Solving, Planning

As the moon grows in light, it is time to support the spells you cast at the new moon through hope, action, and integrating insight as challenges arise. Divine what lies ahead in your moon-magick manifestation journey and how best to prepare and pivot to achieve your dreams. In this reading, you will use tarot or oracle cards to guide your actions in the waxing phase, but you can also use crystals, runes, or meditation if you prefer. Use the insight gleaned to help craft an action plan and see the way forward. You can also choose more than one card for each question, if desired. If you did the Intention-Setting Candle Blessing, you can keep your paper close by to reflect on your goals.

You Will Need:

❯ Tarot deck

Directions:

1. Set the space for meditation according to what works best for you (see Chapter 6).
2. Shuffle your cards. Call out to your spirit guides and say aloud:

   "With the growth of the moonlight, grant me foresight.
   Illuminate for me, the path forward this night."

3. Pull a card using the list that follows, thinking of each question in mind as you choose a card. Each card's question is inspired by each waxing phase, to help you glean the wisdom within the symbolism of each phase.

   ● Waxing Crescent: What should I do to support the manifestation of my spell?

   ● First Quarter: What challenges might arise?

   ● Waxing Gibbous: What insight or advice do I need to integrate for success?

4. Tune into the imagery and symbolism of the cards—are they advising you integrate a certain energy, or to be wary of certain challenges? Let the suits of the cards guide your insight as well. For example, if you receive a Swords card (representing the realm of air in many—but not all—tarot decks), it could be indicating information on your mindset or providing advice about communication—either an action to take or something to watch out for.

5. Use the insight gleaned to guide your path forward—and perhaps also to guide your choices of spells, meditations, rituals, or reflections to help pivot around any roadblocks.

Spark of Hope Candle Spell

Best Lunar Timing: Waxing Crescent, Sagittarius, Winter-Spring Moons

Lunar Energy: Hope, Positivity, Dispelling Negativity

During the waxing phase (especially the waxing crescent), it's time to inspire hope and positivity—whether it's hope in your dreams, yourself, or your life. The waxing crescent's sliver of light reminds us of possibility—that we can always start anew with the limitless potential of the unknown before us. Relight your sense of hope and faith as you light the candle in this spell. It uses coconut, a moon-associated ingredient that promotes spiritual energy, tranquility, and working through transitions. With a sprinkling of wish-blessing nutmeg, lemon to cleanse and uplift, sugar to sweeten, and lavender to soothe, this spell will help you to find your inner light and sense of positivity as it relights your faith.

You Will Need:

- Fresh lemon wheel
- Yellow or white chime candle
- Coconut oil
- Sugar
- Tray or plate
- Dried lavender
- Dried chickweed pieces, optional
- A piece of your own hair
- Matches or lighter
- Sea salt
- Ground nutmeg

Directions:

1. Begin by preparing the lemon wheel. Press the base of the candle through the center to create a hole the candle will fit through, then set the lemon wheel aside.

2. Dress the candle with oil. Anoint it from the top (wick end) to the base, drawing the oil toward your heart and pulling hope, optimism, and positivity toward yourself.

3. Mix together sugar and lavender on a tray, plate, or other flat surface. Advanced practitioners might also like to add chickweed pieces if they have it on hand. Roll the candle toward yourself through the mixture. Some of the mixture will stick to the candle, and some will remain on the tray.

4. Wrap the hair around the candle to bind this energy to you. If it's a short piece of hair, you can simply place it by the base of the candle toward the end of the spell, before lighting the candle, or add it to the mixture you roll your candle through, so that the oil grabs it and it sticks to the candle.

5. Insert the candle through the hole in the lemon wheel, and affix it to the plate by using a match or lighter to lightly melt the bottom of the candle so that it will stick. Using a candleholder is also an option.

6. Sprinkle sea salt on the plate around the lemon—a metaphoric barrier to ground and dispel any negative energy that comes your way. Then sprinkle the remainder of the sugar and lavender atop the lemon wheel, combining their energies to uplift, sweeten, and soothe for positivity.

7. Hold your hands around the candle, visualizing a light of hope within you. Imagine your faith renewed, whether in yourself, your dreams, or a specific spell, or just in general.

8. Light the candle, connecting to the power of the spark, and say aloud:

   "As this light grows, my hope renews.
   The possibility is, my dreams can come true.
   So mote it be, by the light of the waxing crescent moon."

9. Sprinkle nutmeg from 6 inches above the flame, creating little sparks—like the spark of your hope and faith relighting.

10. Allow the candle to burn down, safely and within sight.

Peach Moonstone Meditation

Peach moonstone can help further enhance your sense of confidence and happiness, and it's especially attuned to the moon. While the candle in this ritual burns, you might like to meditate with a piece of peach moonstone in your hand to help inspire optimism and faith in yourself as you visualize your moon spells coming true. Hold your stone and soften your gaze at the flame. Visualize, feel, or imagine breathing in its light with each inhale, then exhale fear, doubt, and worry. Let the fire transform the energy. With each breath, begin to imagine a light of power growing within you, the flame feeding it. Place the stone by the candle base to charge in the spell's power, then keep it with you in the following days.

Cocreation and Cooperation Support Spell

Best Lunar Timing: Waxing Gibbous or Full Moon, Moon in Libra or Aries, Supermoon

Lunar Energy: Cocreation, Magnification, Support

The waxing gibbous moon is a favorable time to push forth and work together, whether combining forces with another, boosting your efforts with the universe, or integrating new themes to propel your intentions to success. If your manifestation requires the assistance of others in any way, use this spell to energize your intentions. With cooperation, the results of your spellwork and intentions can become bigger and better than imagined. Cooperation can mean partnership with specific people (friends, coworkers, peers, customers, audience), with a spirit ally, or with a concept or idea. You can even use this spell to bind a new habit or theme to support your purpose. For example, to seek focus as you finish a project, or even to spark forces for a night of romance with another. You can also use this spell to add a final push of energy to propel your efforts for success at the full moon.

You Will Need:

- ❭ 2 chime candles, colors corresponding to your intention
- ❭ Toothpick, knife, or needle
- ❭ Jasmine absolute oil (or moon, coconut, or corresponding oil of choice)
- ❭ Ground ginger
- ❭ Dried lemon balm
- ❭ Dried jasmine
- ❭ White thread, or thread of color corresponding to your intention
- ❭ Bowl of sugar
- ❭ Matches or lighter

Directions:

1. Engrave each small candle with a name, title, or relevant word or trait. For example, if you want to combine forces with another person, write your name on one candle and your collaborator's name on the other. Or write your name on one candle and a habit, goal, or key word on the other candle.
2. Dress the candles with oil.
3. Mix the ginger, lemon balm, and jasmine on a tray or other flat surface, and roll the candles one by one through the mixture, toward yourself, coating them.
4. Hold the candles together and wrap them with the thread, tying them together as you chant.

   ● For habits or success:

   "With this thread, I bind to me, the ___ that I need."

   ● For harmony, cooperation, or love:

   "With this thread, I bind to me, that we might work in harmony."

5. Stand the candles in the bowl, in the sugar—the sugar should provide a supportive base, enough to hold up the candles and sweeten the energy.
6. If desired, working clockwise, sprinkle any remaining herb-and-spice mixture into the sugar surrounding the candles.
7. Light the candles, thinking of what each one represents. See the two flames burn side by side. Visualize or feel in your body two forces joining together to form something greater than originally imagined. Watch as the sugar lightly melts, like cooking candy. Savor the sweet burnt sugar smell.
8. Let all candles burn safely and within sight.

Binding a Habit for Success

If you are using this spell to bind a habit, you can dress one candle with oil and herbs for the moon and dress the other with ingredients related to your intention. For example, if binding self-love to you, you might dress the second candle with rose oil and dried, crumbled jasmine. See Chapter 5 for suggestions of ingredients for different energetic purposes.

FULL MOON SPELLS

Full Moon Reflection Tarot Reading

Best Lunar Timing: Full or New Moon, Lunar Eclipse

Lunar Energy: Reflection, Insight, Personal Growth

At the time of the full moon, the moon is opposite the sun. Some may feel a push and pull between these forces, creating a sense of conflict or drama of sorts. Others might feel empowered by the moon shining in her full radiance. Reflecting on the balance between these forces can help reveal what needs to be healed, changed, or unblocked to truly bring the potential of your moon spells to life. The reflection questions in this exercise will help you connect to the wisdom of the moon. While this reading is designed for a tarot or oracle deck, feel free to simply meditate on these questions or use your favorite divination method to glean insight instead. Just as the full moon reflects the sun's light, the insight of the cards can reflect back to you the healing and potential of the lunar cycle. You can also cast this reading at the new moon to divine what that lunation ahead might have in store for you.

You Will Need:

❭ Tarot or oracle deck, or other divination tools of choice

Directions:

1. If possible, sit where you can experience the moonlight. You might also like to hold a lunar crystal (see Chapter 5) and tune into its energy.
2. Close your eyes and take a few deep breaths. Exhale tension and worry. Breathe in peace and lunar clarity. With each deep breath, tune more and more into your body, and into any emotions or patterns that may have risen to the surface with the lunation. Recognize them, and breathe them out.
3. Savor (or visualize) the moonlight shining upon you, illuminating the dark and the answers to all your questions. When ready, ponder the following tarot card layout:

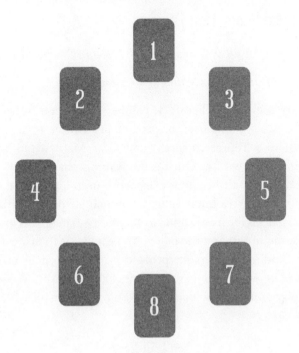

- **Card 1:** What matter or issue is the full moon illuminating for me at this time?

- **Cards 2 and 3:** What do I need to find a balance between?

- **Card 4:** What do I need to release?

- **Card 5:** What do I need to empower or embrace in my life?

- **Card 6:** What is my next course of action?

- **Card 7:** What advice and insight do my spirits guides and ancestors have for me at this time?

- **Card 8:** What is this energy sending me toward?

4. Record any answers or insights in your journal. If desired, follow this activity with any full moon magick (bath, cleansing, etc.) that aligns with your insights.

Moon-Charged Protection Powder

Best Lunar Timing: Full or Waning Moon, Moon in Scorpio or Cancer

Lunar Energy: Cleansing, Protection, Grounding

Salt has many uses in witchcraft. It can be called upon to clear and consecrate space, mark boundaries, or provide protection. It can also be used for grounding or to represent earth on an altar. Many witches cleanse and protect their homes with it. During the waning phase, the cleansing and protective power of salt becomes even more useful, so why not empower some sea salt with extra lunar energy for such purposes? Enhanced with lunar-associated myrrh resin and protective eggshell, this powder combines the powers of salt and the moon. You can use it to protect your home or add it to candle dressings for protection. For a simpler option, forego the myrrh and eggshell and just use the incantation to bless salt to keep on your altar, place under your bed to ward off illness or ill will, or enchant lunar baths.

You Will Need:

❭ Mortar and pestle
❭ Salt, preferably sea salt

❭ Myrrh resin
❭ Eggshell

Directions:

1. Place equal parts salt, myrrh, and eggshell in the mortar. Grind them counterclockwise with the pestle to enchant them with cleansing energy, saying aloud as you do so:

"Charged by the moon as it wanes,
To send unwanted energy away."

2. Pour the powder into a dish and bring it to where the moon's light can touch it.
3. Hover your hands above the dish, tuning into the energy of its contents. Think of the full moon above, shining its light down upon you and the salt.
4. Say aloud, filling in the blank with your intention, such as protection or marking the boundaries of your home:

"Lunar lady, shining bright,
Charge this powder for _____ this full moon night."

5. Stir the powder clockwise with your finger, envisioning the movement empowering it with lunar energy. Leave the powder to charge in the moonlight, and collect it the next morning.
6. Use the powder in your lunar workings as desired. To place a protective barrier around you home, you can cast the powder clockwise around the boundaries of your property, or sprinkle it upon doorways and windowsills.

Moon Water

Best Lunar Timing: Full Moon, Any Moon Whose Energy You Wish to Preserve (Such As Special Eclipses, Supermoons, or Blue Moons)

Lunar Energy: Rejuvenation, Attunement, Empowerment

"Moon water" might sound like a modern buzzword, but witches throughout time have acknowledged the sacred power of water and prayed over it for healing and cleansing and to cast intentions. The moon's special connection to water makes using Moon Water a simple and easy way to connect with it. In this exercise, you'll use the energy of the moon to charge water that you can then use to empower baths; craft sprays to mist the air around you; provide a base for water scrying; clean or bless hands, feet, or magickal tools; or even make magickal ice cubes! Your moon magick could be as simple as drinking Moon Water to connect to the lunar energies. Once you know how to make Moon Water, you can charge water on any favorable astrological occasion to preserve for future use.

You Will Need:

❭ Jar with lid

❭ Purified or spring water

❭ Pen and paper, optional

Directions:

1. If possible, do this in an area where moonlight can touch the water. If that's not possible, you can charge the water on a windowsill that doesn't specifically get moonlight and simply attune the water to the energy of the moon via your intention. It may not always be perfect, but work with what you have!
2. If you have a specific intention for the lunation, think about it now. If not, just reflect on the energy of this given full moon. If you feel

called to, write an intention or word on the piece of paper and place it under the jar, writing-side up.

3. Pour water into the jar, envisioning the moon pouring blessings into your cup. Hold your hands around the jar and imagine the moon in the night sky charging the water for your intention with its light, the charge strengthened by the moon's connection to water. Hold the jar until you feel the water energetically change or respond.

4. With your finger, trace a symbol for the moon—the crescent used in astrology or the Triple Goddess symbol mentioned in Chapter 5—in the air above the water, and gently press the symbol down toward the water with the palm of your hand.

5. Leave the jar out overnight, and collect it in the morning (before sunrise, if possible). Refrigerate and use within a week. Or you can preserve the water using alcohol, such as a splash of vodka, and label with the date, time, and relevant information (such as moon sign). This way, you can use Moon Water from a specific moon in future elixirs and tinctures!

Nourishing Full Moon Bath

Best Lunar Timing: Full or Waning Moon, Moon in Cancer or Pisces, Lunar Eclipse, Supermoon

Lunar Energy: Healing, Rejuvenation, Cleansing

Some full moons call for big rituals, but others might fall during challenging times when you just want to relax and release. Under the blessing of the full moon, let this bath restore and rejuvenate your energy. The salts and eucalyptus will cleanse your energy, while the lemon oil and lemon balm will nourish your body and uplift your senses. With nurturing ingredients, both your energy and skin will feel soft and restored, making you feel like a moon goddess yourself! Use before or after a moon ritual, or as a stand-alone practice. Feel free to substitute your preferred skin-safe lunar essential oils.

You Will Need:

- ☽ Bowl or container
- ☽ ¾ cup sea salt
- ☽ 1 cup Epsom salt
- ☽ ¼ cup baking soda
- ☽ 1 tablespoon dried lemon balm, rose, or other safe moon-associated herb (see Chapter 5 and Appendix B)

Part Two: Spells and Rituals for Every Moon

> 12 drops lemon essential oil

> 6 drops eucalyptus essential oil

> Seashell, optional

> Cucumber slices, optional

Directions:

1. Sit somewhere you can see the moonlight. Place all the needed items before you.
2. With the moon's light blessing each item, add ingredients to the bowl or container: sea salt (like from the ocean tides, which the moon influences), Epsom salt, baking soda, and moon-associated healing lemon balm.
3. Add in essential oils and stir counterclockwise, visualizing the mixture cleansing away unwanted energy.
4. You may charge the mixture overnight under the moonlight in a closed container or use it right away. When ready to use, stir ½ cup of the mixture into a bath of warm water.
5. In the bath, you may use a shell—a symbol of the nurturing ocean— to spoon water over your shoulders and body. Visualize the healing waves of the ocean under the moonlight, cleansing and nurturing your energy.
6. For a touch of youthful rejuvenation, you may wish to sit in the bath with moon-associated cucumber over your eyes. Visualize the bath aglow, the moon's rejuvenating and youthful light soaking through the nourishing salt water into your skin.

Lunar-Charged Cleansing Herbal Bundle

Best Lunar Timing: Full or Waning Gibbous Moon

Lunar Energy: Cleansing, Healing, Release

At the full moon, herbs are abuzz with their full potential and energy. It's the perfect time to craft a cleansing herb bundle, which can then charge with the waning moon to amplify the purifying properties. Cleansing your energy is an important part of preparing for spellwork, and smoke cleansing is one technique for doing that. This recipe makes a rosemary, thyme, and rose petal– or bay leaf–based cleansing bundle to use for smoke cleansing before moon meditations or rituals. The spiritual, clearing, and healing properties of these herbs make for an aromatic, purifying herb bundle to promote the release of negative energy and spiritual attunement under the moon.

You Will Need:

) Fresh rosemary sprigs

) Fresh thyme sprigs

) Twine, thread, or string in a color that resonates with your intention, such as white for cleansing, black for protection, or purple for harmony

) Rose petals or bay leaves

) Fireproof dish or large shell filled with sand

) Matches or lighter

Directions:

1. At the full or waning gibbous moon, gather your items before you in a sacred space. You may wish to work where you can see the moonlight.

2. Before you begin, take a few deep breaths to clear your mind. Smell the fragrance of the herbs and feel grateful for their energy. If you like, take a moment to hold them and feel their essence.

3. When you feel ready, start by bunching the rosemary and thyme sprigs together. Tie once around their base.

4. Now weave or wrap the twine or string upward toward the tip of the bundle, then back down, bunching the herbs together. As you wrap upward, tuck in rose petals or bay leaves, holding them in place as you pull the string tightly.

5. As you wrap, visualize, think about, or feel the moon. Imagine this bundle being empowered with the energy of the waning moon for powerful cleansing in your own life whenever you light it. You may also wish to chant something like:

"As the moon wanes, these herbs are blessed, to cleanse away unwanted banes."

6. When done, knot the twine or string at the base and leave some extra string at the end so you can hang the bundle to properly dry. Visualize the waning moon blessing it. By the new moon, you should have a dried cleansing bundle to use.

7. When ready to use, untie a bit of the twine and retie it a little lower on the bundle so the string doesn't burn. Light the tip of the bundle, and then blow out the flame, leaving smoldering embers. Place it on the fireproof dish or sand-filled shell to snuff out the burning and further the lunar connection.

Part Two: Spells and Rituals for Every Moon

WANING MOON SPELLS

Wax Scrying for Wisdom

Best Lunar Timing: Waning or Dark Moon, Moon in a Water Sign, Lunar Eclipse, Black Moon

Lunar Energy: Reflection, Insight, Psychic Abilities

As the moon begins to retract in light, it's time to reflect. As the astrological body associated with the subconscious, dreams, and inner knowing, the moon is used by many to access psychic information and strengthen divinatory powers. In this scrying spell, you will turn to the moon's illuminating psychic energy to shine a light on what to reflect on and release, and to answer any lingering questions that remain. Take the lessons gained and reflect on what worked and what didn't. This is a way of seeking divine wisdom or insight on what remains ahead.

You Will Need:

❭ Bowl
❭ Water (can be moon-charged water)
❭ Candle
❭ Matches or lighter
❭ Quartz point, optional
❭ Candleholder

Directions:

1. Place the bowl in a place where you can see the moonlight, or in a dark space if you prefer. Pour water into the bowl. With your hands above the water, focus on your intention: insight.
2. Light the candle, connecting to the moon as you do so. Holding the candle upright, say aloud:

   "As the moon's light wanes, this candle's light guides the way.
   Through the art of dripping wax, I receive guidance on the question I ask."

3. Ask your question aloud, stirring the water with your finger or a natural quartz crystal point to get it moving.
4. With the moon's guidance in mind, hold the candle horizontally over the bowl and drip wax into the moving water. Continue dripping, noticing any symbols as you go. As the wax continues to drip, the shapes, letters, or symbols might shift, so be sure to note everything

you see—each image may become an important facet of the end reading. Continue dripping wax until you get a sense that you have dripped enough, or until you notice a significant pause in the flow of wax.

5. When done dripping, place the candle aside in a candleholder to help illuminate the bowl if needed. Look at the moonlight or candlelight reflecting in the water. Soften your gaze, and invite any further information to come to you. Divine what you see in the water and wax.

6. If needing clarity, you can use your breath to move the wax with intention. You can also pick out the big wax blob and look at its underbelly for additional shapes.

7. This can take some practice to interpret. Wax dripping, like tea leaf reading, is a highly subjective and intuitive art, so allow yourself to relax, take your time, and see what you notice without judgment.

Rosemary-Sea Salt Home Cleanse

Best Lunar Timing: Waning or New Moon, Moon in Virgo or Cancer, Solar Eclipse

Lunar Energy: Cleansing, Blessing, the Home

In astrology, the moon is associated with the home. In fact, many witches perform home cleanings, blessings, and protection with the progression of the lunar cycle. Such a regular practice ensures that at least every lunar cycle or month, your home—where you rest, nurture, restore your soul, and also perform your magick—is protected and maintained. In this cleansing and blessing ritual, you revamp the energy in your home, using the power of the waning moon to help release stagnant energy in your space. If you feel called, you can always perform the spell at other lunar occasions, such as during the waxing moon with the aim of increasing good vibes in the home.

You Will Need:

- Bowl
- Moon Water (see Chapter 7)
- Sea salt
- Lemon peel
- Fresh rosemary sprig

Directions:

1. Into the bowl, pour Moon Water, or water you will leave out to be charged by the moon before performing this spell.
2. Counterclockwise, sprinkle in sea salt to dispel unwanted energy.
3. Squeeze the lemon peel (with the outer, yellow side facing the water) to release its aromatic oils, thinking of spreading uplifting lunar energy and joy. Drop the peel into the water, or discard.
4. Use the rosemary sprig to stir the mixture clockwise, envisioning your home environment pristine, protected, and positive.
5. Walk the bowl around your home and use the rosemary sprig to flick drops of water around each space as a water blessing.

Clockwise or Counterclockwise?

You might have noticed the use of clockwise or counterclockwise stirring or sprinkling in this book. In witchcraft and energy work, many practitioners use clockwise movement to bring in energy or invoke, and counterclockwise movement to cleanse. You can use these themes throughout your magick. For a more complex home cleansing, you can go around your home counterclockwise from the front door to cleanse and release (perhaps with your dried herbal cleansing bundle), and then go around once more clockwise to bring in blessings and harmonize.

Snuffing Out Doubt Spell

Best Lunar Timing: Dark, Waning, or First Quarter Moon, Moon in Scorpio or Leo, Waxing Crescent Moon

Lunar Energy: Banishing, Confidence, Release

As you work with the lunar cycle to manifest your intentions, doubts and fears may arise. The dark moon phase is the time to face these hidden emotions and diminish them. You can snuff out fears, worries, and anxiety with this simple candle spell. You can even use this exercise to blow away old habits or energy you are diminishing, such as stress. Blow out and away any woes that are getting in the way of your dreams and prepare the way for powerful magickal manifestation at the coming new moon. Perform this spell once, or repeat as needed, perhaps as a meditation to cleanse your mind before spellwork on days when you are feeling particularly anxious.

You Will Need:

- ❭ Candle in a color that aligns with what you want to banish (or a white candle, in a pinch)
- ❭ Toothpick or needle
- ❭ Your choice of banishing oil and/or herbs, such as black pepper, garlic, or red pepper
- ❭ Candleholder
- ❭ Matches or lighter
- ❭ Protective stone, such as black tourmaline or jet

Directions:

1. Visualize the doubt or fear you are feeling as an external energy. Think about its color, shape, and texture and where in your body you feel it. Realize that it is outside of you and, as such, is manageable. It is not a facet of who you are.
2. Use the toothpick to engrave a word or symbol that represents your emotion onto the candle.
3. Anoint the candle with banishing oil and herbs. Place candle in candleholder.
4. Light the candle and gaze at the flame. Feel it warming the part of your body where you feel the undesired energy. Imagine the warmth loosening the energy so that it moves outside your body.
5. When the energy is loosened from your body, tap into your well of power at your solar plexus energy center, right between the breastbone and stomach.
6. Take hold of the protective stone, and visualize your willpower growing bright and stronger here with each inhale. When you feel empowered, blow away the anxiety and the candle flame with an outward, powerful exhale. Like the candle flame, the energy is extinguished.
7. Now that your power center is aglow, think about what you might wish to work with in the coming lunar cycle, and let it set your soul alight with hope and renewal.
8. Discard the candle if you wish, or keep it around to repeat the spell as desired.
9. You might consider keeping the black tourmaline or jet with you to help ground you and dispel any negative energy that tries to return.

Part Two: Spells and Rituals for Every Moon

Chapter 8

SPECIAL OCCASION MOON MEDITATIONS

From the moon turning red in the night sky, to the sun being blacked out and disappearing in broad daylight—it's difficult to deny the extra-special feeling of magick in the air under such rare lunations. As the moon moves around earth and the earth orbits the sun, sometimes the alignment is just right enough for the two most important celestial objects in our sky to meet and create these special lunar events. Since ancient times, eclipses have been critical moments requiring action and prayer, and in modern times blue moons, black moons, and supermoons add excitement and lunar connection to witchcraft practice. While all of the moon's cycles have always enticed and inspired humankind, these special lunations offer extra-potent times for magick, healing, and manifestation.

Because eclipses and blue and black moons are extra-special lunations, this section includes one meditation for each occasion, and one special spell or ritual aligned to each occasion's overall intention. (You can always revisit these occasions' meaning and magick in Chapter 2.) The zodiacal signs these events happen in add even more nuanced energy. Looking at the lunar phase, the moon sign, the seasonal energy, and your own intentions, you can reference a wide variety of spells and efforts from throughout this book to fully customize a magickal and healing ritual with the moon. Eclipses and supermoons can seem intense at times, but they regularly provide opportunities to propel you to new levels of manifestation and personal growth.

CREATING A PERSONALIZED LUNAR RITUAL

Many of the spells in this book are chants, recipes, or spells you can perform on their own. However, the magick and rarity of these special lunar occasions may inspire you to cast a full ritual, which can incorporate several spells and rites. This way, you can create a customized ritual that truly captures the power and potential of these special occasion moons.

A lunar ritual could be composed of the following:

- Setting the tone (such as with music or incense)
- Cleansing (such as a smoke cleansing with an herbal bundle, a bath, or a selenite stone cleansing)
- Grounding and centering (as covered in Chapter 6)
- A meditation to connect to the lunar energy or glean insight (you'll find many options in this chapter)
- Divination, such as using tarot or oracle cards
- Spells that match your intention (for example, for healing, manifestation, money, or love)
- Leaving items out to charge under the lunar energy
- Grounding and cleansing once again to close out the ritual

If you feel compelled to fully celebrate these special lunar events, consider combining these elements to truly seize the energy of the moment.

LUNAR ECLIPSE MEDITATION AND SPELL

Eclipsed Moon Reflection

Best Lunar Timing: Full Moon, Lunar Eclipse, Dark Moon, Moon in Scorpio

Lunar Energy: Reflection, Shadow Work, Healing

When the moon passes into earth's shadow and turns bloodred, the moon might illuminate hidden emotions and patterns. Use the occasion and this meditation to reflect on your shadow self—the primal part of you that experiences fear, desire, and more—to bring healing. You can use your own set of divination tools to navigate these questions: a pendulum, oracle deck, tarot cards, etc.

You Will Need:

❭ Black moonstone, optional

Directions:

1. Prepare for ritual and meditation as desired (see Chapter 6). Hold your black moonstone, a powerful stone for new beginnings and releasing toxic emotions, and rediscover your power. Breathe deeply into your body and close your eyes.
2. After a few calming and relaxing breaths, visualize the earth, moon, and sun moving in the cosmic backdrop of the stars. The moon moves around the earth as the earth moves around the sun, creating the passage of time—the past that has brought you to the present moment. The sunlight hits the earth, casting a shadow in the cosmos much like you cast a shadow as you walk in daylight.
3. Visualize the moon passing into the earth's shadow, turning red. The moon, which represents your sense of feeling—intuition, emotions, and past feelings and experiences—is discolored by the shadow of earth, the planet you're inhabiting in this lifetime. Turning red, the color of life force, passion, and blood, it illuminates your own shadows—your primal self, wants and needs, past patterns, and bonds that need to be released.
4. Within you, you might feel a flare in your base or root energy center (at the base of your spine) in response—it is often activated by this energy. Tune into that feeling—how this eclipse makes you feel, and what it has revealed that needs healing and attention at this time. Recognizing these darker parts of the self brings the opportunity for revealing old trauma and healing from it.
5. Reflect on the following questions in a grimoire or journal, or perhaps even with tarot or oracle cards. Use the information you uncover to guide further lunar spellwork and healing.

● What is being revealed at this time, and why?

● What cycle or pattern is ending, or what is it time to finally end?

● What is it time to release and fully let go of? What is holding you back?

● What is the potential healing that releasing this can bring?

- Do you notice any suggestions or advice from the spiritual world? (Invite insight from your guides—in the present moment, or perhaps in symbols, messages, and happenings over the coming days.)

6. With answers in mind and illumination gleaned, visualize the moon passing out of the earth's shadow and back to luminous bright white in the cosmos. You, too, will get through this time and shine brighter for (or in spite of) it.

Healing Water Ritual

Best Lunar Timing: Lunar Eclipse; Full, Waning, or Dark Moon; Moon in Scorpio or Pisces

Lunar Energy: Letting Go, Healing, Banishing

Since they carry the energy of the supercharged full moon, lunar eclipses can illuminate important themes and reveal old wounds for healing to bring change in your life. While oftentimes this disclosure can feel intense or sudden, it often has your best interest in mind. Eclipses tend to put you back on your soul path. In this spell, you will burn away old patterns and issues that have been revealed to you. Use the spell for releasing, healing old wounds, forgiving past occurrences, or snuffing out old energy of any kind that you no longer desire. The transformative power of fire, coupled with the soothing and healing of (moon-charged) water, will help you release and wash away what no longer serves you so that you can step forward onto a new path and cleanse your subconscious of repeating patterns.

You Will Need:

❭ Candle
❭ Toothpick or knife, optional
❭ Rose or coconut oil, Moon Oil (see Chapter 7), or other oil of choice
❭ Rose petals
❭ Cauldron or fireproof bowl
❭ Sand or rocks

❭ Water (ideally Moon Water— see Chapter 7, chilled jasmine tea, or water infused with cucumber for healing)
❭ Matches or lighter
❭ Pen and paper, optional
❭ Lemon wedge, optional
❭ 1 teaspoon sea salt, optional

Directions:

1. Use the toothpick or knife to engrave the candle, if desired, with a word or symbol that represents what you are letting go. Anoint candle with oil and dress with rose petals for healing.
2. Melt the bottom of the candle above the center of the cauldron or fireproof bowl, and while the wax is still warm, fix the candle to the bowl's center. Allow it to solidify for a moment as you hold it in place to ensure it's steady.
3. Pour sand or rocks into the bowl, providing a grounding foundation to hold your candle in place.
4. Once the candle is steady, hover your hands around it, thinking of what you are letting go of. Imagine pouring your emotions into the candle.
5. Now gently pour in Moon Water (or jasmine tea, or infused water), stopping about halfway (or less) up the candle. As you do, visualize the water, attuned to and illuminated by the moon, flowing in to heal and cleanse.
6. Light the candle. Notice that its light, while currently bright (like what you are letting go of), is about to be diminished, just like the waning moon's light slipping into darkness.
7. Write down what you are releasing on your slip of paper. You might name old patterns and habits that were revealed during the eclipse meditation, or list fears or feelings that are limiting you. You can write several things or just one—whatever feels right to you.
8. Rip the paper between the words, so that they each habit, fear, or feeling has its own slip of paper. As you do so, visualize tearing away that/those things.
9. Above the water and candle, hold one slip of paper. Thinking of or looking at the eclipsed moon above, say aloud:

   "As the moon is eclipsed, I burn all that's on this list.
   Fire to transform that which I have torn
   With salt to cleanse, and water to mend
   At this lunar eclipse, to my soul do I tend."

10. Set fire to one slip of paper with the candle's flame, and before it burns close to your fingertips drop it into the water. Repeat for as many papers as you have to burn.
11. Watch the candle burn until it is snuffed by the healing waters. Know that the moon is helping you to release the unwanted energy and heal.

Once the flame is extinguished by the moon's healing waters, you may wish to squeeze a lemon wedge into the water, then swirl the water in a counterclockwise direction, undoing that energy or theme from your life.

12. Pour the salt counterclockwise into the water to ground and cleanse the energy, then pour the water onto the earth to neutralize its energy, saying:

"With the waning moon, I cast this energy away.
It no longer plagues me, from this day."

13. Follow this ritual with healing or spellwork to help replace the energy you are releasing with something new and better!

SOLAR ECLIPSE MEDITATION AND SPELL

Solar Eclipse Reflection

Best Lunar Timing: Solar Eclipse; New Moon; Moon in Leo, Aquarius, or Sagittarius; Black Moon

Lunar Energy: Alignment, New Beginnings, Blessing

While a solar eclipse is only visible in certain parts of the world, its energy can be felt and accessed throughout the planet. A supercharged new moon where both the sun and the moon disappear from the sky for a brief moment, a solar eclipse provides a powerful portal to a new pathway in life. Regardless of where you are on earth when the eclipse happens, tune into the wisdom of this divine alignment and reflect on the meeting of these defining celestial forces of life on earth.

You Will Need:

❯ Sunstone and moonstone, optional

❯ Tarot or oracle cards, optional

Directions:

1. Breathe deeply and relax. Hold the sunstone in one hand and the moonstone in the other, then close your eyes.

2. Visualize the moon and sun in the sky, inching closer and closer together. Think upon their themes and energy: The moon represents your emotional and intuitive landscape and is the inner compass that guides your waking consciousness. The sun defines the day, inspires your identity, and cocreates your force, strength, confidence, and radiance.

3. Visualize the moon eclipsing the sun. When the alignment is just right, the mysterious moon steps into power and eclipses the sun. The moment turns the day dark for a blink of an eye, illuminating instead the light within you. The moon and sun are aligned and seemingly disappear—a true blank slate.

4. With this image and reflection in mind, tune into the stones in your hands. Now is a time to reflect on what has been brought to light in your life this eclipse season. What path or restart is your soul guiding you to take?

5. With the insight you've gleaned, visualize the moon moving past the sun and light beginning to reappear. The return of the sunlight lights up a new pathway before you.

Solar Eclipse New Pathways Key Ritual

Best Lunar Timing: Solar Eclipse; New Moon; Black Moon; Moon in Aquarius, Sagittarius, Leo, or Aries

Lunar Energy: New Pathways, Blessings, Opportunities

Eclipse season can bring a rough rollercoaster of up-and-down energy, but it also offers a time to heal, align, and step into new energy. With its supercharged new moon energy, the solar eclipse can help you pursue new paths that are in line with your soul—just keep in mind that sometimes this momentum takes you in unexpected directions! Open the door to a new path and bless your way forward with this door-opening spell. You can use a blank key or a skeleton key from a metaphysical or witch shop, or buy a charm key from a craft store or online. Select a key that you like, that feels magickal, and that matches your intentions!

You Will Need:

> Tarot cards: The World, The Star, and the Two of Wands

> Matches or lighter

> Sandalwood or cinnamon incense

- ❭ Yellow, orange, or red candle
- ❭ White or silver candle
- ❭ Candleholders
- ❭ Key
- ❭ Red ribbon
- ❭ Moonstone and sunstone, optional

Directions:

1. Place the three cards in a row: The Star on the left, the Two of Wands in the center, and The World on the right.

   - The Star represents destiny, alignment, connection with the universe, and vulnerability. It's a reminder that, though the cosmic events or energy of eclipse season can be rough to experience, they're helping you to reconnect to your spiritual path and reminding you to have faith in the universe.

   - The Two of Wands shows you at this moment, pondering and planning the future with the world of possibility in your hands—the path ahead.

   - The World represents the realm of possibility that rests ahead of you, limitless in potential, and the beginning and ending of cycles as one chapter closes and another begins.

2. Light the incense and reflect on the cards and the meaning you glean from this eclipse energy. Reflect on each of these cards at the moment of the eclipse. Think of what you are pursuing, visualize and brainstorm, and connect to that vibrational energy.

3. Place the yellow, orange, or red candle in a candleholder off to the right and the white or silver candle off to the left, both candles behind the cards. These candles represent the forces of the sun and moon, respectively.

4. Hold the key and visualize opening a door to your desired new path. Feel excitement roaring through your body. Light the candles and say:

   "As the new moon and sun align
   I take heed of the signs.
   As the moon eclipses the sun
   A new pathway is begun."

5. Turn the key in the air between the two candles, as though unlocking a door. Thinking of your new pathway, pass the ribbon through the hole in the key and tie it in a knot—a symbol of the string of fate.

6. Pass the key and ribbon through the incense, then set them down before you, between the two candles. Here, the key will charge by the candlelight. If desired, you can place moonstone by the moon's candle and sunstone by the sun's, or hold one in each hand to meditate.

7. Once the candles have burned down, keep the key with you as a charm or on your altar, and use it in future spells related to your efforts. Proceed with spells that match your intentions, or road-opening spells to bless the path ahead. You can even make the key into a blessing charm—by stringing beads or supportive stones on the ribbon—to carry with you for good luck on this new path.

BLUE MOON MEDITATION AND SPELL

Blue Moon Miracle Reflection

Best Lunar Timing: Blue or Black Moon, Moon in Sagittarius or Aquarius, Supermoon

Lunar Energy: Possibility, Expansion, Hope

This reflection will help you connect to the sense of wonder that the blue moon provides and remind you of times when the impossible became possible. You will first consider what you need to use the blue moon for, and then attune your energy to a sense of possibility that you can then channel into your moon magick. You can do this meditation anytime you want to boost your sense of possibility, hope, and positivity before casting a lunar spell.

Directions:

1. Breathe deeply, cleanse, and do whatever you need to do to set the space for moon meditation (see Chapter 6).

2. Ask yourself:

● What themes are arising in my life that could use the magickal support of the blue moon?

● What in my life could use a second chance?

● What are some elements of life that evoke wonder in me?

3. Close your eyes and spend some time visualizing the aspects of life that evoke a sense of amazement within you. Perhaps it's gazing at the sunset or the luminous full moon and starlit sky above. Isn't it stunning that earth is even here and life is possible?

4. Consider what occurrences of chance or rarity have happened in your life. Perhaps you met someone special—a partner, a friend, an animal; perhaps you were chosen for a raffle once, or found $20 in your pocket. Scan all the times past and present when you had this sense of luck. If you feel called, you might write them down in your grimoire for future memory and to boost your morale.

5. Choose one moment that resonates for you—the most powerful one that really makes your heart sing with amazement and happiness. Take yourself back to that time and space. Visualize and feel the energy of that moment and all the little details you can recall. What did you see, smell, hear, taste, and feel? For five solid breaths, breathe that experience into your body, and let the details illuminate within your heart and soul.

6. Bring the energy of that event—that anything is possible—into the present moment. Breathe deeply, feeling a buzz of excited energy tingle throughout your body.

7. Having uplifted your energy by returning to that time and remembering the emotion and moment, carry this feeling into your blue moon–magick workings to help install a sense of possibility.

Blue Moon Bay Leaf Wishing Spell

Best Lunar Timing: Blue or Black Moon, New Moon, Moon in an Air Sign, Moon in Sagittarius

Lunar Energy: Wishes, Manifestation, Luck

The blue moon, whether calendrical or seasonal, symbolizes an extra boost of energy. Use that gift of energy to propel your desires into the world. In this spell, you will use the tradition of wishing with a bay leaf to create your own special spiced lunar ritual. Coupled with ground spices to empower, this spell will help support old intentions or manifest new ones. You can even divine based on how the bay leaf burns and crackles, or instead of burning it, keep the magickally infused bay leaf in your wallet for moon money magick.

You Will Need:

- ☽ Sharpie
- ☽ Bay leaf
- ☽ Moon Oil (see Chapter 7) or oil of choice, optional
- ☽ Ground nutmeg
- ☽ Ground cinnamon
- ☽ Ground ginger
- ☽ Bowl or dish
- ☽ Fireproof dish
- ☽ Matches or lighter

Directions:

1. Use the Sharpie to write your intention on the bay leaf.
2. With your intention in mind, rub the oil on the bay leaf, empowering it with lunar energy, if desired.
3. Mix the ground spices clockwise in bowl or dish, drawing your intentions toward you.
4. Massage the spice mixture onto the bay leaf, infusing it with more power.
5. Above the fireproof dish, set the bay leaf aflame. The flame should sputter out, leaving embers to glow and raise smoke, its incense carrying your intention up to the blessed moon in prayer.
6. You may need to relight the bay leaf a few times. That is okay! Draw on this moon's illumination of second chances, and simply relight and keep the energy going. You can also keep the bay leaf and burn it several times during a waxing phase.

BLACK MOON MEDITATION AND SPELL

Black Moon Starseed Planting Reflection

Best Lunar Timing: Black Moon, New Moon, Moon in Taurus, Solar Eclipse

Lunar Energy: Intention Setting, New Beginnings, Blessings

An extra or repeated new moon of sorts, the black moon gives a chance to replant seeds. What's something that hasn't taken off, or that you need to redo or rebuild? In this meditation, you will reflect on the potent energy of this time. In all her phases, the moon guides when to sow, nurture, and reap, and the black moon offers extra-fertile energy with which to grow many things to fruition. Connect to the energy at hand and attune to the desires you want to take with you into aligned spellwork.

Directions:

1. Close your eyes and take deep breaths. Imagine yourself before a field of dark soil. It is dark out. Despite that darkness, the stars up above twinkle and light your way.
2. Imagine touching the soil with your hands—it is black, fertile, moist—ready and perfect for planting.
3. Look up above—the starlit sky, with no moon in sight, is reminiscent of a million seeds, ready to be planted and born.
4. Tune into the fertile earth energy around you. The sun and moon are aligned, and you have an extra lunation to bring something important into this world. Consider the following questions:

   ● What energy is the black moon repeating?

   ● How can I rework my intentions?

   ● What do I need a second chance in?

   ● Is there anything I want to rebirth in a new and different way?

   ● What intention in my life could use a second burst of supportive energy?

   ● How (if this black moon is astrological, meaning it's the second new moon in a sign season) can I explore this zodiac sign's energy? Why might this energy be presenting in my life right now?

   ● What does the seasonal moon energy offer me?

5. Once you've pondered, decide what you are using this extra new moon for. Visualize a light—like a small glowing gemstone, or even a shooting star—appearing within your hands. Visualize planting this light in the soil and covering it, knowing that as the moon grows full, so will your intention be illuminated.
6. Follow with corresponding spell efforts that match your intentions.

Seed Planting Paper

Best Lunar Timing: New Moon, Black Moon, Moon in an Earth Sign

Lunar Energy: Intention Setting, Nature Connection, Manifestation

The new moon is a time to plant seeds—a metaphor often used for setting goals and intentions for what you wish to manifest with the waxing of the moon. At the time of a black moon, that energy may be doubly so. What better way to plant seeds for your intentions than by crafting your very own moon-magickal seed paper? Embedded with actual seeds along with your words, this seed paper is easy to make and also a great way to recycle and to support bees and wildlife with your moon magick. Bathed in the black moon's prosperous potential, now is the time to bless your efforts to multiply and grow beyond your wildest dreams. You can even share the paper with your family, friends, or coven.

You Will Need:

-) Pieces of recyclable scrap paper
-) Blender
-) Warm water (enough to cover the paper scraps)
-) Strainer
-) Noninvasive seeds of choice
-) Towel or cloth

Directions:

1. Tear the old paper slowly and place pieces into the blender. As you do so, imagine clearing away blockages and stagnant energy that might keep you from your goals—for example, things that have restricted you in the past.
2. Visualizing the moon's dominion over water, pour warm water into the blender, as though the moon is giving her blessing and magick directly to your endeavor. Blend until the paper is broken down, and think upon what you wish to alchemize.
3. Pour the mixture through the strainer over a sink. Press on the mixture to remove excess water, but leave it slightly wet so that it doesn't crumble.
4. Gently massage seeds of your choice (perhaps a native species or a plant that resonates with your intention) into the mixture.
5. Place the cloth on a flat surface, then dump the mixture onto it. Form the mixture into your desired shape and size, and press down gently to remove any remaining water. You can even use cookie cutters to make shapes! Just remember you want to be able to write on the paper.
6. Once one side dries, flip it over to dry the other.
7. Once completely dry, usually about 24 hours later, store in an airtight container or bag. At the new moon, write your intentions on the

paper, then plant the paper in soil. Or give the blank paper to others to share the blessings!

SUPERMOON MEDITATION AND SPELL

Celestial Gravity Meditation

Best Lunar Timing: Supermoon, Full Moon, Lunar Eclipse

Lunar Energy: Power, Lunar Connection, Intention Setting

At the supermoon, the moon comes closer to earth in its orbit, and its pull upon the ocean tides is strengthened. You may also feel a noticeable pull in your own connection with the moon. In this meditation, you will tune into that magnetic energy and carry it with you into your spellwork.

You Will Need:

❭ Cup, preferably one that feels special!

❭ Shells or ocean-related objects, optional

❭ Pitcher or bottle of purified or spring water

❭ Quartz point

Directions:

1. Place the cup before you, and arrange shells or ocean objects around its base to remind you of the moon's influence on the tides.
2. Close your eyes, and breathe deeply. Visualize the moon traveling around the earth and reaching her closest point.
3. As the moon pulls closer, the tides rise in the oceans. Imagine yourself on a beach, with all the sensory elements that accompany that place— the ocean wind, sounds of crashing waves, the smell of salt water, the sound and feeling of sand beneath your toes. Spend a moment basking under the full moon and watching the wild, high tides before you in this meditative mind space.
4. Opening your eyes for a brief moment, pour water into the cup, envisioning the moon's connection with it. Take a sip. Feel it pass through your mouth, and down your throat, and into your body. Water truly nurtures your entire body—after all, about 60 percent of

your body is water. Visualize yourself just like the tides: aglow under the moon, feeling her pull upon your body.

5. Think about the moon's intrinsic connection to you and to earth— how in the early days of earth, the moon's closeness and gravity influenced the tides, causing the oceans to pull from the land and integrate minerals essential for evolution. To this day, ocean creatures are influenced by the tides, and in the wild, creatures live in cycles with the moon; turtles use the moonlight to guide them, newly hatched, to the water. The moon's call beckons and nurtures all.

6. In your meditative space again, visualize the moon above you. Think about the water within you. Your emotions. Your sense of feeling. Liquid traveling through and revitalizing each part of your body. Breathe in the moon's light and power, feeling it grow stronger and stronger within you with each inhalation. Once you feel empowered, you can stop there. However, if you like, you can also empower the water with an intention for more magick.

7. Think about what your intention is. Do you want to imbue a certain intention into your body? Or do you just want to imbue lunar energy into your body?

8. Hover your palms above the water in the cup. Visualize the moon shining down on your hands. Think of your intention, and direct that energy from your hands into the water.

9. Hold this visualization until you sense the water vibrating back toward your hands.

10. Use the quartz point to stir the water clockwise with intention—like the supermoon, quartz magnifies energy.

11. When ready, sip the water, infusing that energy into your body. Visualize your body absorbing the water and being infused with your intention.

12. You can do this whenever you like—perhaps even before beginning a ritual.

Magnified Moon Blessings Bowl

Best Lunar Timing: Supermoon; New, Waxing Gibbous, or Full Moon; Blue Moon; Moon in Libra, Sagittarius, Taurus, or Pisces

Lunar Energy: Attraction, Manifestation, Luck

At the time of a supermoon, you may feel an especially ethereal pull from the moon. With this magnified sense of connection, it's time to multiply the odds in your favor and increase matters of all kinds—whether money, love, or psychic powers. Using the attracting power of sugar, you will create a blessing bowl to use the sense of magnification around the supermoon to draw your desires to you. In this spell, you will echo your sense of a magnified moon to work with lodestones—naturally magnetized stones—to draw your intention to you. Lodestones are a staple in many witchcraft practices and are often sold in witchcraft shops. They are often sold in pairs, but if you see them sold separately, see if you can find a pair yourself by finding two pieces that have natural pull between them. (This also makes a great love spell.) Add coins to increase your money, rose petals to boost your chances with love, or even dice to push the odds in your favor and cast some magick for luck.

You Will Need:

- ❯ Cinnamon stick
- ❯ Bowl, preferably silver-colored or white, or cauldron
- ❯ Sugar
- ❯ Bay leaf
- ❯ Sharpie

- ❯ 2 pieces of lodestone
- ❯ Object that represents your intention, such as a dollar bill for money or rose petals for love
- ❯ Matches or lighter

Directions:

1. Perform the Celestial Gravity Meditation (described just before this spell) to tune into and feel connected to the moon. You might also want to drink water that has been charged ahead of time under her ethereal light.

2. Cleanse your magickal items and set them before you. Reflect on the round shape of the bowl and its reflective properties—its kinship with the moon. Acknowledge that it is a vessel (much like an offering cup) to bless and contain your efforts for favorable outcomes.

3. With the round moon in mind, hold your cinnamon stick like a wand and drag it around the outer lip of the bowl three times, saying aloud:

   "Like the moon grows, good luck do I know.
   When I roll the dice, the moon blesses me thrice."

4. Fill your bowl or cauldron with a generous layer of sugar for attracting your desires toward you. Sugar is known for its ability to

allure the object of any desire. You can also mix in the Moon Dust Blessing Powder (see Chapter 7).

5. On the bay leaf, with the Sharpie, write what you are drawing toward you. Place the leaf in the bowl, nestling it in the sugar with the word facing you.

6. Then, nestle in symbols for what you are manifesting, such as coins, dice, rose petals, or other small objects, throughout the bowl. As you "plant" them in the sugar, visualize your manifestations growing and multiplying any effort you put in.

7. Hold the two lodestones separately, thinking about what you wish to attract. Visualize luck drawing toward you and slowly move the lodestones together. Whisper your intention to them, then place them in the bowl, atop the bay leaf, together. Hold your hand above the bowl, further empowering it with your intention.

8. Trace the cinnamon stick around the bowl again three times, repeating the chant. With a lighter, light the cinnamon stick and blow the flame out to produce an ember, as you would with incense. Now you have a spiced aromatic for manifestation to draw your desires to you. As the embers produce smoke, say:

"As the supermoon magnifies my lunar call,
With these magnetized stones, my desires to me are drawn."

9. The cinnamon stick will only burn for a short time before the embers go out, but you can snuff it in the sugar if needed. You can relight it each day as you continue drawing your goals to you, and even refresh the bowl by adding more objects to it each week. For example, if your intentions have to do with money, on a Friday (Venus's day), add an additional coin or bill if desired, a symbolic act of multiplying your abundance.

Chapter 9

SEASONAL MOON SPELLS

The seasonal energy of each lunation cycle holds enhanced power and potential for your moon magick. In the cold of winter, the moon illuminates the long nights; in spring, she brings renewal and sensuality. The summer moons reflect the growth of the sun for play, personal power, and positivity. During harvest season, the full moon allows agriculturalists to work well into the night and witches to cast late-night lunar spells. People past and present have celebrated, crafted, and cast spells with the seasonal energy of the moon, and now you can too.

In this chapter, you will find a selection of seasonal moon spells to strengthen your lunar magick. Celebrate the July moon with Herb Moon Prophecy Tea, or create Beltane Beauty Facial Ice Cubes to enchant and nourish your skin. Summon abundance with the Pentacles Prosperity Protection Spell, or tap into the wisdom of ancestors and witches past with the Witch's Mirror Ancestor Moon Meditation. Once you feel confident in the magick and rituals of the seasonal moon spells, you can add additional layers to your moon magick. If you like, alter your spells for specific moon phases or moon signs by incorporating different crystals or herbs (use Chapter 5 and Appendix C as guides). The abundant power of seasonal moons awaits.

WINTER MOON SPELLS, RITUALS, AND RECIPES

Lemon and Clove Moon Blessing Charms

Best Lunar Timing: Moon in Sagittarius, New Moon–Full Moon

Lunar Energy: Blessings, Gratitude, Joy

Making pomander balls and dried orange wheels is a common winter solstice practice for blessings. Transform this into a lunar practice and meditate on the year of moons ahead with these cloved lemon wheels. Lemon is a wonderful cleansing ingredient, and it also happens to be associated with the moon and joy! With the addition of whole cloves (associated with Jupiter) for luck, spirituality, and abundance, these charms are a great way to bless your home and lunar goals, and a great gift to give to friends and family. Create as many lunar charms as you like, or create 12 or 13—one for each of the full moons in the year ahead.

You Will Need:

- ❭ Baking sheet
- ❭ Parchment paper
- ❭ 1 large lemon
- ❭ Knife
- ❭ 8–13 whole cloves per charm
- ❭ Ground nutmeg
- ❭ Ground cinnamon
- ❭ Bay leaves (1 for each charm)
- ❭ Toothpick or scissors
- ❭ Ribbon

Directions:

1. Preheat the oven to 200°F. Line the baking sheet with parchment paper.
2. Take a moment to decide what your approach will be. Do you want to create a blessing charm for each lunar cycle for the year ahead, or just create general lunar charms to give as gifts? This will influence how many slices and cloves you may need.
3. Hold your lemon, thinking of the moon, her cycles, and what awaits you in the year ahead. Lemon, which is associated with the moon, is not just purifying but also invokes love, joy, and inspiration.
4. Cut the lemon into slices about ¼" thick (the thinner, the faster it will dry out), thinking of the blessings of the year opening up to you.
5. Squeeze the ends of the lemon over a drain, dripping cleansing lemon juice and draining away unwanted energy. Rinse your hands and discard or compost the lemon ends.
6. Count out whole cloves for each lemon slice. To make a charm that represents one lunar cycle, use 8 cloves—one for each lunar phase. To create a year-long moon blessing charm, use 12 or 13 cloves on a single lemon wheel, each clove representing one of the year's full moons. If you wish, refresh your knowledge of the lunar cycle (see Chapter 2), or have a reference note handy to remind you of each lunation's themes (see Chapter 3).

7. Think about the year ahead—perhaps a specific intention you wish to come into being, general blessings for yourself or your home, or a person you might be gifting the charm to. You could even think of a separate intention for each lunation.

8. Poke a clove into the flesh of a wheel, then add cloves, equally spaced, until you've added all desired cloves, one for each phase or one for each moon. The result is like a wheel of the lunar cycles of the year or the phases of one lunation. Clove is associated with Jupiter, invoking luck and abundance. Think on that as you poke each clove into the lemon wheel.

9. Mix together the nutmeg and cinnamon. Sprinkle a pinch on each side of the lemon slice, adding more blessings. Place on the baking sheet.

10. Repeat for as many lemon slices as you'd like.

11. Stick the baking sheet in the oven for 6–7 hours, turning the lemon slices every 2 hours until dehydrated.

12. Once done, let cool. For each charm, write a wish, intention, or name (if the charm is a gift for someone) on a bay leaf.

13. With a toothpick or scissors, poke a hole through each lemon wheel and one through each leaf, and weave a leaf to each wheel with ribbon. Hang the charm on your altar, above a doorway, or somewhere else in the home, or give it as a gift of blessings.

Hermit Winter Moon Meditation

Best Lunar Timing: New or Dark Moon; Moon in Scorpio, Sagittarius, or Cancer

Lunar Energy: Introspection, Inner Guidance, Spiritual Growth

When the seasons of growth end, in winter, we turn inward to find introspection and rekindle our inner light. Your internal lantern, along with the moon's light, shines the way forth and illuminates matters of the soul. The Hermit tarot card reflects the theme of turning and journeying within, so it's a useful accompaniment to this meditation. Meditate and connect with the moon at this time to find your inner guiding light.

You Will Need:

❭ Cloak or blanket, optional
❭ Tarot card: The Hermit
❭ Black, rainbow, or blue moonstone, or quartz point
❭ Candle
❭ Matches or lighter

Directions:

1. Sit somewhere you are comfortable—if possible, where you can see the moonlight. Cover yourself with a blanket for warmth if needed and reflect on the solemn light within the sky.
2. Place The Hermit card before you. Notice the imagery of the hermit carrying a stick, his lantern guiding his passage through the snow.
3. Take hold of your moonstone or quartz point—your metaphorical "staff" supporting your reflection and journey—and gaze or think upon the moon, the lantern guiding your internal journey.
4. Close your eyes and visualize yourself walking through snow. What is currently frozen, covered, or at rest in your life?
5. As you walk in the snow, look up and see the moon, your celestial lantern, illuminating a pathway forward. Follow the pathway, your cloak or blanket protecting and warming you along the way. Continue walking forward until you see what the moon is leading you toward.
6. When insight is achieved, open your eyes and light the candle before you. Imagine that it is a guiding light for the winter moons to come. You can keep the crystal on you for continued support in whatever is revealed to be a key theme for you, for the winter moons.

Wolf Moon Knot Magick Garland

Best Lunar Timing: Moon in Capricorn or Cancer, Full or Waning Gibbous Moon

Lunar Energy: Strength, Connection, Prosperity

Knots bind strongly, and they can be used in magick for a similar purpose. The Wolf Moon and Capricorn moon summon themes of strength in numbers, connection, and abundance for winter survival and thriving. Use the power of knots in this ritual to help you forge strong bonds, strength, and prosperity under the winter moons. Hang the finished product as an altar decoration, above your bed, above a doorway, or on your solstice tree or hearth—wherever you feel it will keep and bring in blessings. If at some point you do not wish to keep it around, burn it as an offering for blessings.

You Will Need:

❭ Matches or lighter

❭ Prosperity incense, such as cinnamon, clove, or patchouli

- ⟩ Needle
- ⟩ Several bay leaves
- ⟩ Green embroidery string or cord
- ⟩ Sharpie, optional
- ⟩ Additional decorations, such as juniper, hawthorn, or cranberries, optional

Directions:

1. Light the incense. Use a needle to poke a hole in each bay leaf so that you can easily weave your string or cord through it.
2. If desired, write intentions, words, or names on the bay leaves with the Sharpie. If working with family or another group (for example, as a craft for Yule), have each person write their own wish on a bay leaf.
3. Take the string in hand. Think about your intention—are you strengthening a circle of support with spirit allies, friends, a coven, or family members? Are you strengthening your energy? Inviting abundance into your life?
4. Keeping your intention in mind, make a knot at one end of the string to symbolize a tight bond of strength and connection. Say aloud:

"With each knot, a bond I form.
I tie abundance, connection, and strength with this cord."

5. Thread the other, unknotted end of the string onto the needle. Now thread a bay leaf onto the string and tie another knot after it. Continue knotting and saying the chant, placing your blessing bay leaves in between knots. Thread and tie on additional decorations as desired.
6. When you've achieved your desired length, pass the cord through the incense, then charge it under the full moon's light for blessings.

Candlemas Crescent Moon Candle

Best Lunar Timing: Waxing Crescent, Full, or New Moon; Blue Moon; Moon in Sagittarius or Aquarius

Lunar Energy: Inspiration, Renewal, Hope

Traditionally, at Candlemas (also called Imbolc), candles are lit to guide spring back. The daylight is slowly growing now, just like the newborn light of the waxing crescent moon, and hope is in the air. The act of lighting a candle evokes themes of inspiration, inner renewal, and purification. In this activity, you'll create a candle to light during the lunar cycle near

Imbolc, inviting the moon to relight your hope and purify your energy in time for the spring moons of growth. These candles also make lovely gifts. Beyond seasonal foliage from around your home, you can incorporate violet flowers for hope or bay leaves for wishes.

You Will Need:

- ☽ Iron
- ☽ Parchment paper
- ☽ Pillar candle

- ☽ Dried flowers or leaves: blades of grass, dried herbs, rosemary, or whatever is available to you in this season

Directions:

1. Set iron on lowest setting. Up to medium if needed.
2. Cut the parchment paper to a little larger than the candle so that you can comfortably wrap it around the candle, and also hold it and keep your hands a safe distance from the iron. Arrange flowers and leaves on the parchment paper in the order you'd like them to appear on the candle.
3. Roll the parchment paper around the candle so that the foliage you chose touches the candle.
4. Use the iron on the outside of the parchment paper to warm (but not melt) the candle wax and allow the flowers and greenery to stick to the outside of the candle. Alternatively, if need be, drip wax from another candle onto the decorations to make them stick.
5. Discard the parchment paper and leave the candle to rest and charge under the waxing moonlight around the time of Imbolc.
6. At the full moon, light the candle to remind you of the growth of light coming and the blessings of the spring moons.

Seed Moon Blessing

Best Lunar Timing: New or Waxing Crescent Moon, Moon in Taurus, Moon in a Water Sign, Black Moon

Lunar Energy: Blessings, Growth, Garden Magick

During the Seed Moon and the growing of light following Imbolc, it's prime time to bless seeds, metaphorical and literal, for success. The spring moons are on their way, and the energy is ripe for new ideas to begin to grow. The new moon, too, is known as a time for blessing seeds. Use this blessing to enchant seeds for your lunar and energetic gardens. Perhaps you can start your moon witch's garden and lunar gardening practice at the next new moon!

You Will Need:

- ❫ Seeds you will plant, or Seed Planting Paper (see Chapter 8)
- ❫ 1 half eggshell, cleaned and dried
- ❫ Candle
- ❫ Matches or lighter

Directions:

1. Place the seeds or seed paper in a clean, dry half eggshell. Eggshells symbolize rebirth and protection, and they contain minerals that can nurture plants.
2. Light the candle. Keep it nearby, notice its glow, and feel the warmth of its light. You can use your Candlemas Crescent Moon Candle (see instructions in this chapter) if you like.
3. Place your hands above the seeds in the eggshell, and visualize a stirring of energy and light within them, warmed by the light of the candle. Say aloud:

"Warmth of the growing light of spring,
Blessings to these seedlings bring,
That as each grow on their own time,
Abundance and plenty bless their vines."

4. Once you feel the seeds are blessed, let the candle burn all the way down.
5. Once the candle is down, plant your seeds in soil and grind up the eggshell to sprinkle over them for nutrients, blessing, and protection.

Nurturing the Seeds of Your Lunar Intentions

Remember that the right weather, water, and pruning are part of the growth cycle, and the same philosophy applies to your lunar spells and magick. While not every seed (or intention) will grow to fruition, proper nurturing with the right beliefs, actions, and timing can grow many things under the moon to prosperity.

SPRING MOON SPELLS, RITUALS, AND RECIPES

Flower Moon Sugar

Best Lunar Timing: New or Full Moon; Moon in Pisces, Taurus, or Libra

Lunar Energy: Sweetening, Positivity, Blessings

Celebrate the growth of the spring moons and attract what you desire with this simple infused sugar recipe. The spring moons bring a focus on growth, beauty, and renewal. This is the time to perform spells related to love, positivity, and prosperity. Use Flower Moon Sugar to enchant recipes, drinks, or sugar spells; to dress candles; as a rejuvenating, sweetening sugar scrub; or even to give as a blessing gift to sweeten a connection with someone.

You Will Need:

❭ 8-ounce or pint jar with a lid

❭ ½–⅓ cup fresh or dried edible flowers, such as blossoms of violet, lilac, rose, elderflower, gardenia, chrysanthemum, chamomile, or other herbs (strong flower scents like lavender will need less, whereas subtler floral scents like rose could need more)

❭ About 1 cup granulated sugar

❭ 1 large lemon, optional

❭ Peeler, optional

Directions:

1. At the new moon, gather flowers, sugar, and lemon. (You can save the inside of the lemon for making lunar lemon bars or spring cocktails or mocktails.) If using fresh flowers, make sure they are dry and not wet.
2. Think about the themes of the spring moons, your intentions, and the blessings you are invoking.
3. Peel 2 strips of lemon peel. Place a layer of lemon peel at the bottom of the jar to cleanse away unwanted energy and bring joy. You'll only want enough to create a layer, and not necessarily stack them, so you may need to cut the peels in half. Cover with ½" layer of sugar.
4. Add a layer of flowers to invite and enchant blessings, and cover with sugar again.

5. Repeat, layering lemon, sugar, and then flowers. For a blend, you can alternate with different edible flowers, such as one layer of rose, one layer of lavender, one layer of violet. As you do so, reflect on the attractive and beautifying energy of flowers and sugar and how they can sweeten the energy in your life.
6. Close the jar and let the sugar infuse and charge from new moon to new moon, or full moon to full moon (about 4 weeks).
7. Blend to remove clumps. Store in an airtight container, and the sugar can last about 3 months. However, the longer it sits, the flower essence may dissipate. Store in freezer to keep fresh longer.

Maple Moon Money Jar

Best Lunar Timing: New–Full Moon; Blue Moon; Moon in Taurus, Capricorn, or Sagittarius

Lunar Energy: Money, Love, Abundance

The Sap Moon (or Sugar Moon) is called that because maple sap is usually collected at this time. Since it's associated with longevity, abundance, love, and money, maple is a perfect ingredient for creating a spell jar to bring luck and abundance over the long term. Do note that, just as sap moves slowly, maple magick can take time, but its results are long-lasting. In this spell, you will make a maple spell jar, just like you would a honey or sugar jar (which can be replacements if you don't want to use maple). Since maple syrup can be expensive, you might wish to choose a small jar.

You Will Need:

❭ Jar with lid
❭ Lucky bills or coins
❭ Maple syrup (enough to fill the jar)
❭ Pen and paper, or Seed Planting Paper (see Chapter 8)

❭ Dried jasmine
❭ 3 cinnamon sticks
❭ Green candle
❭ Pinch of ground cinnamon
❭ Matches or lighter

Directions:

1. Place the bills or coins inside the jar.
2. Fill the jar halfway full with maple syrup.
3. On the paper, write your intention.

4. Focus on your intention and blow on the paper, then fold it toward yourself and place it in the maple syrup.

5. Sprinkle in ¾ of the dried jasmine (setting aside a pinch to dress the candle) and push in the cinnamon sticks. Fill the rest of the jar to the top with syrup. Close the jar.

6. Anoint the candle with a bit of maple syrup.

7. Roll the candle toward yourself through a mixture of dried jasmine (the pinch you set aside) and ground cinnamon, drawing abundance and money toward you.

8. Affix the candle atop the lid of the jar, then light it. Visualize abundance coming your way.

9. To maintain the spell (since sap can move slowly), burn a candle atop the jar regularly. Choose the timing that works best for you—perhaps every new and full moon, or every Monday (moon day), or even Thursday (Jupiter's day) or Friday (Venus's day). Ideally, you'd burn a new candle once a week for as long as you'd like to maintain the spell.

Pink Moon Blush

Best Lunar Timing: Full Moon; Moon in Libra, Cancer, Leo, Capricorn, or Taurus; Supermoon

Lunar Energy: Love, Glamour, Personal Power

Nothing brings to mind the youthful, enchanting energy of spring moons quite like fresh, glowing cheeks—there is no better time than the month of the Pink Moon to create an enchanting blush. In this spell, you will create your very own natural blush powder, which also doubles as powder for love, beauty, and power in magick. You can use this recipe as makeup if you like, or mix it with water (as needed) to create a magickal paint for drawing sigils on paper, or sprinkle to dress candles. This way, you can use the powder on aligned spell candles, and also wear it on your cheeks for some glamour magick. The instructions here make a pink-red blush. However, feel free to customize this based on your skin tone or preferences, adding more or less of the following to your liking: beet root powder for a dark pink; powdered rose petals for red-pink; powdered hibiscus for burgundy-red; turmeric for orange; ground ginger for light gold; cocoa for brown. Arrowroot powder acts as the base for consistency for the blush, but is white and will greatly lighten whatever you put in it.

You Will Need:

- 1½ tablespoons beet root powder
- 1 tablespoon arrowroot powder
- ¼ teaspoon ground turmeric
- ¼ teaspoon ground ginger
- ¼ teaspoon ground cinnamon
- ½ tablespoon cocoa powder
- Powdered hibiscus, rose, and/or additional amounts of other powdered ingredients to vary recipe to your skin tone and preference, optional
- Jar with lid or other sealable container

Directions:

1. Under the light of the Pink Moon or any full moon, sprinkle in beet root powder (for a pink, and for love and fidelity), arrowroot powder (for spiritual cleansing), turmeric (for power and a rich, gold-orange glow), ginger (for power), cinnamon (for quick manifestation and power), and cocoa powder (for warmth) into jar.
2. Close the jar and shake (this is the best way to really mix the powders thoroughly). Test on the back of your hand or with a drop of water on paper (to test as a magickal paint), and add more of the aforementioned and/or optional ingredients to get to desired tone and color.
3. Once finalized, stir clockwise with intention, thinking about the beauty and power of the spring moons, and leave in a sealed container under the full moon to charge. Keep in a sealed container, and ideally use within 3 months.

Beltane Beauty Facial Ice Cubes

Best Lunar Timing: Full Moon; Moon in Libra, Pisces, Cancer, Scorpio, or Leo

Lunar Energy: Beauty, Sensuality, Rejuvenation

The spring moons often bring plenty of dew and rain, making it a favorable time for moon-blessed water recipes. Create these cooling Moon Water ice cubes to soothe your skin and energy or to use in sensual play with a partner under the Beltane moon. Packed with lunar beauty and healing ingredients, these can help you relax after a moon ritual, cool down during the coming summer heat, or to tighten up and enchant your skin with lunar beauty! Make sure to use organic ingredients for a safe and happy skin-soother.

You Will Need:

- 1 cup Moon Water made at the spring full moon (see Chapter 7)
- 2 tablespoons fresh or dried rose petals
- 1 tablespoon dried lemon balm, optional
- Cucumber slices
- Aloe leaf, optional
- Ice cube tray

Directions:

1. Set Moon Water (enough for your ice cube tray) to boil. Meanwhile, place rose petals and lemon balm (if using), in a heat-safe container with a lip for easy pouring, such as a Pyrex measuring cup. Pour boiling water over rose petals and lemon balm to infuse.
2. Let cool, then add cucumber slices and the gel from the aloe leaf, if using. Infuse in the refrigerator overnight.
3. The next day, strain out the cucumber slices and discard. Pour the mixture into an ice cube tray and let freeze.
4. Once frozen, they are ready to use! Massage into skin—which might be chilling—but will feel rejuvenating and sensual! Follow with your moisturizer to hydrate.

Makeup-Setting Spray

You can easily turn the Beltane Beauty Facial Ice Cubes recipe into a lunar-enchanted facial mist or makeup-setting spray! Simply add aloe, do not freeze the water, and filter the infused water into a spray bottle. The spray will stay fresh in the fridge for about a week. To make it last longer, add a preservative, such as glycerin.

Milk Moon Flower Bath

Best Lunar Timing: Moon in Cancer, Libra, Taurus, or Pisces; Full Moon; Supermoon; Blue Moon

Lunar Energy: Rejuvenation, Peace, Beauty

Milk is often associated with goddesses and the moon, and it's long been used in baths—most famously Cleopatra's. With the full Milk Moon's spring energies of rejuvenation and beauty, now is the perfect time to create a moon milk bath and feel like a moon god or goddess. With the addition of rose, lavender, and your favorite flowers, you'll be surrounded by the energies of this full moon and infuse your aura with spring moon beauty, peace, and lunar glow. You can also use this as a love bath to share with a partner.

You Will Need:

-) Jar with lid
-) 1 cup powdered milk
-) ¼ cup cornstarch
-) ½ cup baking soda
-) 10 drops lavender essential oil
-) ¼ cup dried rose petals
-) ⅛ cup dried violet or other safe flower of choice

Directions:

1. In jar, mix together all ingredient. Close the jar and shake thoroughly to mix. As you do so, use the movement to visualize raising youthful, excited energy (like a fresh flower blooming) into the mixture.
2. Set aside and fill bathtub with water.
3. Add ½ cup of mixture into bath, or more if desired.
4. Clockwise with your hand, stir, visualizing the moon illuminating it. Say aloud:

   "Ethereal light of the milk moon,
   Enchant my energy in this nurturing cocoon."

5. Disrobe, get in the bath, and enjoy the nurturing energy and scene. Sip Lunar Loose-Leaf Flower Tea (see Chapter 10) for added flower moon magick, and think upon your intentions for the moon. Store rest of mixture for future use, and use within 1 month.

SUMMER MOON SPELLS, RITUALS, AND RECIPES

Strawberry Moon Happiness Honey Syrup

Best Lunar Timing: Moon in Libra, Cancer, or Leo; Full Moon

Lunar Energy: Happiness, Peace, Love

With plentiful seeds, strawberries are a great magickal ingredient for both abundance and fertility. The fruits themselves are associated with happiness, joy, harmony, and love. Whether invoking love with a partner, inviting happy abundance, or inspiring harmony between yourself and another, this jar spell is perfect for this lunation cycle.

You Will Need:

- Fresh strawberries, enough to loosely fill desired jar
- Knife
- Dried lavender
- Toothpick
- Jar with lid
- Honey, enough to fill the jar

Directions:

1. Hold the strawberries, thinking of happiness and love and how the energy of these berries resonates in tandem with their namesake moon. Eat one, if inspired.
2. With the knife, cut off the head of the strawberries and core out part of the center. Fill the center of each strawberry with lavender, as though filling your own mind and center with peace.
3. With the toothpick, lightly engrave the outside of the strawberries with your intention(s), your name, or (if invoking commitment) the name of your partner. Place the berries in the jar so that they loosely fill it (leaving space for honey).
4. Sprinkle in a generous amount of extra lavender (about 1 tablespoon per ½ cup of honey), just like the Strawberry Moon rains down joy and harmony.
5. Pour the honey over the strawberries in the jar, sweetening the energy and welcoming your desires to you. Close the jar and store in fridge, shaking every other day or so to make sure the infused strawberry juices spread throughout the honey.
6. Infuse for 2 weeks, until the next new moon. Test to see that the flavor is just right! Then use in drinks, fruit salads, teas, or lunar lemonades to share with friends or partners, or even in a honey jar spell (similar to the Maple Moon Money Jar, but with honey) for happiness and love.

Mead Moon Magick

The Strawberry Moon is also called the Honey Moon and the Mead Moon. If you want to inspire love and happiness within yourself or another, drink a sip of mead (if of legal drinking age) as you craft the jar to further enchant the energy of this spell. You can even serve a glass to a lunar deity of your choice as an offering. If you want to share your happiness, you could share a glass of mead under this magick moon, perhaps accompanied by some honey-glazed strawberries or strawberry-based fruit salad. What a perfect way to celebrate the abundance, happiness, and love of this summer moon!

Summer Solstice Moon Circlet

Best Lunar Timing: Full Moon, Moon in Leo or Sagittarius, Supermoon

Lunar Energy: Power, Abundance, Blessings

Resonating with the full moon themes of celebration, fun, positivity, abundance, and manifestation, the solstice is a time of power. The fae are awake, too, and the midsummer sun and the beaming ethereal full moon that appears closest to solstice keep all of life abuzz, both day and night. In this activity, you'll create a flower circlet and use it to surround and crown a blessing candle, wear upon your head, or place on the water (as many witches do for Kupala, the Slavic celebration of the summer solstice). (You could also create a circlet with seasonal foliage to adorn a Candlemas candle.) After your solstice celebration, you can dry the circlet and use it as a wall hanging to bring positivity, luminosity, and blessings any time of year.

You Will Need:

- Long, pliable sticks or branches
- Moon Water (see Chapter 7)
- Dried, fresh, or artificial seasonal flowers or foliage
- Ribbon, assorted colors and lengths, optional

Directions:

1. Place the branches in a bucket of Moon Water to soak and soften. When they are bendable, weave the sticks into a large wreath or crown. Reflect on the full cycle of the moon and sun as you do so.
2. When you have a stable circle, begin to weave in flowers and foliage. Consider adding flowers and foliage from a nature walk, or choose greens, or yellow, orange, red, purple, or white flowers for the colors of harvest and of the season. If you're planning to use this as a wall hanging, you might arrange the flowers into a crescent moon within the circlet. Think about flowers coming to their full bloom under the moon and sun. Many herbs and flowers come into fullness under the summer full moons—integrating them in the circlet, think upon the moon's nurturing energy growing these plants to fruition, alongside the sun and earth.
3. Once you like the arrangement of flowers and greenery, allow the circlet to rest if the branches are still wet.

4. When ready to use, you might place the circlet upon your head as you dance in celebration underneath the full moon nearest the summer solstice. Then, you might place the circlet upon the water. Or, rest the circlet around a small candle (making sure the circlet won't catch fire) such as the Candlemas Crescent Moon Candle, to celebrate the herbs and flowers coming to fullness and your own power blossoming under the summer moons. When the candle is done burning, you can attach a trail of ribbons for a crescent moon wall hanging.

Herb Moon Prophecy Tea

Best Lunar Timing: Moon in a Water Sign, Moon in Sagittarius, Dark–New Moon, Full Moon, Blue Moon

Lunar Energy: Psychic Insight, Peace, Wisdom

Celebrate the spiritual insights and personal power available now with this delicious tea. Whether this moon calls itself Buck Moon, Wort Moon, Thunder Moon, or Herb Moon, herbs and their magickal properties are at their peak now. Attune to the herbal energies of this time for blessings and psychic downloads. Sip the tea while divining, meditating, or watching summer storms for insight. Make sure to use food-grade (and, if possible, organic) flowers and herbs.

You Will Need:

) 5 ounces water
) 5 fresh sage leaves
) ½ teaspoon dried lavender
) Teacup
) ½ tablespoon honey, or to taste
) 1 fresh rosemary sprig
) Tarot cards, optional

Directions:

1. Set water to boil.
2. Place all herbs except the rosemary sprig in a teacup. Smell their aroma and hover your hands above them, acknowledging and tuning into the wisdom of these herbal allies.
3. Pour in hot water. Add in honey to taste, perfect for a summer moon harvest tea. Let steep for 5 minutes, then strain.
4. Stir clockwise with the rosemary sprig, noticing its resemblance to a lightning bolt in its length and formation. Invite flashes of insight into the tea as you stir, infusing the hot tea with clarifying rosemary.

Part Two: Spells and Rituals for Every Moon

5. Meditate and read tarot cards as you sip, and invite blessings and psychic prophecy under the Herb and Thunder Moon of summer.

Harvest Moon Grain Gratitude Offering

Best Lunar Timing: Full or Waning Gibbous Moon, Moon in Virgo, Supermoon

Lunar Energy: Gratitude, Abundance, Protection

The first harvest is a time to celebrate and invoke abundance for the coming harvest moons—but also to give back. Create an offering of gratitude, attract prosperity, and request protection for the remaining harvests with this cornmeal mixture. Use it to line the outskirts of your property, leave in the soil as an offering, fill an abundance jar, cover a candle as dressing, or pack a corn husk poppet or charm bag.

You Will Need:

) Cornmeal

) Dried blue cornflowers

) Onion powder

) Dried basil

) Grains, such as barley or oats

Directions:

1. Under the Lammas or Harvest Moon, mix all ingredients together, thinking on their properties: cornmeal for abundance and prosperity, cornflower for peace, onion for protection and money, and basil for protection and wealth. The grains represent the harvests of the past, which are the seeds for future abundance.

2. While mixing, say:

   "Harvest moons come, the grain fields glow.
   Around me, prosperity and abundance grow."

3. Leave the mixture in a bowl or jar to charge under the moon. Visualize the earth aglow with these blessings.

4. Scatter the mixture around your property for protection, and as an offering for the land and ancestor spirits around you.

Pentacles Prosperity Protection Spell

Best Lunar Timing: Moon in Capricorn, Virgo, or Taurus; Full or Waning Gibbous Moon

Lunar Energy: Abundance, Protection, Financial Security

Grain is an important form of sustenance for many cultures across the globe, which has led to various customs related to the harvest. At this point, it is time to fill your stores (both energetically and financially) to prepare for the coming turn of the season and decline of the year. Like the waning gibbous moon, you can share and reflect, but also begin to slowly retreat within and protect your own energetic resources to grow and change through autumn and winter moons and lunar cycles. Depicting a king holding on to his coins, the Four of Pentacles can help you grow, reserve, and protect your resources. With this grain jar spell, call upon the theme of the season (grain) and this card's symbolism to help you save money and reflect on how you can begin to turn within, and reserve some of your own energetic resources after the limitless growth of spring and summer.

You Will Need:

> Tarot card: Four of Pentacles
> Jar with lid
> Grains of choice (oats, rice, wheat, barley, corn)
> Sharpie
> Bay leaf
> 4 copper pennies or other coins

Directions:

1. Meditate on the Four of Pentacles: The king holds on to each coin to reserve his resources for secured abundance. Place your jar atop the card and fill it halfway with your choice of grains, a symbol of the abundance of the harvest moons.
2. With the Sharpie, write your intention on the bay leaf. Place the leaf and 1 coin in the jar, then fill it the rest of the way with grain. Close the jar, which is now your own personal magickal grain reserve, whether for finances or reserving your energy.
3. Sit down and place a coin under each foot and one atop your head. Hold the jar to your chest.
4. Visualize what you are reserving—whether money and abundance to make it through a time of scarcity or the coming change of seasons,

or your energy. Visualize it becoming real, and say aloud, filling in a name for today's moon:

"___ moon, I hunger no more.
Complete are my energy, money, and food stores.
With some to keep and some to share,
I have all I need and plenty to spare."

5. Breathe abundance and energy into your body, and feel safe, secure, and surrounded by plenty. Store the jar on your altar, and repeat the meditation and light a candle atop it anytime you need more abundance for your stores.

More Money Magick

Use the three coins for the Prosperous Property Jar Spell (see Chapter 10).

AUTUMN MOON SPELLS, RITUALS, AND RECIPES

Mabon Moon Tarot Meditation

Best Lunar Timing: Waning, Last Quarter, or Dark Moon; Moon in Scorpio or Libra

Lunar Energy: Reflection, Shadow Work, Balance

At the autumn equinox, the cycle of the seasons turns toward the darker part of the year. Now the moon's light is ever more prominent, guiding your passage, insight, and reflection through the seasons of release and rest. Embrace the journey and call upon your inner moon to guide the way with this tarot meditation.

You Will Need:

❱ Tarot card: The High Priestess
❱ Pomegranate or pomegranate seeds, or pomegranate juice (in a pinch)
❱ 1 dark lunar stone (such as black moonstone), optional

❱ 1 light lunar stone (such as moonstone or selenite), optional

Directions:

1. Sit before your moon altar with The High Priestess card and the pomegranate.
2. If incorporating the stones, place the darker stone in your left hand and the lighter one in your right, to represent the dark and light of the moon. Breathe deeply, tuning into their energy.
3. Think about the symbolism of the pomegranate. It calls to mind the story of the goddess Persephone, a spring maiden who was stolen away to the underworld, where she ate 6 pomegranate seeds and was therefore forced to spend 6 months of every year as queen of the underworld, a yearly journey that gave rise to the seasons. The pomegranate also symbolizes abundance, rebirth, creativity, and magick.
4. Now turn your attention to The High Priestess tarot card, which shows the balance of light and dark, represented by the correspondingly colored pillars on either side. The priestess is unafraid to dip into the wisdom of the shadow or the higher self at any moment; she knows the wisdom available in both. A crescent moon rests at her feet, denoting her intuition and the power of the moon through all its phases. Like the growth and waning of moonlight, and the seasons of the year, there is a time for light, and a time to retreat within the dark. What are you feeling called to reflect or work on in the darker part of the year?
5. Continue to reflect on the symbols and imagery before you. With her cycle of light and her journey through the Wheel of the Year, the moon shows us that both dark and light are necessary. Your inner intuition and the moon are both there to guide your way.
6. Open the pomegranate, its red color a symbol of blood, life, and sacrifice—but also abundance. Give thanks for this wonderful seasonal treat. Mindful of the decline of the year, count out 6 pomegranate seeds and set them aside as an offering. Alternatively, pour pomegranate juice for yourself, and a small amount for an offering.
7. Eat some seeds as a magickal snack while contemplating abundance and the cycle of life. Close your eyes and visualize your inner moon guiding the way through anything.

Wine Moon Sweet Tea

Best Lunar Timing: Moon in Pisces or Scorpio, Waning Gibbous Moon, Lunar Eclipse

Lunar Energy: Abundance, Prosperity, Psychic Energy

Celebrate the Wine Moon and the harvest energies of plenty with this moon's namesake ingredient—grapes. Grapes are packed with moon-magick potential, since they're associated with the moon and are used as a magickal treat to invoke luxury, abundance, and mental powers, or transformed into wine to commune with the gods. Combining grapes with jasmine and honey (a great harvest moon treat), this sweet tea is a great way to invite psychic visions while you meditate with the moon and summon prosperity. (Remember to work with food-grade flowers and, if possible, organic ingredients for a safe and earth-friendly tea.)

You Will Need:

- 4½ ounces water
- 3 large red seedless grapes
- 1 large blackberry
- ½ tablespoon dried jasmine
- ½ tablespoon honey
- Moon Water ice cubes (see Chapter 7), optional
- Jasmine incense
- Matches or lighter

Directions:

1. Set water to boil. As you do so, wash the grapes (perhaps with Moon Water). Think on the moon, the decline of the year, and the alchemy of grapes turning into wine and energy, of intention turning into prosperity.
2. In the bottom of a glass, muddle the grapes and blackberry.
3. Add jasmine, pour in the hot water, and allow to steep for 5–10 minutes.
4. Stir honey in clockwise, giving thanks for the harvest work of hardworking bees and inviting sweet abundance, wisdom, and psychic visions to come to you.
5. If you like, you can drink this tea hot. Or allow it to chill in the fridge or freezer, or pour over Moon Water ice cubes and stir.
6. Enjoy while burning jasmine incense to invite prosperity and invite psychic insight as you meditate, reflect, or summon visions.

Wine Moon Offering

Pour an offering of wine (if you are of legal drinking age) or grape juice into a glass, as an offering to wine-associated deity Dionysus during the Wine Moon for a plentiful harvest. Leave out, then pour into earth a few days later.

Moonfire Releasing Rebirth Ritual

Best Lunar Timing: Waning or Dark Moon, Moon in Scorpio, Lunar Eclipse

Lunar Energy: Banishing, Release, Rebirth

Samhain and its corresponding Blood Moon or Hunter's Moon are often called the witch's new year. This is a powerful time to banish old limiting and unwanted energy and cleanse in preparation for the rebirth at the winter solstice. Under the full moon, alchemy is possible, and this energy is only magnified by the seasonal themes. Burn away old memories, bad habits, and old ties or repeating patterns under the power of the Blood Moon with this simple burning ritual. As the Blood Moon's energy heralds, sacrifice and release must precede a rebirth. The corresponding myth and bloodred color of pomegranate is perfect for reflecting on such themes of sacrifice and the cycle of life and transformation. For a special lunar ritual, you can perform the Mabon Moon Tarot Meditation (see this chapter) beforehand.

You Will Need:

❱ Pen and paper
❱ Cauldron or fireproof bowl
❱ Matches or lighter
❱ Pomegranate juice

Directions:

1. Fold the paper in half. On one half, write things you'd like to banish, change, or let go of. On the other half, write things that you'd like to manifest in place of those things you are banishing.
2. Rip the paper in two to symbolize cutting away the unwanted energy.
3. In your cauldron or fireproof bowl, burn the half of the paper that lists things you wish to change. Say aloud as you watch the flames:

"As the full moon waxes and wanes, life is constantly remade.
Moonfire, burn what no longer serves, ashes to new things give birth."

4. Let the powers of the alchemical full moon and of fire transform old energy into ashes, to allow room for the new—just as a wildfire prepares the way for new foliage to grow.

5. Once that half of the paper is burned, pour into the ashes some of the pomegranate juice—a seasonal ingredient and symbol of sacrifice, blood, and transmutation. The juice adds nutrients to your offering to the earth.

6. Use your finger to anoint the positive paper with the pomegranate-ash mixture as a sign of sacrifice, of commitment and transmutation. Keep the paper in a sacred space as a reminder of the Wheel of the Year and what you wish to bring to life.

7. Pour the rest of the pomegranate and ash mixture into the earth as a nourishing offering.

Prosperity Pumpkin Spell

Best Lunar Timing: Full or New Moon; Moon in Cancer, Sagittarius, or Scorpio

Lunar Energy: The Home, Luck, Abundance

Pumpkin is the ingredient of the season, and it also happens to be associated with the moon and lunar abundance! Transform the tradition of carving pumpkins and putting in lights, to send away unwanted visiting spirits but guide familial ones back home, into a spell to bring abundance and good fortune. With this sacred pumpkin spell right by your front door, new blessings will come to your doorstep. You can also try using moon-associated melon (such as watermelon) if performing this spell out of season.

You Will Need:

- ❯ 1 large pumpkin
- ❯ Tools to carve the pumpkin
- ❯ Granulated sugar
- ❯ Ground cinnamon and/or sandalwood powder, or Moon Dust Blessing Powder (see Chapter 7)
- ❯ Green, gold, or white candle
- ❯ Moon Oil (see Chapter 7)
- ❯ Handful of poppy seeds
- ❯ 5 bay leafs and/or cinnamon sticks
- ❯ Matches or lighter
- ❯ Offering of food or drink for spirits, optional

Directions:

1. Carve your pumpkin so that it has a removable top, is hollowed out, and has a face or design like a jack-o'-lantern. If desired, set aside

pumpkin seeds to roast for a snack, future spells, offerings, or for use in recipes.

2. Pour in a generous layer of sugar inside the bottom of the pumpkin, enough sugar to support a candle.

3. Sprinkle a spiral of ground cinnamon or sandalwood powder atop the sugar inside the pumpkin—starting from the face/holes of the pumpkin, and spiraling inward to the center of the sugar. This powder spiral will guide good fortune and spirits to the central candle you'll place in the next few steps. You can also use the Moon Dust Blessing Powder (see Chapter 7) for this.

4. Dress a green, gold, or white candle with Moon Oil (see Chapter 7) and cinnamon or sandalwood (or both) or the Moon Dust Blessing Powder (see Chapter 7). Think upon drawing abundance and good fortune to you as you do so.

5. Where the spiral stops, nestle the candle. Use a candleholder, if needed.

6. But, we also want to guide mischievous energy and misfortune *away* this Samhain moon night! Poppy seeds are associated with the moon, and have dual purpose: They are often used to cause confusion (because of poppy's association with opium), but also associated with luck, dreams, and prosperity. Take a handful of poppy seeds and sprinkle them counterclockwise around the outermost edge of the sugar and along the inside of the pumpkin wall, to confuse unwanted energy, but still invite prosperity.

7. Lay cinnamon sticks or bay leafs atop the sugar (or alternate both) at a firesafe distance around the candle, pointing them out from the center candle like a star.

8. Say aloud:

"With the blessing of pumpkin and this candle's guiding light
Guide to me good luck and fortune, this Samhain/Blood/Hunter's Moon
   night.
Let all misfortunate, ill meaning eyes and spirits be deterred away
But those who bless and bring goodwill, to this home, find their way."

9. Light the candle and, if safe, replace the pumpkin top. Keep by your door to invite prosperity from good spirits and be sure to keep an eye on it for fire safety. If desired, you might leave an offering for the spirits that come and bring blessings. Be wary of the sugar attracting ants!

Witch's Mirror Ancestor Moon Meditation

Best Lunar Timing: Moon in Scorpio or Pisces, Waning or Dark Moon, Lunar Eclipse

Lunar Energy: Gratitude, Reflection, Spirits

The descent into the darker part of the year brings a time for reflection and also for connections beyond the veil. The moon is a guardian of the past, and through her power, you can access the wisdom of your ancestors or witches past. Connect to the other side and welcome wisdom, visions, and knowledge with this simple meditation. As a sign of gratitude, you might like to prepare an offering plate of food or treats for ancestors or spirit guides that you encounter.

You Will Need:

❭ Candle
❭ Matches or lighter
❭ Mirror
❭ Veil or lace, optional

❭ Dried rosemary sprig
❭ An offering, such as food or drink

Directions:

1. Breathe deeply and relax your mind. Cleanse your energy and the energy of the space. Light the candle and place it in front of the mirror.
2. If desired, place a veil or lace over your head.
3. Light the rosemary in the candle flame to produce a soft smoke, saying:

   "By the light of Samhain (or Hunter's or Blood) moon, ancestors I call to commune.
   Guardian moon of the past, your wisdom and visions I seek at last."

4. Hold the rosemary between you and the mirror as you softly gaze into the mirror. Wait patiently and see what visions, thoughts, or ideas come to mind, or watch for illusions produced by the interplay of candlelight and smoke. If stuck, call upon the moon again and tune into your intuition.
5. Afterward, use the rosemary smoke to cleanse your energy and give thanks for the insight. Leave offering out for ancestors or spirits that came through, and discard the next day or a few days later.

Chapter 10

MOON SIGN SPELLS

As the moon moves through her phases, she also moves through the zodiac signs. In each sign, her energy takes on a different flavor and personality, illuminating emotions and intuition and empowering moon magick in unique ways. Utilizing the power of her movement through the zodiac signs can help you not only cast more powerful spells, but also work with specific themes of life that the moon calls you to ponder for healing and change.

In this chapter, you will find two special spells, rituals, or recipes for each moon sign. Each of these does especially well under the given moon sign, but they also can be cast at a variety of other lunar occasions. Furthermore, each moon sign has more magickal potential and themes beyond what's shared here. To find a wider variety of workings for your intentions, revisit Chapter 4 to refresh your memory on each moon sign's magickal potential, and select what suits your needs best from the wide array of spells throughout Part 2. Open the road and set new habits for success with the Road-Opening Clove Spell, or practice Moonlit Bibliomancy to glean information when the moon is in Gemini or Sagittarius. Whatever sign the moon is in, there is a spell to help you live a moon-magickal life.

MOON IN ARIES

Energy and Vitality Waxing Crescent Crystal Layout

Best Lunar Timing: Waxing Crescent Moon; Moon in Aries, Virgo, or Capricorn; Solar Eclipse

Lunar Energy: Action, Vitality, Determination

The energy of the moon in Aries can be fruitful for boosting vitality and for determination and success in goals—as long as it is directed with intention. In magick, clear quartz is often used to program, direct, and magnify energy. During the waxing crescent, you'll direct your energy via specific goals and actions, and in this spell a clear quartz point helps you focus your energy toward your goal. Along with other Aries-related stones (carnelian for vitality and passion, bloodstone for endurance and determination), the clear quartz in this simple crystal healing layout and meditation will boost your energy and sharpen your focus on your new moon intentions. This is a powerful practice to support your goals throughout the lunation cycle, to use as a simple new moon or waxing crescent meditation, or even to charge a quartz point for use in lunar rituals.

You Will Need:

❭ Bloodstone

❭ Carnelian

❭ Clear quartz point

Directions:

1. Decide where you want to perform this crystal layout. You will be laying down, so you may want to lay on your bed, or perhaps you feel more adventurous and want to do it where you can experience the moonlight. The new moon also rises and sets with the sun, so you can even perform in the morning, outside during the waxing crescent moon. Set your stones nearby, within arm's reach, and lie down.

2. Close your eyes and breathe deeply. Inhale peace and focus, exhale random thoughts and unwanted energy. Place the bloodstone on your heart and the carnelian an inch or so below your navel. Hold the quartz point in your nondominant hand, directing the point up your arm.

3. Feel the weight of the stones on your body. Visualize light pouring down from the cosmos, through you, and deep into the earth's core, so that you are both grounded and connected to the cosmos.

4. Then, think on your intention—what it looks and feels like. Let the possibility excite your heart, your center of giving and receiving. Breathe in the moonlight, envisioning it igniting a lunar-inspired flame or spark within your body where you feel the most excitement toward your purpose. With each inhale, envision that energy and fire growing bigger and brighter.

5. Bring the quartz point to your heart. Point the quartz inward to draw and direct energy to your heart center, toward your passion. Hold it

there, envisioning the crystal directing energy for vitality with your intention in mind.

6. Slowly draw the quartz and your hand down toward your navel, where the carnelian rests. Hold it there, and continue visualizing feeding the flame of energy and passion.

7. Once you feel the energy activated within your body, move the crystal point down, visualizing moving the energy down your body to ground the energy into reality and spread the vitality throughout your system.

8. Move the crystal to your dominant hand, with the quartz point now pointing outward, directing energy out into the world. Keep your visualization as you hold on to the quartz, imagining it focusing and magnifying energy for the desired intention. Tune into and accept the energy of the bloodstone and carnelian.

9. Hold the meditation for at least a few minutes longer, or as long as you'd like, and repeat it regularly if you like. Keep the quartz with you and use it in aligned ritual work; hold on to the carnelian to continue feeding vitality toward your goal.

Road-Opening Clove Spell

Best Lunar Timing: Moon in a Fire Sign; New, Waxing, or Full Moon; Solar Eclipse

Lunar Energy: Road Opening, Success, Habits

When casting new moon intentions, you may at times find the pathway is blocked. Banish unwanted obstacles and unblock stalled projects with this road-opening lunar spell. Cast it at the new moon to clear the pathway, or at the full moon to encourage success. Under the Aries moon, this spell will help you break through barriers for victory and start healthy habits; under the Sagittarius moon, it will invoke luck and opportunities; while in Leo, it will bless your endeavors with creativity and success. Regardless of when you cast it, this spell will invite the moon to illuminate and bless your path forward.

You Will Need:

❱ Small white standing candle

❱ Matches or lighter

❱ Pen and small piece of paper

❱ 1 orange

- ❯ Knife
- ❯ Ground ginger
- ❯ Ground cinnamon
- ❯ Needle or toothpick
- ❯ Whole cloves

Directions:

1. Light the candle and write your intention on the small piece of paper.
2. With a knife, cut a hole in the top of the orange. Reflect on orange's association with the fire signs and its energies of road opening, success, joviality, and inspiration.
3. Roll your intention paper up tightly, thinking of the moon clearing a pathway forward. Sprinkle the paper with ground spices and push the paper into the center of the orange, through the opening you just cut.
4. Starting at the bottom of the orange, use the needle or toothpick to poke a swerving clockwise pathway upward and around to the top of the orange. (The holes will allow the cloves to easily poke into the citrus.)
5. Hold the cloves. Visualize moving successfully toward your goal, and one by one, poke a clove into each hole along the pathway you made. As you poke them in, imagine each clove as a habit or facet that is necessary to support the endeavor.
6. Think of your intention, and of the moon growing from new to full. Visualize a pathway and opportunities opening up for your goal or intention. As you do so, say aloud:

"Lunar light, clear the way, victory I shall have this day."

7. Seal the top of the orange with wax dripped from the candle, and let the candle burn down within sight.
8. Alternatively, push the candle's base into the orange and let the candle burn there. Just be sure you secure the orange to stand upright, and burn it within sight.
9. When the candle is done burning, you might bury the orange outside as an offering to the earth, keep it on your altar for a few days, or preserve it by drying it out in a bag of more ground spices for 3 weeks to make a good luck charm.

MOON IN TAURUS

Eggshell Blessing Powder

Best Lunar Timing: Moon in Taurus, Virgo, or Cancer; Blue Moon; Black Moon; New Moon

Lunar Energy: Abundance, Moon and Earth Connection, Blessings

Eggshells are filled with nutrients that are good for soil—plus, they're often powdered for protection spells in witchcraft. The Taurus moon is a favorable time to cast spells to nurture intentions' growth. But Taurus's stubborn energy also includes standing firm in your values and protecting your desires and space. Create your own blessing powder to connect to the power of nature and of the moon, to give rise to fertile and abundant ground for prosperity, to protect your seedling ideas in the early stages of their growth, or to protect the boundaries of your home while giving thanks to the earth and moon's cycles of abundance. Feel free to replace the flowers mentioned here with flowers of your own choosing, or whatever you have on hand.

You Will Need:

❭ Eggshells

❭ Mortar and pestle

❭ Dried blue cornflower

❭ Dried lavender

❭ Dried rose petals

❭ Dried violets, optional

Directions:

1. Grind the eggshells with the mortar and pestle. As you do so, think about the protective energy of the moon and the egg, and also their nurturing energy for plants.
2. Sprinkle in your dried flowers and grind them up too. Contemplate their energies of blessing and peace.
3. On the new or full moon, sprinkle the powder clockwise on the earth outside your home, or even in a nearby park. As you do so, say:

   "Flowers, eggs, and the moons of spring,
   Protect this home/seedling and only blessings bring."

4. Visualize the eggs and moon creating a protective barrier around your home—a shell that only allows positive energy in.

Apple Seed Spell

Best Lunar Timing: Moon in Taurus or Capricorn, New Moon, Black Moon, Solar Eclipse

Lunar Energy: Prosperity, Long-Term Growth, Success

In the earth sign Taurus, the moon-blessed land is fertile and ready to grow the seedlings of your desires into long-term results. With ingredients calling upon Taurus's ruler, Venus (namely apple and rose), you will summon long-lasting success, stability, and abundance. With the Apple Seed Spell, you will call down the power of prosperous Taurus and the nurturing energy of the moon to see your intention through from seed to abundant tree.

You Will Need:

- 1 apple
- Knife
- Firesafe plate
- Green candle (chime candle or small standing candle)
- Moon Oil (see Chapter 7) or honey
- Ground cinnamon
- Dried rose petals
- Matches or lighter

Directions:

1. Cut the apple in half horizontally so that it shows a five-pointed star in its core.
2. Remove the seeds, set them aside, and cut a slice about ⅛" thick from one of the halves. Place the apple slice in the center of the plate. (Alternatively, you can use an entire apple half for the spell, as long as it will stand upright.)
3. Anoint the candle with Moon Oil or honey.
4. Visualizing the moon growing from new to full and your intention manifesting alongside it, sprinkle cinnamon and rose petals onto a small plate. Roll the candle so the dried mixture sticks to the side of the candle.
5. Stand the candle in the middle of the star in the apple slice, clearing away any apple bits in the way so that the candle stands securely upright. If needed, melt the bottom of the candle with a flame to affix it. Sprinkle any remaining cinnamon and rose petals on the apple and on the plate.
6. Working clockwise, place the apple seeds around the apple on the plate, then hover your hands above the candle. Think about your intentions.

Speak them aloud and visualize them coming to life—like apple seeds germinating and growing into tall, durable, and fruitful trees.

7. When you feel the energy is charged up, light the candle and let burn all the way down. When finished, you may decide to keep the apple seeds on your altar in a jar to continue feeding them, or plant them in the earth.

MOON IN GEMINI

Social Butterfly Body Glitter

Best Lunar Timing: Moon in Gemini or Libra, Full Moon

Lunar Energy: Charm, Communication, Glamour

Sometimes you might need a little push to go out and socialize or stand out in a crowd. The full moon, especially in an air sign, is the perfect time to perform magick related to this goal. Let your inner social butterfly (or lunar moth) take flight with this simple shimmering ointment. With the moon's blessing, you can gracefully connect with anyone through conversation. For best results, make this under a Gemini or Libra moon. Use before networking events or speeches, or even for wooing through your words. Alternatively, you can skip concocting your own and do the incantation and anointment with perfume, lotion, or body glitter you already own.

You Will Need

- ❭ 2 tablespoons coconut oil
- ❭ Small container
- ❭ Toothpick
- ❭ Sparkly eye shadow or highlighter (preferably blue or white)
- ❭ 2 drops peppermint essential oil
- ❭ 5 drops jasmine essential oil

Directions:

1. Set your items before you on your altar or under the moonlight. Spoon coconut oil (which is associated with the moon) into the container.
2. With a toothpick, lift up a tiny amount of eye shadow (you can always add more). Think of butterflies or lunar moths flying, their wings shimmering in the moonlight, as you add it in and stir the eye shadow to evenly mix into the coconut oil.

3. Drip in essential oils. Peppermint is a great choice for communication, while jasmine is great for lunar enchantment and charm.
4. Mix the concoction clockwise, close the lid, and leave out to charge under the moonlight.
5. To use, stand before a mirror and see yourself shining with moonlight. Say:

   "Blessed by the moon's light,
   My words as enchanting as a butterfly in flight."

6. For a subtle, lunar-like sparkle, use the glittered oil to anoint your collarbones, under your ears, or your throat (a powerful Gemini location).

Bluebird Communication Spell

Best Lunar Timing: Moon in an Air Sign, Full or Waxing Moon, Supermoon

Lunar Energy: Communication, Information, Messages

Few can resist the magnetic call of the full moon. Usher forth communication under her light and summon messages from someone you share a close bond with, or receive recognition or word on a project you've poured your heart into. Using a feather (like those on Mercury's winged feet), you will enchant your preferred method of communication to receive news. You can even bless a device for clear communication or to summon word from an old connection during Mercury retrograde. Whether under the Gemini, Aquarius, waxing, or full moon, let the moon's light keep the pathways of communication open—and, like birdsong, call information to you.

You Will Need:

> Tissue
> Moon Oil (see Chapter 7), optional

> Communication device you wish to bless
> Feather, preferably blue or gray
> Bell

Directions:

1. Stand before the item you are blessing. Anoint the tissue with a very small amount of oil.
2. Use the tissue to safely and lightly anoint the edges or protective case of your object clockwise, visualizing the moon waxing toward full.
3. Hold the feather and think of what you are calling toward you.

4. Visualizing the full moon above, calling forth communication, use the feather to trace the object three times. While you do this, say aloud:

"Birds of a feather, flock together.
Like the bluebird sings, ____ to me does ring."

5. Chant once, thrice, or until you feel the energy ring.
6. Put the feather down and ring the bell around your messaging device. Visualize the device ringing with a message.

MOON IN CANCER

Harmonious Home Moon Simmer Pot and Kompot

Best Lunar Timing: Moon in Cancer, Libra, or Taurus; Full Moon

Lunar Energy: Harmony, Home Blessing, Luck

The moon in Cancer is a great time to spruce up your home. Enchant the air around you with a harmonious, warming aroma with this apple-peel simmer pot spell. Plus, the recipe duals as a kompot (an Eastern European drink with water, sugar, and fruits) by just adding sugar, once the simmer pot has done its work! Just as baking in the home fills the air with spices and enticing smells, simmer pots use warm water and fragrant ingredients to aromatize your home. Apple is a common ingredient for these pots, and it also happens to have been used in the past for divination—an apple peel was tossed over the shoulder, and in landing it was said to take the shape of a letter indicating who the thrower might marry. Pear evokes longevity, abundance, and love. Craft this simmer pot under the Libra moon for harmony and love, Taurus for abundance, or Cancer for a nurturing home environment.

You Will Need:

- 1 apple
- Peeler
- Pot
- 3 cups Moon Water (see Chapter 7) or purified or spring water
- Knife
- ⅛ teaspoon ground nutmeg
- 1 pear, sliced
- 1 small lemon, sliced
- 3 bay leaves
- 2 cinnamon sticks
- ⅓ cup granulated sugar, optional

Directions:

1. Peel the apple while thinking of an intention or question. Try to peel it in one go, but if the strip of peel breaks into pieces, that is fine too.
2. With your eyes closed or looking over your opposite shoulder, toss the peel into the pot. Divine any symbols or information you see once the peel lands.
3. Giving thanks for the insight, fill the pot with Moon Water. Cut apple and add to pot. Add in nutmeg, pear slices, lemon slices, and bay leaves, stirring clockwise with the cinnamon stick, thinking of filling the home with a moon-blessed intention.
4. Turn on the stove, place the pot on it, and bring it to a gentle simmer. Allow your home to fill with aroma, and turn off the stove when satisfied. You can strain out the solids and keep the water as an offering, or divine more symbols from the leftover ingredients in the pot.
5. If you want a soothing kompot drink, once about 1 cup of the simmer pot has evaporated, you can stir in sugar and let boil for 30 more minutes before it's ready to serve—just make sure pear and apple is fully soft.

Cancer Moon Crystal Healing Ritual

Best Lunar Timing: Full Moon, Moon in Cancer or Pisces, Lunar Eclipse

Lunar Energy: Healing, Peace, Release

When the moon is in Cancer, you might feel particularly vulnerable. As the moon travels in its home sign, the crab, it can heighten your feelings both psychically and emotionally, revealing wounds or even emotional burnout. Tune into the moon's power over the oceans and water and cleanse away unwanted energy with this lunar crystal healing ritual. In this session, you will use some selected stones to tune into your inner moon and emotions and cleanse away energetic debris.

You Will Need:

❯ Selenite
❯ Bowl, hollow geode, or shell filled with water (Moon Water works well too—see Chapter 7)

❯ 7 stones, 1 for each energy center (whatever stones you like and have on hand), optional
❯ 6–7 pieces of mother-of-pearl

Directions:

1. Pass the selenite through your aura. (You can add a smoke cleanse if you'd like, using the herbal bundle from Chapter 7.) Breathe deeply, place the vessel of water between your feet, and lie down.
2. Lay a stone at each of your body's energy centers: crown, third eye, throat, heart, solar plexus, sacrum, and root.
3. Place a piece of mother-of-pearl between each stone and its neighbor or atop each energy spot if not using additional stones, to help the symbolic flow of water through the body.
4. Continue breathing deeply, and imagine the moon's power over water, pulling at earth's tides to flow just as the moon pulls at you. Emotional currents may flow around you in the same way.
5. Visualize water coming down from the moon and through you. It flows from your head through your body, down your legs and feet, picking up emotional debris along the way, and into the vessel. Lie with this visualization—the healing power of water and the moon rushing through you, cleansing your energy.
6. Stay here as long as you like. When you feel ready, remove the stones. Then get up and pour the water down a drain or onto the earth to neutralize the energy it's carrying.

MOON IN LEO

Mirror Meditation

Best Lunar Timing: Full Moon; Moon in Leo, Scorpio, Libra, or Aries

Lunar Energy: Inner Worth, Identity, Confidence

As the moon moves around the earth, she reflects the sun's light. With this activity, you can use the illuminated night to reflect on your internal warmth and the qualities that you radiate out to others. You'll meditate on your own inner light and how it reflects out into the world. Perform this meditation when the moon is in Leo to reflect on your inner warmth and confidence, or during the Scorpio moon using a bowl of Moon Water instead of a mirror to ponder your ego and inner truth. Use the Libra moon to perform this meditation to find your inner beauty, or the Aries moon to reflect back courage to take the action you want. You can also use this as a glamour magick ritual to work on reflecting qualities you aspire to, such as courage, charm, and more.

You Will Need:

> Mirror
> Moon Water (see Chapter 7)
> Candle
> Matches or lighter
> Rosewater or Moon Water spray, optional

Directions:

1. Sit before the mirror. Anoint the perimeter of the mirror with Moon Water.

2. Close your eyes and take three deep breaths in and out, thinking of the ethereal moon up above, pulling at your heart and emotions. Visualize your own inner light—steady like a flame—within your center, ignited by the moon. Open your eyes and set the candle between you and the mirror. Light it and soften your gaze.

3. Breathing deeply, notice how the mirror reflects the candlelight, magnifying the light and making the space behind you even brighter. Think about what parts of you are and aren't reflected out into the world, and let these thoughts illuminate the landscape of your life. What do you want others and the mirror to see? What do you want to project into the world?

4. With this in mind, look into the mirror. Visualize your own internal light burning steady like the candle. Breathe deeply, visualizing that light growing brighter. With each breath in, breath in the power of the ethereal moon and visualize it feeding your internal light. That internal light grows brighter and brighter, until it expands outside your body, then even outside your aura. You can even use your fingers to pull this energy out from your center and around you into your energy body. Continue until you feel fully empowered. Then visualize your light reflected back at you by the mirror.

5. Feeling charged up and aglow, spritz the area around you (your aura) with Rosewater or Moon Water. Put out the candle. Repeat this meditation daily, or as needed with the moon, for a regular reminder of what you're putting out into the world.

Power of Reflection

The moon is a mirror. In this spell, you witnessed the power of the mirror—beyond reflecting back your visage, it can be used to spread light throughout a room. This is the power of reflection—you can reflect, amplify, and magnify the energy around you, or reflect unwanted energy back to the sender. With this power, like the moon, you can influence the world around you. You can work with mirrors as a form of protection magick, as well as for imagery and glamour.

Candlelight Creativity Spell

Best Lunar Timing: Full or Waxing Crescent Moon; Moon in Leo, Aquarius, Gemini, or Sagittarius

Lunar Energy: Creativity, Ideas, Inspiration

In Leo, the moon ignites our inner creativity and inspiration. From poets to musicians, the moon has inspired both language and great works of art. Let the moon in this fire sign light the way toward new ideas with this simple candle and incense spell. Using moon-associated jasmine or sandalwood to uplift your mind—and the spark of inspiration of a candle flame—you will invite insight. To focus on the mind, cast this spell while the moon is in an air sign: Gemini for information or Aquarius for genius or new plans. At the Sagittarius moon, this spell can help relight hope and summon new philosophies to guide your way. Under the Leo moon, it invites inspiration. You can also perform it at the new moon to invite ideas and solutions with the waxing phase, or during the full moon to channel inspiration and genius.

You Will Need:

❯ Matches or lighter
❯ Jasmine or sandalwood incense
❯ Gold, orange, or yellow candle
❯ Moon Oil (see Chapter 7) or magickal oil of choice
❯ Candleholder
❯ Ground cinnamon, optional

Directions:

1. Light the incense and turn down the lights in your space to a soft setting.
2. Anoint the candle with oil. Pass the candle through the incense smoke and set it in the candleholder. Place the candle right behind the incense so that the smoke rises between you and the candle.

3. Close your eyes and visualize the moon rising above, full and luminous. It illuminates the dark landscape before you, lighting a way forward.

4. Open your eyes and light the match or lighter—the spark of an idea—as you say aloud:

"Bright inspiring moonlight,
Grant me creativity and insight."

5. Light the candle. Taking deep breaths, soften your gaze above the candlelight and smoke. Discern visions in their combined movements, or let the light and incense spark creativity as you open your mind to the moon's guidance. For added energy, sprinkle cinnamon a safe distance above the candle's flame, causing little sparks like stars, a magickal metaphor for igniting your own spark of creativity.

MOON IN VIRGO

Lemon Cleansing Solution

Best Lunar Timing: Waning, Full, or New Moon; Moon in Virgo, Capricorn, or Cancer

Lunar Energy: Cleansing, Protection, Clarity

The moon is associated with the home, and there's no better time to clean house than in analytical, organized Virgo! Get organized and cleanse away unwanted energy with this easy-to-make, all-natural Lemon Cleansing Solution. Empowered by the moon, you can use this as an all-purpose cleaner, or add to floor-wash solution or laundry to help purify and spruce up the home with cleansed, rejuvenated energy. While you're at it, try to declutter! Getting organized and making space will allow blessings to flow in.

You Will Need:

- ❭ Jar with lid
- ❭ 1 cup white vinegar
- ❭ 1 cup purified or spring water (or Moon Water—see Chapter 7)
- ❭ 1 large strip of lemon peel
- ❭ Knife or toothpick
- ❭ 1 teaspoon sea salt
- ❭ 5 rosemary or sage sprigs

> ❯ 10 drops of essential oil of choice, optional (see Appendix C)

> ❯ Citrine
> ❯ Spray bottle

Directions:

1. Perform at the full moon, to charge with the waning moon. Mix together vinegar and water in jar.
2. On the white rind side of the lemon peel, with a knife or toothpick, draw the waning crescent moon for cleansing and banishment. Then face the outer, yellow part of lemon rind over the vinegar and water, and squeeze the lemon peel to spritz its oils into the container. Drop it in to infuse to promote cleansing and lunar joy.
3. Sprinkle in sea salt for cleansing, grounding, and protection.
4. Use a rosemary sprig to stir the mixture counterclockwise, visualizing the mixture cleansing away unwanted energy. Then stir clockwise, visualizing a happy, purified home. Add all rosemary sprigs to the jar, along with any essential oils you want, and close the lid.
5. Leave the solution out to charge under the moonlight. If desired, set the citrine stone out to charge in the moonlight on the full moon (but be sure to grab it before sunrise—citrine can gradually lose color in sunlight).
6. The next morning, collect the jar and the citrine stone. Let the cleaning mixture infuse for 1 week with the waning moon. Then, transfer to spray bottle, discarding rosemary and lemon rind (unless you want to keep those in). Drop in citrine to promote positive energy. Then use it around your home as an all-purpose cleaner to add a touch of cleansing moon magick! Just be wary of using vinegar on certain surfaces, such as granite.

More Home Moon Magick

While cleaning the home, put the Harmonious Home Moon Simmer Pot and Kompot (see this chapter) on the stove to add an enchanting scent to your home!

Moon Broom Dolly

Best Lunar Timing: Full, Gibbous, or Waning Gibbous Moon; Moon in Virgo

Lunar Energy: Gratitude, Blessing, Dedication

Dedicate yourself to a new habit, idea, or your lunar witchcraft practice and give thanks to the land by my making a broom-shaped "corn dolly." Despite their name, these braided or woven figures are made of stalks of wheat or other small grains, not corn. (They're called corn dollies because of the Old English word for grain, "kern.") In European pagan tradition, harvesters craft a corn dolly to create a home for the corn spirit as the last stalks of grain are harvested. The practice has evolved into a variety of beautifully woven and braided straw creations. Plus, the broom shape is great to cleanse and bless the home! Make your own to give thanks and create a hearth and kitchen decoration, or hang over your door for abundance blessings and protection. If inspired, you can venture into the realm of making more intricate versions by researching more complex styles of braiding online.

You Will Need:

> 9 hollow stalks of grain, such as wheat, grain heads intact

> Moon Water (see Chapter 7) or jasmine tea

> 2 lengths of red ribbon

Directions:

1. Soak stalks in Moon Water or jasmine tea for 15 minutes. When they are pliable, bundle the stalks and tie them together with a ribbon right at the base of the grain heads. Softly separate the stalks into 3 bunches of 3, that you might braid all 9 together.

2. Slowly braid the stalks, weaving in the ends of the ribbon as you go (red is the color of life force). As you do so, think upon what you might like to dedicate yourself to, or even a simple dedication to your craft. Think on the spirits of the land, too, who provide you with sustenance so that you might harvest.

3. Stop braiding before you get to the ends, and tie the stalks together with the second ribbon to preserve the braiding. Notice how the grain splays out like a broom. If you feel called to, use the remainder of the ribbon to tie a bow, or attach any charms.

4. Bless the doll under the full moon's light, and then bring it into your home. Hang it in your kitchen or on your harvest altar. In some traditions, the corn dolly from the previous harvest is burned at Imbolc, at the start of spring, and its ashes are returned to the field to nurture the next year's grain. You can also simply repeat this craft every year, burning the old dolly once you have made one anew.

MOON IN LIBRA

Lunar Lip Scrub

Best Lunar Timing: Moon in Libra, Cancer, or Gemini; Full, Waxing Crescent, or Gibbous Moon

Lunar Energy: Glamour Magick, Communication, Beauty

Enchant your words and strengthen your beauty with this Lunar Lip Scrub. The moon illuminates both inner and outer beauty, and its impact on language—from "moonstruck" to "lunatic"—is clear. Use the beautifying energy of the moon to enchant your lips and words. Create this lip scrub under the Libra moon for harmonious and diplomatic words, under Cancer for nurturing conversations and self-care, or under Gemini for youthful appearance and clever words. Take care to use food-grade and, if possible, organic ingredients here. Use regularly as a lip scrub to enchant your use of language, communication, and beauty.

You Will Need:

- ❯ Generous pinch lemon zest
- ❯ Small jar with lid
- ❯ ⅛ cup granulated sugar
- ❯ 1½ tablespoons coconut oil
- ❯ ½ teaspoon ground nutmeg
- ❯ 2 drops peppermint essential oil
- ❯ 2 drops jasmine essential oil

Directions:

1. Place lemon zest into jar, visualizing your words evoking positive responses.
2. Add sugar, sweetening your words, then add moon-associated coconut oil, nutmeg, and essential oils.
3. Stir together clockwise, thinking of the luminous, beautifying moon up above.
4. Close the jar, and leave to charge under the full moon's light.
5. Use regularly one to three times a week, visualizing your lips shaping harmonious, enchanting words.

Mirror Beauty Blessing

Best Lunar Timing: Moon in Libra, Cancer, Leo, or Taurus; Full Moon

Lunar Energy: Beauty, the Home, Self-Love

Libra, symbolized by the scales of balance, has a keen eye for the beauty in all things, all people, and all situations. Enchant your home with this energy so that all might see their inner beauty staring back at them. In this spell, you will charge rose and cardamom water under the Libra moon to create a potion to bless the mirrors in your home. This is a great working to enhance self-love, as well.

You Will Need:

- Bowl
- Dried or fresh rose petals
- Ground cardamom
- Distilled or spring water
- Cloth

Directions:

1. Place bowl outside under the light of the moon. Add in rose petals and sprinkle in a generous pinch of cardamom.
2. Hover your hands above the ingredients, breathing in their aroma and feeling the buzz of their energy underneath your palms, enhanced by the moonlight. Think on the moon's connection with beauty (which is enhanced in Libra) and the soul. Visualize the moon charging these items to bring out inner beauty.
3. Pour water into the bowl, and say aloud:

"Like the moon reflects the sun's radiance, and water reflects the light
Bless this potion, so that all see beauty within their sight."

4. Leave the bowl to charge in the moonlight. The next day, dampen the cloth with the water. Wash the edges of each mirror in your house with this blend, repeating the chant as you do so.

MOON IN SCORPIO

Banishing Freezer Jar Spell

Best Lunar Timing: Dark or Waning Moon, Moon in Scorpio, Lunar Eclipse

Lunar Energy: Banishing, Protection, Suspension

The moon disappears from the night sky a few days a month, and there are matters in our lives that must similarly be put to bed. Suspend bad habits, negative thoughts, or unwanted energy with this freezer jar spell. A freezer spell is a simple, easy, and direct way to pause a situation or energetically protect yourself. Using the power of the lessening waning moon, the moon's power over water, and banishing ingredients, you will freeze and pause unwanted circumstances that put you or your dreams in harm's way.

You Will Need:

-) Freezer-safe jar with lid
-) Water
-) Ground black pepper
-) Sea salt
-) Pen and paper
-) Item or image to represent what you are suspending (such as candy to stop a sugar addiction)
-) Ground red pepper
-) Black candle
-) 1 lime
-) Matches or lighter

Directions:

1. Fill the jar ¾ of the way with water, leaving space for the water to expand when frozen. Stir black pepper and sea salt into it counterclockwise, then leave the jar overnight under the waning moon (preferably quarter or waning crescent moon, as it wanes into the dark moon) to infuse and charge with banishing, cleansing, protective, and grounding energy.

2. The next night, (ideally the first night of the dark moon, before the new moon) write what you are freezing on the piece of paper, whether the name of a harmful person, a bad habit, or a situation you want to stop. Fold the paper away from you, visualizing the situation at hand going away. Place the piece of paper in the jar, add in any related symbols, and close the lid.

3. Dress the black candle with lime juice, then roll it away from you in a mixture of black pepper, red pepper, and salt. Affix the candle to the top of the jar and burn it.

4. Once the candle is done burning, place the jar in the freezer. Leave it there temporarily, until you are able to clear the energy, as defrosting it can allow the banished energy to appear back in your life. To affirm the energy, follow this with cleansing work or cord cuttings. Once you are sure the situation is over, you can throw it away somewhere far from your home, or thaw and pour the water at a crossroads.

Ovomancy Reading Ritual

Best Lunar Timing: Moon in Scorpio, Dark Moon, Solar Eclipse, Lunar Eclipse

Lunar Energy: Divination, Psychic Insight, Spirituality

The moon can stir up our fears and our inner darkness—but that's not something to be afraid of. While they can feel uncomfortable in the moment, these emotions offer insight and messages that are important for your healing and manifestation journey—messages you can recognize and then release. This is a good time to practice your psychic and intuitive skills to read into the state of your energy and spirit, and perhaps guide you on what spellwork to do to aid you. Ovomancy is the act of using egg—a magickal ingredient that is often also used for cleansing rituals—to scry, or to divine information. The psychic, cleansing, and rebirth-related energy of eggs fits perfectly in Scorpio (whose alternative symbol is the phoenix). Cast this spell under the Scorpio moon to illuminate your hidden truths, or under the dark moon to tune into your spiritual state.

You Will Need:

❭ 3 eggs, room temperature
❭ Drinking glass
❭ Lukewarm Moon Water (see Chapter 7)
❭ Sea salt

Directions:

1. From the 3 room-temperature eggs, select one that calls to you when you think on your question. If the other 2 eggs haven't been out too long, you can put them back in the fridge.
2. Fill the glass almost all the way up with Moon Water, visualizing the moon, through her power over water, offering healing and reflection to you now.
3. Thinking of the question or matter at hand, hold the egg. Under the lunar light (if the moon is full), close your eyes and breathe deeply.
4. Focus on the question at hand. Allow any grief or doubts you have to come to the surface, tuning into your sense of feeling. Run the egg gently over your skin, especially anywhere you feel those emotions or fears as you think upon your question. Then breathe and blow out any further lingering energy into the egg.

5. Crack the egg over the water, visualizing breaking the unwanted energy and getting to the heart and message of the matter.

6. Watch how the egg falls and lands in the water. Look at the shapes and the yolk. Notice if anything calls out to you, then set aside the glass for 10–15 minutes. The egg's status in the water will shift over that time, providing a better reading.

7. After 10–15 minutes have passed, you might notice the white of the egg now having a distinct formation—that means it's time to read the egg. Like most intuitive arts, this is highly subjective. Always trust your personal symbolism, and remember that as you practice, you will understand what you see more.

8. See what you can make sense of with your egg. How does the yolk rest in the glass—is it centered or to one side? Is it uneven? How do the wisps of egg white appear—are there multiple strands pulling in different directions? Some read the yolk as the physical body, and the white as the spiritual or energetic body. You can look online for more in-depth guidance on symbols, but remember that your guides are giving you signs and symbols that make sense to your interpretation. Keep your question in mind as you read.

9. When done, sprinkle sea salt into water and discard the egg. Use your reading to guide you as to further spellwork. For example, if your reading showed your energy pulled in many directions, follow this ritual with any of the cleansing lunar spells within this book.

MOON IN SAGITTARIUS

Moonlit Bibliomancy

Best Lunar Timing: Moon in Sagittarius or Gemini; Full, New, or Dark Moon

Lunar Energy: Psychic Insight, Information, Messages

Bibliomancy is the art of using books to divine information. And the moon in Sagittarius often invites us to expand our sense of optimism and belief. Seek wisdom from the moon using the tools you already have at your fingertips—even this very book! With the moon in Sagittarius's association with prophecy and higher education, or the Gemini moon's favoring of information and research, there is no better time to try your hand at this art. Scrying takes time to master, as it requires sharp discernment and trust of your intuition. So keep trying until you are familiar with the feelings, signs, and symbols of your intuition. Once you are confident, you can use bibliomancy again and again to guide messages, reflections, meditations, and insights, and even to help you decide what spell to cast.

You Will Need:

> Incense, such as jasmine, sandalwood, or opium/poppy
> Matches or lighter
> A few books

Directions:

1. Begin by clearing your mind with a few deep breaths.
2. Light the incense, visualizing the smoke rising to the bright moon.
3. With a book before you, soften your gaze. Ask your question aloud and visualize the moon illuminating the book.
4. With your gaze still softened, slowly flip through the book. Say aloud:

"The full moon allows me to see,
Knowledge now does come to me."

5. Alternatively, during the dark or new moon, you can replace the first line with:

"In darkness, the light of truth can be seen."

6. As you flip the pages, listen to your natural inclinations. Perhaps you imagine the moon above shining on a specific page, or feel an urge to stop.
7. Stop at or open to a page. Pause to read, or go a step further, using your finger to point to a passage, sentence, or word before beginning to read.
8. Read and interpret the meaning, whether symbolic, literal, or metaphorical.

Once in a Blue Moon Coin Talisman

Best Lunar Timing: First Quarter Moon, Moon in Sagittarius or Pisces, Blue Moon

Lunar Energy: Chance, Luck, Opportunities

With its zodiac sign ruled by Jupiter, the planet of expansion, luck, and opportunities, the moon in Sagittarius is a great opportunity to invite chance and blessings to your side. Using a coin—whether it calls to mind tossing a coin for luck or feeling fortunate to find one on the ground—you will create your own lunar-blessed charm so that no matter which way the coin falls, it always lands on your side. Charged under the Sagittarius moon or—to add a further sense of luck—the blue moon, this is a talisman of luck that you can create and bless for yourself. Keep it with you at times when you need chance to turn your way, or leave it on your altar to use in spells or meditation when you need a little bit of luck.

You Will Need:

- 2 clean, shiny quarters
- Strong glue (such as superglue)
- Ground nutmeg
- Ground clove
- Ground cinnamon
- Jasmine incense, optional

Directions:

1. Start by cleansing the coins in soap and water—who knows where they've been!
2. Think of the full blue moon above—a rarity and a blessing. Visualize the moon illuminating the coins with luck and blessings.
3. Apply the glue to the tails side of each coin. Sprinkle a tiny amount of lucky nutmeg, clove, and manifestive cinnamon on each side, then press the coins together so that no matter which way the coin would land, a heads side would face up.
4. Hold the coins, blessed with spices, together with your hands to strengthen the bond. As you do so, close your eyes and say:

   "No matter which way the coin falls, no matter the labor;
   Like the luck of the blue moon, it always lands in my favor."

5. Visualize the moon blessing your efforts.
6. Run the money through jasmine incense for extra blessings, if desired.
7. Leave the talisman out in the moonlight to charge overnight. You can also maintain the spell's energy over time by passing the coin through lunar incense each full moon.

MOON IN CAPRICORN

Prosperous Property Jar Spell

Best Lunar Timing: Moon in Capricorn or Taurus, Waxing Moon, Supermoon

Lunar Energy: Money, Property, Boundaries

With the moon's power over the home and ability to nurture growth of all kinds, moon magick is a great way to bless your home, workspace, or altar to bring in plenty. Many witches bury pennies in the four corners of their property to lay the boundaries of their space and bring blessings—this is another type of coin-based spell. Whether you work from home, are building a business, or want to watch your wealth build up, perform this spell during the new to waxing moon and create a firm foundation for your prosperity.

You Will Need:

❯ Green or gold candle
❯ Moon Oil (see Chapter 7) or store-bought prosperity oil
❯ Ground cinnamon
❯ Ground nutmeg
❯ Jar with lid, big enough to hold the candle
❯ 5 pennies
❯ 1 nickel, 1 dime, 1 quarter, and 1 dollar bill
❯ Matches or lighter
❯ Cinnamon sticks, bay leaves, or money-drawing stones such as pyrite or green aventurine, optional

Directions:

1. Dress the candle with Moon Oil or prosperity oil, and on a plate, roll it toward yourself through a mixture of cinnamon and nutmeg.
2. Affix the candle in the center of the bottom of the jar. Anoint all coins with the same oil, and place 4 of the pennies around the outside of the jar in a diamond or square shape. Sprinkle the area with cinnamon and nutmeg, if you like.
3. Hover your hands around the spell setup and above the unlit candle, visualizing your intention. Feel the resonance of the coins and candle. Say aloud:

"As the moon ebbs and flows, my wealth, evergreen, nonstop grows."

4. Repeat until you feel abuzz with energy.

5. Visualize money growing and sprouting around your home, abundance being realized, and blessings flowing to you. One by one, drop the remaining penny, nickel, dime, and quarter in the jar, around the candle. Place the dollar bill under the jar.
6. Light the candle and let it burn safely all the way down. When done, place or bury the 4 pennies that surrounded the jar at the four corners of your home or property, and place the dollar bill inside the jar. Add in cinnamon sticks, bay leaves, or stones. Close the jar and place it somewhere visible.
7. As you find spare change or small bills, add them to the jar. Refresh the jar energetically as needed with incense and candles to continue calling money your way.

Cinnamon Ladder for Success

Best Lunar Timing: Moon in Capricorn, Taurus, Virgo, or Sagittarius; Waxing or New Moon

Lunar Energy: Success, Goals, Achievement

Strengthen your will and resolve to reach your goals with this enchanting cinnamon stick witch's ladder. In witchcraft, a witch's ladder is a magickally knotted or braided rope crafted and infused with intention, often with charms woven in. While these often look like beautiful blessing cords, other types of witch's ladders include sticks and feathers. With the moon in Capricorn it's an ideal time to work with the metaphor of "climbing the ladder" for achievement in your goals. In this knot magick ritual, you will bind your intentions, goals, and aspirations and climb the steps toward your goal. You can even use driftwood or sticks selected on a moonlit nature walk for an ocean- or forest-themed witch's ladder!

You Will Need:

❭ Long piece of natural twine, string, or desired cord
❭ Cinnamon sticks, enough to represent each important aspect of your goal
❭ Charm, such as a crescent moon, feather, stone, or bead, optional
❭ Bay leaf, optional
❭ Sharpie, optional

Directions:

1. Fold the string in half and knot it close to the halfway point, leaving a little loop (for hanging) and two long strands (which you'll use to tie on your ladder's rungs).
2. Think about the different steps and important aspects of your goal. Each cinnamon stick can represent one part of the goal, a theme (such as focus), or just your growing abundance and success.
3. Thinking of your intention, tuck and center the first cinnamon stick between the two strings, nestled up to the knot. Visualize affirming your goal, and tie a knot around the cinnamon stick. Ensure it is secure.
4. Several horizontal cinnamon sticks will form the bars of your witch's ladder, with the strings knotted around the center of each stick to hold them. After securing your first stick, add knots to create as little or as much space as you'd like before the next one. Then tie in another cinnamon stick, and so on.
5. As you work, focus on what each stick represents, and tie knots affirming and strengthening your resolve. You can say the following chant as you work:

"I climb the ladder of success,
My determination knows no rest.
I reach the summit of my goal(s),
My pathway lit by my moonlit soul."

6. Continue until you've added all the cinnamon sticks desired to represent your goals. You can leave the strings loose at the bottom or tie on a final charm if desired. With the Sharpie, you can even write your intention on a bay leaf to hang on the ladder as a blessed intention.
7. Hang the ladder where it will strengthen your energy and remind you of your aspiration. Feel free to charge it every full moon until you reach your goal.

More Cinnamon Moon Magick

Some cinnamon sticks can be softened in water to slowly unroll. To add another dimension to your ladder, heat Moon Water, pour it over the cinnamon sticks, tuck something (such as a bill or piece of paper) inside each, and roll them back into shape to dry.

MOON IN AQUARIUS

Waning Crescent Cleansing Candle Spell

Best Lunar Timing: Waning Moon, Moon in Aquarius or Virgo, Moon in a Water Sign, Lunar Eclipse

Lunar Energy: Cleansing, Inspiration, Banishing

The Aquarius moon can shed light on restrictive connections, identities, and outdated ideas that are preventing you from truly manifesting with the moon. Using lemon, the moon's citrus, you will wash away unwanted ties, unfavorable energy, and limiting labels, and refresh your spirit to venture into a new future and greener pastures. Perform this at the Aquarius moon to sever limiting ideas and invoke inspiration and vision for the future, at the Pisces moon to heal old wounds, at the Cancer moon to cleanse your home, or during any waning moon phase to release what no longer serves you.

You Will Need:

-) 1 lemon
-) Knife
-) White candle
-) Ground rosemary
-) Sea salt
-) Matches or lighter

Directions:

1. Cut the lemon in half, visualizing cutting away unwanted energy. Cut the end off of one of the lemon halves so that it has a small flat end and will stand up. Set aside the uncut half for later.
2. Anoint the candle with lemon juice and roll it away from yourself through a mixture of rosemary and some of the cleansing sea salt.
3. Insert the base of the candle into the wider side of the other lemon half, and push it in so that the candle is supported and affixed to the lemon. Set aside.
4. Carry the other lemon half and a handful of sea salt or a bowl of salt water around your home counterclockwise. Squeeze lemon juice down all of the drains, and sprinkle sea salt or salt water to banish unwanted energy from your space and your life.
5. Now that your home is cleansed and blessed, light the candle held up by the lemon. Visualize the light warming and renewing the home or your energy, severing unwanted ties or energy.

6. Sprinkle a circle of sea salt clockwise around the candle, visualizing a circle of protection around yourself and your inner light as you do so.
7. Let the candle burn in sight, perhaps while taking a moon bath or using New Moon, New You Sea Salt Scrub (see Chapter 7). The candle will burn down into the lemon, and the juice should extinguish the flame, just as it will extinguish unwanted energy. If not, snuff the candle.

Smoke Scrying Visionary Incense

Best Lunar Timing: Moon in an Air Sign, Moon in Sagittarius, Waxing Gibbous or Full Moon, Lunar Eclipse, Black Moon

Lunar Energy: Wisdom, Visions, Freedom

When it comes to manifesting with the moon, there are times when we need to think outside the box and free our sense of possibility to manifest something perhaps even better than we'd imagined. This incense ritual can prevent a limited mindset from getting in the way of your moon magick, cleanse unwanted thoughts and energy, and invite insight and vision. Since Aquarius is a sign of the future, this spell does well under the Aquarius moon for freedom, vision, and foresight. In a pinch, you can perform it with just the rosemary sprig or your favorite incense.

You Will Need:

) Dried peppermint
) Dried lavender
) Cauldron or fireproof bowl
) Dried rosemary sprig
) Matches or lighter

Directions:

1. Place equal parts peppermint and lavender in the cauldron or fireproof bowl, breathing in their refreshing aromas as you do so.
2. Think about what you are seeking insight about, cleansing away, or freeing yourself from, or focus on the limitless, futuristic Aquarius moon up above.
3. Take your rosemary sprig in hand, a metaphorical representation of lightning (with which Aquarius is associated) and genius, and a great herb for the mind and clarity.
4. Stir the herbs in the bowl with the sprig clockwise three times, thinking upon your intention.

5. Leave the rosemary sprig in and safely set the herbs aflame. You may need to blow out the flame or use your breath to keep the embers that provide smoke alive and consistent. But that's okay—air is Aquarius's home element. Just breathe with intention, using your breath to fuel the embers for smoke.

6. As the smoke arises, soften your gaze. Experience your mind and sense of vision rising to higher matters with the rising of the smoke—to a plane of wisdom and possibility beyond what you thought possible, to freedom.

7. For smoke divination, note the flow and movement of the smoke or incense, and any shapes you might see. You can also waft the smoke around your body for cleansing, freeing yourself from limiting thoughts and restrictive bonds or patterns.

MOON IN PISCES

Soothing Wounds Aloe Moon Spell

Best Lunar Timing: Moon in a Water Sign, Moon in Libra, Full or Waning Crescent Moon, Lunar Eclipse

Lunar Energy: Healing, Reconciliation, Harmony

The moon will at times reveal wounds and magnify tensions, but she will also always offer a time to release and heal them. Aloe is the perfect ingredient for mending magick, because it's associated with the moon and used in magick for both healing and protection. Under the ethereal moonlight, you will petition this plant ally to aid in healing a wound or mending a rift between yourself and another. Grab a fresh aloe leaf from your grocery store and cast this spell with the moon—when the moon is in Pisces, the spell is especially suited to soothe old wounds and invite harmonious healing; during the waning cycle to lessen wounds; and in Cancer to reconcile rifts and bring closeness.

You Will Need:

❭ Pen and small piece of paper
❭ Moon Oil (see Chapter 7), optional

❭ Aloe leaf
❭ Knife
❭ Dried rose petals

Directions:

1. Under the moonlight, write on the paper your intention or what you are healing. If mending the rift between yourself and another, write your name on one side of the paper and theirs on the other. Dab the paper with healing Moon Oil if desired.
2. Cut a slice of aloe leaf, just the right size for the paper, when folded, to fit inside. As you cut, think on getting to the heart of the matter. (You can save the rest of the aloe for other moon magick, such as a beauty salve, or to hang above your door for protection.)
3. Thinking of the moon illuminating what needs to heal, cut a small hole in the gel inside the cut leaf.
4. Sprinkle the rose petals on the paper. Fold the paper toward yourself several times, bringing healing. Push the paper into the hole in the leaf.
5. Go outside under the moonlight. Hold the leaf in your hands and say:

"Aloe leaf, with inner gel to soothe,
And a protective leaf with a shell that's toothed.
Heal this wound and make things smooth,
That nothing more can wake this wound."

6. Bury the aloe leaf in the earth.

Lunar Loose-Leaf Flower Tea

Best Lunar Timing: Moon in Pisces, Cancer, or Taurus; Blue Moon; Lunar Eclipse

Lunar Energy: Psychic Powers, Peace, Divination

Nothing is quite as relaxing and soothing as a sip of tea. This special mixture allows you to commune with nature spirits under the moon to uplift your senses, soften your disposition, and offer psychic insight. You can even divine insight from the tea leaves if you want! Sip while the moon is in Pisces for psychic information and to reflect on how to go with the flow, or share a cup under the light of the Libra moon for harmony. Regardless of when you enjoy this tea, its color-changing properties, cleansing citrus, and soothing honey are sure to unwind your mind. This recipe calls for a blend of floral ingredients and herbs, but in a pinch, a minimum of rose, butterfly pea flower, and clove will work just as well. As always, make sure the flowers and other ingredients you use are food-grade (organic if possible).

You Will Need:

❯ Purified or spring water (or Moon Water—see Chapter 7)

❯ 1 teaspoon dried rose petals

❯ 1 tablespoon dried butterfly pea flower

❯ ½ teaspoon dried lavender

❯ 1 teaspoon dried jasmine

❯ ⅛ teaspoon ground clove

❯ Cup, preferably a wide-mouthed teacup for easier reading

❯ Lemon wedge

❯ 1–2½ tablespoons honey

❯ Cinnamon stick

Directions:

1. Set water to boil. Combine the flowers and clove as you wait. If wishing to divine psychic insight, leave the leaves loose in the cup. Otherwise, place them in a tea strainer.

2. As you wait for the water, tune into the energy of the blossoms, thinking of the moon awakening their energy. Think about your question or intention.

3. Pour in hot water, visualizing the moon's power filling your cup. Smell the aroma of the floral steam, enjoying it as it raises your awareness, and let the tea steep for 5–7 minutes.

4. Continuing to focus on your intention, squeeze the lemon wedge into the tea. The combination of lemon and butterfly pea flower will cause the tea to change color. Use the cinnamon stick to stir in honey, clockwise, to taste, keeping your intention in mind.

5. When ready, sip your tea under the moonlight as you use tarot or oracle cards or think about how you can regularly unwind with the moon. With each sip, concentrate on your consciousness rising, connecting with spirits of nature, and tuning into the cosmic flow.

6. When the tea is nearly gone, leave a little bit of liquid at the bottom of your cup. Thinking about your intention or question, swirl the cup three times, then flip the cup upside down onto a paper towel. Many of the herbs will fall out, but many will also stay attached to the cup.

7. Divine insight from the herbs left in the cup for insight, if desired. Tea leaf reading is a highly subjective art, so practice, relax, and trust yourself without judgment until your skills strengthen. You can look up tasseography (or tea leaf reading) guides online.

Chapter 11

MOON DEITY SPELLS

To ancient peoples, the moon was a deity. Astrologers sat atop ziggurats in ancient Sumeria mapping the movements of the moon, and Egyptians petitioned the waxing crescent for fertility. They invoked abundance, healing, and magick with the cycles of the moon. To this day, many people still celebrate and meditate to moon gods and goddesses. You, too, can connect to these deities to empower your magick.

In this section, you will find spells inspired by a handful of the lunar deities mentioned in this book. Weave your own lunar wheel of fate and create something from nothing like Arianrhod, or inspire writing like the self-actualized god Thoth. Connect to the abundance of the waxing crescent by meditating with the moon god Nanna, or stir your own cauldron of herbal lunar wisdom like Cerridwen. One of the many magickal qualities of the moon is that it's a doorway to the past. Let these ancient deities lead you through that door and inspire, motivate, and encourage you.

Thoth Lunar Inspiration Petition Spell

Best Lunar Timing: Waxing Crescent or Full Moon, Moon in Pisces, Moon in an Air Sign

Lunar Energy: Clearing, Inspiration, Focus

An Egyptian god associated with the moon, Thoth is a patron of scribes, writing, and magick of all kinds. Just like he weighs the heart against a feather for judgment in the afterlife, Thoth reminds us that if we are to be channels of divine information and inspiration, our hearts must be clear. Attune to Thoth and clear what weighs on your heart, to help make the way for inspiration. Whether you're writing a spell, a poem, or other creative work, or even clearing your mind for focus and creation before ritual or work, use this spell to invoke lunar insight and inspiration from a master of it.

You Will Need:

❭ Incense, such as myrrh

❭ Matches or lighter

❭ Feather

Directions:

1. Light the incense. Breathe onto it with intention and feed its embers with your gentle breath.

2. Run the feather through the smoke. Then use the feather to cleanse energy from your heart, using it like a fan to waft away any stuck energy from your heart. You can also use your hands instead of a feather, plucking and moving energy away from your heart. As you do so, say:

"I cleanse my heart, that I may be free/clear, to channel my art."

3. Repeat three times, as you continue fanning or plucking.

4. Once you feel cleansed, look at the full moon (or imagine it). Reflect on Thoth and his ability to create something—even himself—from nothing. Breathe the celestial light into your body, lifting your energy.

5. Touch the feather to your forehead as you close your eyes and say aloud:

"As you weigh hearts against the feather,
To me writing inspiration do weather."

6. Sit in meditation or stop and keep the feather near you as you return to work. You can also anoint your writing instrument or computer with it.

Selene Sleep Sachet

Best Lunar Timing: Full Moon, Moon in Pisces or Cancer

Lunar Energy: Visions, Dreams, Rest

The moon goddess Selene was an amorous lover, and at the end of the lunar cycle would visit her lover Endymion in his eternal youthful slumber.

The moon is often thought to rule the realms of sleep, where we obtain messages and symbols. Invoke visions and a peaceful beauty rest with this Selene Sleep Sachet. Use it to help bring ancestor messages and other visions in your sleep, and let the moon provide the answers you seek.

You Will Need:

❭ Cucumber
❭ Bowl
❭ Short selenite wand
❭ Dried jasmine
❭ Dried mugwort pieces, optional
❭ Poppy seeds
❭ Dried rose petals, optional
❭ 1 star anise
❭ Sachet bag in a dreamy color (silver, white, purple, or blue)

Directions:

1. The night before the spell, collect seeds from the cucumber—perhaps setting the rest aside for a later snack or to use in Beltane Beauty Facial Ice Cubes (see Chapter 9) or in infusions. Allow the seeds to dry in the moonlight.

2. On the night of the spell, focus on the moon goddess Selene. She once was invoked in magickal rituals and considered a matron of moon lovers and all who cast magick under her illumination. Look at the bowl, its shape round like the moon's. Encircle it with the selenite wand, then lightly tap the bowl's side three times.

3. Visualizing the celestial moonlight raining down blessings, sprinkle each herb and flower into the bowl with intention: jasmine and mugwort for psychic dreams; poppy seeds for peaceful, psychic sleep; and rose petals for love and spirituality.

4. Make a little hole in the center of the herb blend. Place the cucumber seeds there.

5. Say aloud:

"Under the power of the moon goddess Selene, here I plant the seeds,
That in my dreams, the information that I seek, I shall receive."

6. Drop the star anise atop the cucumber seeds, a symbol of celestial blessing.

7. Transfer the mixture to the sachet and place the selenite wand inside. Leave to charge under the blessing of the full moonlight.

8. Whenever you wish to receive a prophetic dream or enchant through the realm of sleep (such as with astral or psychic travel), take the selenite out of the bag and touch it to your forehead while holding

the sachet in the other hand. Make your request aloud, and hold the selenite there for a moment, visualizing and affirming your intention in your body. Then close the bag and place it under your pillow. Hold the selenite wand as you fall asleep.

Cerridwen Cosmic Cauldron of Wisdom

Best Lunar Timing: Full or Dark Moon; Moon in Sagittarius, Leo, or Aquarius

Lunar Energy: Inspiration, Wisdom, Scrying

Cerridwen keeps the cauldron of the stars, a never-ending source of wisdom, knowledge, and magick. But in order to brew truly cosmic potions, the cauldron must continuously be stirred. Just as when you want to manifest your magickal efforts in the world, you must continue to feed them. In this spell, you will burn herbs and feed the flames to receive information, wisdom, or inspiration to transform a situation and alchemize it. You can also use this spell to smoke scry.

You Will Need:

❭ Dried lemon balm
❭ Dried jasmine
❭ Dried mugwort
❭ Cauldron or fireproof bowl
❭ Crystal, wand, spoon, pen, or stylus (for stirring)
❭ Pen and paper or bay leaf, optional
❭ Matches or lighter

Directions:

1. Add each herb to the cauldron or fireproof bowl, one by one, thinking of your intentions and the herbs' magickal properties: lemon balm for healing and success, jasmine for prophecy and fortune, and mugwort for psychic powers.
2. Using a crystal, wand, special spoon, or even pen or stylus (if using the spell to inspire writing), stir the herbs clockwise. Say aloud as you do so:

"Like Cerridwen at her cauldron, I stir and stir
Wisdom and insight to me do occur
That I might transform the situation at hand.
The answer I seek, shall come to land."

3. If you wish, you can write your request on a piece of paper or a bay leaf and add it to the cauldron.
4. Set the herbs aflame. Feed the fire with your steady breath, focusing on your intention. You may need to relight the herbs.
5. Use the smoke from the embers to consecrate your body, a sacred item, or to scry for symbols in the smoke to find wisdom or inspiration.

Arianrhod Silver Wheel Spell

Best Lunar Timing: Full, New, or Waxing Moon; Solar or Lunar Eclipse; Blue or Black Moon

Lunar Energy: Power, Manifestation, Blessing

Arianrhod's name may mean "silver wheel," which likely refers to the moon. Some believe she may have also been associated with weaving, weaving the tapestry of life. Inspired by this namesake, you will weave your own silver wheel imbued with moon magick. You can use it for a specific spell or intention, or think of it as a protection charm or craft for the lunar year.

You Will Need:

❯ Candle
❯ Incense
❯ Matches or lighter
❯ Colored thread or yarn representing your goal(s) or intention(s)

❯ Silver thread or yarn
❯ 4 sticks, considering size you want your wheel

Directions:

1. Light the candle and incense. Hold the colored threads representing your goal, thinking of your intention, and pass them through the incense.
2. Use the silver thread or yarn to bind 2 sticks together to form a cross—symbolizing polarity, and two opposites meeting together, and the four quarters of the moon. Repeat for the other two.
3. Bind the two pairs together crosswise, representing the crescent and gibbous phases and defining the spaces among the four quarters. The wheel's center, where the four sticks cross, will be thick, but it will be the inception point of your magick, like the inception point of the universe.

4. With the silver thread anchored at the center, slowly weave over and under the sticks, pushing the thread to the center to make a tight pattern. As you weave over and under each stick, think about the balance of the light moon—reality and the waking world, consciousness—and the dark moon—the underworld, the ethereal realm of spirit, and the yet undefined.

5. As you weave, say aloud:

"I weave the silver wheel, the tapestry of life.
I weave into this wheel, my desires this full/new moon night."

6. Add in a thread representing your goal, and continue weaving. Visualize weaving your intention into reality. Like Arianrhod the Silver Wheel, you weave and create your own fate and making matter from working with the moon.

7. Add in more threads, if you like, to represent your goals, or themes or traits that might be necessary. For example, to weave the life of your dreams you might include one thread for finances, one for travel, one for love, etc. Continuing weaving, repeating the chant, by candlelight.

8. When done, tie off the threads (if you want you can tie them in a loop for hanging). Leave the wheel to charge by the moon, perhaps surrounded by lunar crystals. You can hang it up, use it on your altar to charge other items, or use it as a protection or manifestation charm.

Hekate Crossroads Petition

Best Lunar Timing: Dark, Waning, or New Moon; Moon in Scorpio

Lunar Energy: Insight, Transitions, Personal Power

There are times when you might feel lost and overcome by darkness or the unknown that lies ahead. But just like the moon is reborn at this time, even in darkness, you can find new pathways. Call upon the wisdom of the goddess of the dark moon and the crossroads and let her torch light a new way forward. In this spell, you will petition Hekate to help you solve your problems.

You Will Need:

) Candle

) Matches or lighter

) Offering for Hekate, such as 3 garlic cloves, a pomegranate, onion, or lavender

Directions:

1. Perform at night, outside, once the sun has gone down if possible. If you cannot perform this spell outside, you can visualize it inside, in a safe space.
2. Light the candle.
3. Like Hekate holding the torch at a crossroads, hold the lit candle in your hand. Think about a crossroads: It's a place where pathways meet, from which you could go in any direction. Ideally, you'd use a three-way crossroads, but it could be an intersection at a traffic light, or a garden pathway that diverges into three or more separate routes. (Hekate is also associated with doorways!)
4. Place an offering for Hekate in a safe location at a crossroads and say:

"Maiden, mother, and wise crone
Hekate of the key and crossroads,
Who in the dark of night, a torch does hold,
Reveal to me, which way I should go OR
A solution/justice to ____ (name of issue) she does sow."

5. Close your eyes, inhale Hekate's power, then blow out through your mouth, making a small whistle and blowing out your candlelight. Turn and walk away without looking back.
6. Pay attention for signs on your way home, in your dreams, or over the next 24 hours—Hekate rules the dark of night, so your answer may come when the moon is not visible. Be especially aware of dogs barking.

Hekate's Key Pendulum

Hekate is heavily associated with keys. You can place a key on a red string or cord to use as a pendulum to invite her to guide your divination and insight.

Artemis's Aim Victory Spell

Best Lunar Timing: Waxing Crescent Moon; Moon in Sagittarius, Cancer, Capricorn, or Aries; Solar Eclipse

Lunar Energy: Determination, Dedication, Success

Greek goddess of the hunt, little escapes Artemis's aim. Her chastity is perhaps a metaphor for completeness and dedication only to oneself. Her bow is like the crescent moon, and thus she illuminates the way forward. Harness her focus and aim and take a shot in the dark with this Artemis's Aim Victory Spell. In this candle spell, you will use rose petals, a stick, a bay leaf, and thread to lay out your own symbolic lunar bow with which to shoot toward success.

You Will Need:

❯ Candle

❯ Oil of choice

❯ Candleholder

❯ Cinnamon stick or other stick

❯ Sharpie

❯ Bay leaf

❯ Dried or fresh rose petals

❯ Silver thread, ribbon, or yarn

❯ Red thread, ribbon, or yarn

❯ Matches or lighter

Directions:

1. Dress the candle in oil and place it in the candleholder, then hover your hand around the candle and concentrate on your intention. Visualize the candle lit, its light guiding the way like a fiery moonlit arrow in the dark, heading toward your goal and/or destination. The candle will act as the tip of the arrowhead.

2. Place the cinnamon stick, or perhaps a stick gathered from a moonlit walk, in line with the candle, as the shaft of the arrowhead.

3. With the Sharpie, write your intention on the bay leaf. Place it at the end of the stick like the feathers that steady an arrow's path through the air.

4. Arrange the rose petals into a bow shape, like the crescent moon, so that the arrow looks ready to take aim.

5. Twist the silver and red thread or yarn, the colors of the moon and of fate or life force, into a single strand, and place it to represent the string of the bow.

6. Visualize Artemis taking aim in the night. Pretend to draw your own arrow, thinking of your intention and Artemis. Say aloud:

"Mistress of Hunt, little escapes your aim.
Guided by the light of the moon, whether it waxes or wanes,
Your sharp arrow guides the way.
Grant me success in ___ this day."

7. Release your imaginary arrow, sending it piercing through the night, shot from a moon-blessed bow. Now light the candle.
8. Allow the candle to burn down, keeping it within sight. If you like, leave the items out and burn them at the full moon in a lunar ritual.

Diana Oak Protection Charm

Best Lunar Timing: Full or Crescent Moon; Moon in Virgo, Taurus, or Cancer

Lunar Energy: Protection, Wisdom, Empowerment

Before being identified with Artemis, Diana was an ancient woodland spirit of Italy. Invoked in magick throughout time, she is a goddess of magick, witchcraft, and all things wild. She's especially known for empowering and protecting disadvantaged peoples. Connect to her rousing energy to create this charm for protection so that wherever you go, you have the shelter and wisdom of trees to guide you.

You Will Need:

❭ Small piece of wood from local tree or oak
❭ Knife

❭ Natural offering, such as Eggshell Blessing Powder (see Chapter 10)

Directions:

1. If you can, collect the oak you'll need during a moonlit walk through some trees, and conduct this ritual in the woods at night at the full moon or any time in the lunar cycle. Otherwise, any wood you collect from a forest will do, and you can visualize the woods from indoors if need be.
2. Close your eyes to meditate and connect to Diana's energy.
3. Carve a crescent moon into the wood, then lay it on the ground. Say aloud:

"Diana, goddess of the witches
Of the wild woodlands and the wolves

*All that's aglow under the moon when full
Empower and strengthen me with your pull
As you guide and protect all under your rule."*

4. Place in front of you a natural offering that will disintegrate with time and not harm the wildlife.
5. Decorate the wood as desired. You can use the Pink Moon Blush (see Chapter 9), adding some water to a small amount of the powder to turn it into a paint to paint the moon or protective sigil on the wood. Leave it under the full moon to charge, and keep it on your person thereafter. Hold the wood anytime you need protection or her guidance. Alternatively, you can place oak shavings in a sachet bag along with a wolf or moon charm to keep with you.
6. When it's time to replace the wood charm, set it aflame in a fireproof container as an offering to Diana.

Maiden, Mother, Crone Lunar Blessing

Best Lunar Timing: All Lunar Times

Lunar Energy: Attunement, Blessing, Lunar Power

The phases of the moon have long been associated with the Triple Goddess and various lunar deities. The waxing crescent represents the maiden, the full moon the mother, and the waning and dark moon the crone. Each phase has an archetypal energy from which wisdom can be gleaned. Attune to the phases of the moon and call upon the specific blessings of these archetypes. Perform this ceremony as a ritual for blessings, or before or after spellwork to empower your intention.

You Will Need:

- Water or corresponding moon drink
- Cup
- Selenite wand

Directions:

1. Notice your drink of choice glistening in the light of the moon (or, alternatively, a candle), and pour it into your cup. Think about how the moon rules liquid, impacting its energy.
2. Hold the cup in your left hand and the selenite wand in your right.

3. Focus on your intention—whether it's something you are manifesting with this lunar cycle or just a connection with the lunar goddesses.

4. Holding the cup at chest level, slowly raise the selenite wand, like the moon rising across the sky. As you move the selenite wand in an arc, think of the lunar phases and say aloud:

"Maiden, Mother, Crone
At the new moon, may my potential be sown
Maiden, Mother, Crone
And with the waxing moon, its potential grow
Maiden, Mother, Crone
Full moon, grant me my boons/or my power I shall know
Maiden, Mother, Crone
Waning moon, all matters I know/truth I be shown
Maiden, Mother, Crone
At the dark moon, unwanted matters disowned."

5. Move the selenite in a circle around the outside of the cup (being sure *not* to dip it into the drink, as selenite is water soluble and would make the liquid unsafe to drink) three times. Put the selenite down and sip the drink, concentrating on the moon's connection to water and the tides.

Kwan Yin Pearls of Wisdom–Inspired Meditation

Best Lunar Timing: Moon in Libra, Pisces, or Cancer; Waning, Crescent, or Dark Moon; Lunar Eclipse

Lunar Energy: Transitions, Inner Guidance, Peace

Like the cycle of the moon, life is full of transitions and changes. A bodhisattva of compassion and mercy, Kwan Yin has spread in popularity and is celebrated today as a goddess to many. While perhaps not a moon deity directly, she is often depicted with the enlightened moon at her back or sitting upon a crescent moon. Just like many pray to her for blessings and to aid in tough times, the moon can help with the turbulent flow of life. In this ritual, you will tune into the wisdom of the pearl (or other ocean-related stones), also associated with Kwan Yin, for a charm to help you make it through tough times. You will also use herbs and a tarot card that can help with this energy, although they are not necessarily associated with Kwan Yin.

You Will Need:

> Pearl, ideally, or a stone or shell from a beach, or water-related crystal (such as aquamarine), or jade
> Tarot card: Six of Swords
> Bowl

> Dried lavender
> Dried rose petals
> Dried chamomile
> Dried lemon balm
> Drawstring bag

Directions:

1. Take hold of the pearl or your chosen stone and tune into its energy. Close your eyes and visualize the pearl, hardened over time, a gem of beauty safely enclosed in an oyster amidst the wild ocean tides. It's a reminder that the tides of life can help refine the beauty of the soul.

2. Open your eyes and place the Six of Swords before you. The card depicts two figures, one of them cloaked, beginning a sea journey, departing the shore with their heads down, crouched over. It depicts a sense of loss and sadness—a forced or necessary journey. The key is the figures do not have their heads up—they are focused solely on what they are leaving and not what they are heading toward.

3. Reflect on your own situation. Like the moon, life is full of phases and transitions, and sometimes you are forced to move on. Envision that the goddess Kwan Yin rests above the people in the sailboat upon a crescent moon. A crescent moon can mean hope while waxing, or inspire peace and surrender when waning. As you look upon her in this visualization, ask for her aid.

4. In looking toward her for aid, you keep your head high and focused on the future—on a better shoreline that awaits you. Sometimes change results in something better than you dreamed of, and as a lunar witch, you can make it so.

5. Place the bowl atop the card.

6. One by one, sprinkle the herbs in the bowl: lavender for peace, rose to draw in beauty, chamomile for calm, and lemon balm for healing and success. Place the pearl atop the pile of herbs atop the card, envisioning it as the glean of Kwan Yin's lunar light guiding you forward.

7. Hover your hands above the bowl. Envision yourself in the boat pictured on the card—but lifting your head high toward Kwan Yin

and this pearl-like moon for a smooth journey, the fierce ocean wind blowing away negative energy. Ahead, a rich shoreline of blessings and a brighter future await. Say aloud:

"As one cycle ends, a new one begins.
I accept and embrace gracefully the blessings each transition brings."

8. Breathe in, then, relaxing your body, exhale. Put the herbs in the bag, nestling the pearl inside as well. Keep the bag with you, and hold the pearl for wisdom and insight in times of need. Feel free to smell the magick of the herbs at any time, repeating the chant. Remember the rich shoreline ahead.

Nanna Guided Meditation for Fertility

Best Lunar Timing: Moon in Taurus, Crescent Moon, Black Moon

Lunar Energy: Prosperity, Fertility, Manifestation

The cow is an ancient symbol of fertility and abundance. Often associated with lunar deities, its horns symbolize the fertility of the crescent moon, and its milk is associated with the spiritual energy and sustenance the moon provides. Nanna, the ancient Sumerian moon deity, was often associated with cows, as a cowherd or as a seated old man with a lapis lazuli beard. In this meditation, you'll connect to this ancient symbol, to the abundant energy of the waxing crescent moon, and to the vibration of abundance and what you wish to manifest. You can perform this as a meditation without the suggested tools, or integrate them for a ritual experience. You can also combine this with the Milk Moon Flower Bath from Chapter 9, to have a lunar milk-filled ritual.

You Will Need:

❯ Bell
❯ Cup

❯ Milk of choice
❯ Lapis lazuli

Directions:

1. Prepare for meditation as desired (see Chapter 6). Place the bell, cup, and milk before you. Take hold of the lapis lazuli and close your eyes. Breathe deeply into your body and tune into its energy.

2. Visualize that you are in a wide-open pasture, a broad landscape laid out before you. The starlit sky illuminates the fields and life all around.

3. You notice a cow moving forward ahead of you, in the distance, and feel called to follow it.

4. As you follow the cow, notice the change in scenery around you— the movement of nature in the whispers of the night's wind. Feel the movement of the air against your skin and the movement and glistening of life all around.

5. The cow guides you to a circle of blooming flowers, then stops and turns around. Its horns are luminous, glowing like the crescent moon against the stars in the sky.

6. Gaze into the cow's eyes, which are glowing like stars. See what messages they have for you. What do you wish to come to fullness?

7. Sit in the circle, and notice the abundance of the flowers all around, the power of the cow's lunar horns shining upon you. Think upon what you wish to manifest. Visualize the lunar light shining brighter upon you, blessing your intention.

8. Open your eyes, thinking of the moon's blessing. Pour the milk, like liquid moonlight, into the cup. Lift up the cup in a toast to the moon, and take a sip. If you wish, leave the remaining milk outside as an offering.

9. Keep the lapis lazuli on your person until your aspirations manifest, or charge it out in the light of the full moon.

Appendix A

MOON SPELLS BY INTENTION

In this section, you will find suggested spells based on theme. Keep in mind that each lunation impacts us all differently at different times. In working with the moon, you will learn to tune into your inner senses and develop your intuition. Look for a theme or intention in this list that interests you, then reference what spells in the book might aid you. Above all, though, let your inner moon guide you.

- **Abundance and Prosperity:** Magnified Moon Blessings Bowl; Wolf Moon Knot Magick Garland; Seed Moon Blessing; Maple Moon Money Jar; Harvest Moon Grain Gratitude Offering; Pentacles Prosperity Protection Spell; Wine Moon Sweet Tea; Prosperity Pumpkin Spell; Eggshell Blessing Powder; Apple Seed Spell; Prosperous Property Jar Spell; Nanna Guided Meditation for Fertility

- **Banishing:** New Moon, New You Sea Salt Scrub; Moon-Charged Protection Powder; Lunar-Charged Cleansing Herbal Bundle; Rosemary–Sea Salt Home Cleanse; Snuffing Out Doubt Spell; Healing Water Ritual; Moonfire Releasing Rebirth Ritual; Banishing Freezer Jar Spell

- **Beauty and Glamour Magick:** Lunar Lip Scrub; Milk Moon Flower Bath; Pink Moon Blush; Lunar Loose-Leaf Flower Tea; Beltane Beauty Facial Ice Cubes; Moon Water; Nourishing Full Moon Bath; Social Butterfly Body Glitter; Mirror Meditation; Lunar Lip Scrub; Mirror Beauty Blessing

- **Blessing (in general; and for specific efforts):** Intention-Setting Candle Blessing; Moon Dust Blessing Powder; Rosemary–Sea Salt Home Cleanse; Blue Moon Miracle Reflection; Blue Moon Bay Leaf Wishing Spell; Lemon and Clove Moon Blessing Charms; Wolf Moon

Knot Magick Garland; Candlemas Crescent Moon Candle; Seed Moon Blessing; Flower Moon Sugar; Summer Solstice Moon Circlet; Harmonious Home Moon Simmer Pot and Kompot; Moon Broom Dolly; Arianrhod Silver Wheel Spell; Maiden, Mother, Crone Lunar Blessing

- **Cleansing and Purification:** Lunar-Charged Cleansing Herbal Bundle; Candlemas Crescent Moon Candle; Waning Crescent Cleansing Candle Spell; Moonfire Releasing Rebirth Ritual; New Moon, New You Sea Salt Scrub; Nourishing Full Moon Bath; Rosemary–Sea Salt Home Cleanse; Healing Water Ritual; Cancer Moon Crystal Healing Ritual; Lemon Cleansing Solution

- **Communication:** Social Butterfly Body Glitter; Bluebird Communication Spell; Lunar Lip Scrub

- **Habits:** New Moon, New You Sea Salt Scrub; Road-Opening Clove Spell; Banishing Freezer Jar Spell

- **Happiness; Peace; and Harmony:** Harmonious Home Moon Simmer Pot and Kompot; Spark of Hope Candle Spell; Flower Moon Sugar; Milk Moon Flower Bath; Strawberry Moon Happiness Honey Syrup; Cancer Moon Crystal Healing Ritual; Lunar Loose-Leaf Flower Tea

- **Healing Energy:** Moon Water; Nourishing Full Moon Bath; Cancer Moon Crystal Healing Ritual; Soothing Wounds Aloe Moon Spell; New Moon, New You Sea Salt Scrub; Lunar-Charged Cleansing Herbal Bundle; Milk Moon Flower Bath

- **The Home:** Moon Dust Blessing Powder; Moon-Charged Protection Powder; Rosemary–Sea Salt Home Cleanse; Wolf Moon Knot Magick Garland; Harmonious Home Moon Simmer Pot and Kompot; Lemon Cleansing Solution; Mirror Beauty Blessing

- **Hope:** Spark of Hope Candle Spell; Blue Moon Miracle Reflection; Candlemas Crescent Moon Candle

- **Inspiration:** Spark of Hope Candle Spell; Candlemas Crescent Moon Candle; Candlelight Creativity Spell; Thoth Lunar Inspiration Petition Spell; Cerridwen Cosmic Cauldron of Wisdom

- **Love and Romance:** Cocreation and Cooperation Support Spell; Maple Moon Money Jar; Pink Moon Blush; Beltane Beauty Facial Ice Cubes; Milk Moon Flower Bath; Strawberry Moon Happiness Honey Syrup

- **Luck:** Moon Dust Blessing Powder; Blue Moon Miracle Reflection; Blue Moon Bay Leaf Wishing Spell; Magnified Moon Blessings Bowl; Once in a Blue Moon Coin Talisman

- **Manifestation:** Intention-Setting Candle Blessing; Moon Dust Blessing Powder; Moon Oil; Cocreation and Cooperation Support Spell; Solar Eclipse New Pathways Key Ritual; Blue Moon Miracle Reflection; Blue Moon Bay Leaf Wishing Spell; Seed Planting Paper; Magnified Moon Blessings Bowl; Seed Moon Blessing; Road-Opening Clove Spell; Apple Seed Spell; Arianrhod Silver Wheel Spell; Nanna Guided Meditation for Fertility

- **Partnership and Cooperation:** Cocreation and Cooperation Support Spell; Wolf Moon Knot Magick Garland; Strawberry Moon Happiness Honey Syrup; Soothing Wounds Aloe Moon Spell

- **Power:** Moon Water; Milk Moon Flower Bath; Moon Oil; Celestial Gravity Meditation; Pink Moon Blush; Milk Moon Flower Bath; Summer Solstice Moon Circlet; Herb Moon Prophecy Tea; Arianrhod Silver Wheel Spell; Diana Oak Protection Charm; Maiden, Mother, Crone Lunar Blessing

- **Problem-Solving/Decisions/Clarity:** Moonlit Bibliomancy; Cerridwen Cosmic Cauldron of Wisdom; Waxing Moon Reading; Full Moon Reflection Tarot Reading; Wax Scrying for Wisdom; Smoke Scrying Visionary Incense; Hekate Crossroads Petition

- **Protection**: Moon-Charged Protection Powder; Pentacles Prosperity Protection Spell; Banishing Freezer Jar Spell; Diana Oak Protection Charm

- **Psychic/Intuition and Divination:** Wax Scrying for Wisdom; Full Moon Reflection Tarot Reading; Moon Oil; Waxing Moon Reading; Full Moon Reflection Tarot Reading; Herb Moon Prophecy Tea; Wine Moon Sweet Tea; Ovomancy Reading Ritual; Moonlit Bibliomancy; Smoke Scrying Visionary Incense; Lunar Loose-Leaf Flower Tea; Selene Sleep Sachet; Cerridwen Cosmic Cauldron of Wisdom

- **Reflection and Spirituality:** Full Moon Reflection Tarot Reading; New Moon Alignment Crystal Meditation; Waxing Moon Reading; Full Moon Reflection Tarot Reading; Wax Scrying for Wisdom; Healing Water Ritual; Solar Eclipse Reflection; Blue Moon Miracle

Reflection; Black Moon Starseed Planting Reflection; Hermit Winter Moon Meditation; Milk Moon Flower Bath; Mabon Moon Tarot Meditation; Ovomancy Reading Ritual

● **Rejuvenation and Renewal:** Lunar Lip Scrub; Pink Moon Blush; Lunar Loose-Leaf Flower Tea; New Moon, New You Sea Salt Scrub; Spark of Hope Candle Spell; Nourishing Full Moon Bath; Beltane Beauty Facial Ice Cubes; Milk Moon Flower Bath; Candlemas Crescent Moon Candle

● **Shadow Work:** Eclipsed Moon Reflection; Snuffing Out Doubt Spell; Healing Water Ritual; Hermit Winter Moon Meditation; Mabon Moon Tarot Meditation; Hekate Crossroads Petition

● **Spirits and Ancestors:** Harvest Moon Grain Gratitude Offering; Prosperity Pumpkin Spell; Witch's Mirror Ancestor Moon Meditation; Moon Broom Dolly

● **Strength; Dedication; and Focus:** Wolf Moon Knot Magick Garland; Energy and Vitality Waxing Crescent Crystal Layout; Mirror Meditation; Moon Broom Dolly; Artemis's Aim Victory Spell

● **Success:** Wolf Moon Knot Magick Garland; Intention-Setting Candle Blessing; Cocreation and Cooperation Support Spell; Solar Eclipse New Pathways Key Ritual; Blue Moon Bay Leaf Wishing Spell; Prosperity Pumpkin Spell; Road-Opening Clove Spell; Cinnamon Ladder for Success; Artemis's Aim Victory Spell

● **Transitions:** Eclipsed Moon Reflection; Spark of Hope Candle Spell; Snuffing Out Doubt Spell; Eclipsed Moon Reflection; Healing Water Ritual; Hermit Winter Moon Meditation; Mabon Moon Tarot Meditation; Hekate Crossroads Petition; Kwan Yin Pearls of Wisdom–Inspired Meditation

● **Wishes:** Once in a Blue Moon Coin Talisman; Intention-Setting Candle Blessing; Moon Dust Blessing Powder; Blue Moon Bay Leaf Wishing Spell; Seed Planting Paper; Lemon and Clove Moon Blessing Charms

Appendix B

MOON ASSOCIATIONS

This section outlines a list of general correspondences for the moon. This is by no means an exhaustive list, but just suggestions for when you might be looking for that perfect moon-associated ingredient. You can reference Chapter 5 for more info on some of these correspondences. Remember, this also doesn't include seasonal or moon sign energy influences—it's just a quick and fast reference. Always go with what works best for your intention, and remember that everything on earth grew under the nurturing moon.

- **Ingredients:** Aloe, Blueberry, Camphor, Chickweed, Coconut, Cucumber, Egg, Eucalyptus, Gardenia, Grape, Grapefruit, Honesty (plant), Iris, Jasmine, Lemon, Lemon Balm, Lily, Melon, Milk, Moonwort, Myrrh, Papaya, Passion Flower, Pea, Pear, Poppy, Potato, Pumpkin, Sandalwood, Willow, Wintergreen

- **Crystals, Metals, Minerals, and Gems:** Aquamarine, Beryl, Chalcedony, Clear Calcite, Marble, Moonstone (all varieties), Mother-of-Pearl, Opal, Pearl, Quartz, Sapphire, Selenite, Silver

Appendix C

MOON SIGN ASSOCIATIONS

Here are ingredients and stones I suggest based on the energy of when the moon passes through a certain sign. You can use this to help modify spells in the text. Keep in mind, there are many correspondences. Always use what is best for you, and reference official correspondence texts, too, for more input. Also, not everything mentioned here is used or explored in this book—there's a vast array of minerals and ingredients. For a breakdown of the energies of some ingredients, reference Chapter 5.

ARIES MOON

- **Themes:** Passion, Vitality, Action, New Beginnings, Health, Physicality

- **Ingredients:** Allspice, Basil, Blackberry, Cherry, Cinnamon, Clove, Ginger, Olive, Pepper, Peppermint, Poppy, Rhubarb, Rosemary, Thyme

- **Stones/Crystals/Metals/Minerals:** Bloodstone, Carnelian, Citrine, Clear Quartz, Fire Opal, Garnet, Green/Red Aventurine, Hawk's-Eye, Pyrite, Red Jasper, Rhodonite, Ruby, Sunstone

TAURUS MOON

- **Themes:** Wealth, Security, Prosperity, Values, Self-Worth

- **Ingredients:** Apple, Apricot, Banana, Barley, Blackberry, Cardamom, Cherry, Hibiscus, Oat, Passion Fruit, Peach, Pear, Raspberry, Rhubarb, Rose, Rye, Sage, Thyme, Vanilla, Violet

- **Stones/Crystals/Metals/Minerals:** Chrysocolla, Emerald, Green Calcite, Lapis Lazuli, Lepidolite, Peridot, Pyrite, Rhodonite, Rose Quartz, Ruby, Rutilated Quartz, Selenite

GEMINI MOON

- **Themes:** Communication, Ideas, Learning, Connecting, Writing
- **Ingredients:** Almond, Anise, Bergamot, Caraway, Dill, Fennel, Hazel, Lavender, Marjoram, Mint, Parsley, Pear, Peppermint, Pomegranate, Rosemary, Walnut
- **Stones/Crystals/Metals/Minerals:** Amazonite, Aquamarine, Blue Apatite, Blue Lace Agate, Chrysocolla, Citrine, Clear Quartz, Fluorite, Hawk's Eye, Orange Calcite

CANCER MOON

- **Themes:** Emotions, Personal Development, Intuition, the Home
- **Ingredients:** Aloe Vera, Apple, Calendula, Chamomile, Coconut, Cucumber, Dill, Jasmine, Lemon, Lemon Balm, Maple, Oak, Papaya, Poppy, Pumpkin, Rose, Violet, Watermelon, Wormwood
- **Stones/Crystals/Metals/Minerals:** Amethyst, Chrysocolla, Citrine, Clear Quartz, Jade, Labradorite, Moonstone, Mother-of-Pearl, Opal, Pink Chalcedony, Rose Quartz, Ruby, Selenite, Sodalite

LEO MOON

- **Themes:** Creativity, Friendship, Fun
- **Ingredients:** Anise, Cacao, Calendula, Chamomile, Cinnamon, Clove, Coffee, Dill, Grapefruit, Honey, Juniper, Lavender, Nutmeg, Oak, Olive, Orange, Pineapple, Raspberry, Rosemary, Saffron, Walnut

- **Stones/Crystals/Metals/Minerals:** Amazonite, Amber, Carnelian, Citrine, Garnet, Onyx, Orange/Yellow Calcite, Peridot, Rhodochrosite, Rose Quartz, Ruby, Sardonyx, Sunstone, Tiger's Eye

VIRGO MOON

- **Themes:** Details, Organizing, Community

- **Ingredients:** Almond, Aloe Vera, Barley, Bergamot, Caraway, Dill, Fennel, Lavender, Maple, Marjoram, Nutmeg, Oak, Parsley, Peppermint, Rosemary, Salt, Violet, Walnut

- **Stones/Crystals/Metals/Minerals:** Amazonite, Amethyst, Apatite (Gold, Blue), Aquamarine, Blue Lace Agate, Carnelian, Chrysocolla, Citrine, Fluorite, Green Aventurine, Hawk's Eye, Kyanite, Peridot, Sapphire, Smoky Quartz

LIBRA MOON

- **Themes:** Harmony, Connection, Aesthetic, Beauty, Art

- **Ingredients:** Aloe Vera, Apple, Apricot, Barley, Cherry, Maple, Marjoram, Oat, Passion Fruit, Peach, Raspberry, Rose, Rye, Spearmint, Strawberry, Sugar, Thyme, Vanilla, Violet, Wheat

- **Stones/Crystals/Metals/Minerals:** Amethyst, Aquamarine, Bloodstone, Celestite, Citrine, Emerald, Jade, Lapis Lazuli, Lepidolite, Rhodochrosite, Rose Quartz

SCORPIO MOON

- **Themes:** Passion, Sensuality, Power, the Occult, Psychic Abilities

- **Ingredients:** Allspice, Basil, Blackberry, Clove, Dill, Gardenia, Ginger, Pepper, Peppermint, Pomegranate, Saffron, Vanilla, Violet

- **Stones/Crystals/Metals/Minerals:** Aquamarine, Bloodstone, Carnelian, Garnet, Labradorite, Obsidian, Ruby, Smoky Quartz, Turquoise

SAGITTARIUS MOON

- **Themes:** Optimism, Philosophy, Guiding Beliefs, Hope, Luck, Expansion
- **Ingredients:** Anise, Clove, Coffee, Elder (berry or flower), Ginger, Juniper, Maple, Nutmeg, Oak, Rose, Rosemary, Sage
- **Stones/Crystals/Metals/Minerals:** Amber, Amethyst, Apophyllite, Citrine, Emerald, Garnet, Herkimer Diamond, Labradorite, Lapis Lazuli, Lepidolite, Ruby, Sodalite, Star Sapphire, Turquoise

CAPRICORN MOON

- **Themes:** Determination, Longevity, Money, Tradition, Achievement, Career
- **Ingredients:** Barley, Beet, Cinnamon, Corn, Cranberry, Elder (berry or flower), Jasmine, Poppy, Thyme, Vinegar
- **Stones/Crystals/Metals/Minerals:** Bloodstone, Carnelian, Clear Calcite, Clear Quartz, Fluorite, Garnet, Hematite, Malachite, Obsidian, Onyx, Ruby, Serpentine

AQUARIUS MOON

- **Themes:** Vision, the Future, Humanitarianism, Freedom, Independence, Revolution, Rebellion
- **Ingredients:** Almond, Anise, Apple, Cherry, Hazelnut, Lavender, Marjoram, Olive, Peppermint, Rosemary, Sage, Violet

- **Stones/Crystals/Metals/Minerals:** Amethyst, Angelite, Aquamarine, Blue Sapphire, Clear Quartz, Fluorite, Garnet, Herkimer Diamond, Labradorite, Selenite, Turquoise

PISCES MOON

- **Themes:** Healing, Peace, Psychic Abilities, Collective Unconscious, Going with the Flow

- **Ingredients:** Aloe Vera, Anise, Blueberry, Clove, Jasmine, Lavender, Maple, Nutmeg, Poppy, Sage

- **Stones/Crystals/Metals/Minerals:** Amethyst, Angelite, Aquamarine, Bloodstone, Blue Lace Agate, Celestite, Fluorite, Fuchsite, Jade, Labradorite, Lapis Lazuli, Moonstone, Mother-of-Pearl, Rhodochrosite, Selenite, Turquoise

BIBLIOGRAPHY

Bacon, Bennett, Azadeh Khatiri, James Palmer, Tony Freeth, Paul Pettitt, and Robert Kentridge. (2023). "An Upper Palaeolithic Proto-Writing System and Phenological Calendar." *Cambridge Archaeological Journal* 33, no. 3 (August 2023): 371–389. https://doi.org/10.1017/S0959774322000415.

Boland, Yasmin. *Moonology: Working with the Magic of Lunar Cycles.* Carlsbad, CA: Hay House, 2016.

Cajochen, Christian, Songül Altanay-Ekici, Mirjam Münch, Sylvia Frey, Vera Knoblauch, and Anna Wirz-Justice. "Evidence That the Lunar Cycle Influences Human Sleep." *Current Biology* 23, no. 15 (July 2013): 1,485–1,488. https://doi.org/10.1016/j.cub.2013.06.029.

Cunningham, Scott. *Cunningham's Encyclopedia of Magical Herbs.* Woodbury, MN: Llewellyn Publications, 1985.

———. *Cunningham's Encyclopedia of Wicca in the Kitchen.* Woodbury, MN: Llewellyn Publications, 1990.

Forrest, Steven. *The Book of the Moon: Discovering Astrology's Lost Dimension.* Borrego Springs, CA: Seven Paws Press, Inc., 2010.

Illes, Judika. *Encyclopedia of Spirits: The Ultimate Guide to the Magic of Fairies, Genies, Demons, Ghosts, Gods & Goddesses.* New York: HarperCollins E-Books, 2010.

Kynes, Sandra. *Llewellyn's Complete Book of Correspondences: A Comprehensive & Cross-Referenced Resource for Pagans & Wiccans.* Woodbury, MN: Llewellyn Publications, 2013.

Main, Douglas. "Why Oysters Close on the Full Moon—and More Odd Lunar Effects on Animals." *National Geographic,* April 17, 2019. http://nationalgeographic.com/animals/article/lunar-cycles-full-moon-effects-on-wildlife.

Mark, Joshua J. "Nanna." In *World History Encyclopedia,* December 7, 2022. http://worldhistory.org/Nanna/.

Morrison, Dorothy. *Everyday Moon Magic: Spells & Rituals for Abundant Living.* Woodbury, MN: Llewellyn Publications, 2004.

Norevik, Gabriel, Susanne Åkesson, Arne Andersson, Johan Bäckman, and Anders Hedenström. "The Lunar Cycle Drives Migration of a Nocturnal Bird." *PLOS*

Biology 17, no. 10 (October 15, 2019): e3000456. https://doi.org/10.1371/journal
.pbio.3000456.

Palmer, M.S., J. Fieberg, A. Swanson, M. Kosmala, and C. Packer. "A 'Dynamic'
Landscape of Fear: Prey Responses to Spatiotemporal Variations in Predation
Risk Across the Lunar Cycle." *Ecology Letters*, 20: 1,364–1,373. https://doi
.org/10.1111/ele.12832.

Rosicrucian Egyptian Museum. "Deities in Ancient Egypt—Thoth." Accessed
October 17, 2023. https://egyptianmuseum.org/deities-thoth.

US Department of Commerce, National Oceanic and Atmospheric
Administration. "What Are Spring and Neap Tides?" NOAA National Ocean
Service. Accessed October 17, 2023. oceanservice.noaa.gov/facts/springtide
.html#:~:text=A%20spring%20tide%20is%20a,without%20regard%20to%20
the%20season.

Wayman, Erin. "How the Moon's Light Affects Animals." *Science News*, July 8,
2019. www.sciencenews.org/article/moon-animals-light-behavior-lunar-phases.

White, Tom S. "3 Ways the Moon Affects Wildlife." *Discover Wildlife*, May 11,
2022. www.discoverwildlife.com/animal-facts/ways-moon-affects-wildlife/.

INDEX

MAGICKAL GUIDES FOR THE
MODERN-DAY WITCH!